In the Eye of the Hurricane

Ellis Amdur, M.A., N.C.C., C.M.H.S.

Skills to Calm and De-escalate Aggressive and Mentally Ill Family Members: 2nd Edition

An Edgework Book
www.edgework.info

Notes and Notices

Eye of the Hurricane: Living with Family Members Suffering from Mental Illness, 2nd Edition

Ellis Amdur, M.A., N.C.C., C.M.H.S. – 2011, Edgework Books

ISBN: 978-0-9823762-3-2

A Message to My Readers
I am committed to sharing the best of my years of experience and study. I ask that you express your respect for these intentions by adhering strictly to the copyright protection notice you'll find below. Thank you for your vigilance in respecting my rights.

Notice of Rights
All rights reserved. No part of this book may be reproduced or transmitted in any form by any means, electronic, mechanical, photocopying, recording, or otherwise, without the explicit prior written permission of the author.

Limited Liability and Disclaimer
This book is informational only. This is not a treatment or counseling manual. The information presented is not a guide for family member treatment, nor is it meant to provide a substitute for consultation about treatment with professionals. Readers interested in advice pertaining specifically to their family member must contact your family member's treatment team, or their supervisors. No professional-client relationship is created through the use of this guidebook. Notwithstanding your purchase of this book, you agree to make a safety, medical, or treatment plan with the help of professions who specialize in the condition(s), syndromes, or mental illnesses that your family member is suffering.

In purchasing this guidebook, you agree that you will hold Edgework: Crisis Intervention Resources PLLC, harmless from all claims arising out of or related to your access or use of, or inability to access or use, this book or the information contained herein.

The information in Edgework: Crisis Intervention Resources PLLC guidebooks is provided for general information only and provided "AS IS" to the fullest extent permitted by law, including, but not limited to, any implied warranty of fitness for a particular purpose. Edgework: Crisis Intervention Resources PLLC makes no warranties about the accuracy, completeness, or timeliness of the content, services, text, graphs, and links appearing in this guidebook.

Credits
Photographs by: Dreamstime.com
Illustrations by: Shoko Zama
Design: Soundview Design Studio

Contents

In Gratitude vii
Introduction ix

Section I	**Centering: Standing with Strength and Grace in Crisis Situations** 1
Chapter 1	It's Hard to Stay Centered in a Hurricane...3
Chapter 2	"I've Got All the Time I Need": Hurrying Slowly 5
Chapter 3	Enhancing Empathy: I've Got You Under My Skin 7
Chapter 4	The Texture of Relationship: Honing Your Intuition 9
Chapter 5	It's Not Personal Unless You Make It So 15
Chapter 6	Circular Breathing: Be the Eye in the Center of the Hurricane 21
Chapter 7	The Intoxication and Joy of Righteous Anger 29
Chapter 8	A Fair Witness 31

Section II	**Communication with Those with Intense, Unusual, or Eccentric Styles** 33
Chapter 9	Tell It Like It Is: Communication with Concrete Thinkers 35
Chapter 10	Rigid Personality (Asperger's Syndrome, "High Functioning Autism," and Other Similar Disorders) 37
Chapter 11	Information Processing and Retention: Consolidating Gains...................................41
Chapter 12	Coping with Stubborn Refusals 43
Chapter 13	Stuck: Coping with Repetitive Demands, Questions, and Obsessions 45
Chapter 14	The Need for Reassurance 47
Chapter 15	Dealing with Individuals with Pronounced Mood Swings 49
Chapter 16	Moving Past the Past 51
Chapter 17	"Would You Just Get off Your Rear End?" Coping with Lack of Motivation...............53
Chapter 18	"If There Is a Problem, That Would Be Your Fault": Useful Tactics for Dealing with Symptoms of Paranoia and Persecution 55

Section III	**A Consideration of People Who Behave in Ways that Cause Strife Between Themselves and Other Family Members** 59
Chapter 19	Borderline Personality Disorder and Splitting...61
Chapter 20	Bad Intentions: Recognizing the Strategies of Opportunistic and Manipulative Family Members 67

Section IV	**Communication with Those with Severe Mental Illness or Other Conditions that Can Cause Severe Disability**	73
Chapter 21	Struggling in a Fog: Dealing with the Symptoms of Disorganization	75
Chapter 22	Dropping Stones in a Well: Latency	81
Chapter 23	Withdrawal from Intoxicating Substances	83
Chapter 24	Psychosis: Delusions and Hallucinations	85
Chapter 25	Communication with Someone Who is Experiencing Delusions or Hallucinations	89
Chapter 26	Welcome to the Rollercoaster: Tactics for Dealing with Symptoms of Mania	99
Chapter 27	Communication and De-escalation with Elderly Family Members	103
Section V	**Suicide**	105
Chapter 28	Why Would You Suspect Your Family Member is Suicidal?	107
Chapter 29	The Essentials of Intervention with Someone You Believe Might Be Suicidal: Who Should Ask the Questions and What Should You Say?	109
Chapter 30	The Four Questions	111
Chapter 31	Further Discussion with Your Loved One When They are Suicidal	115
Chapter 32	Self-Mutilation and Parasuicidal Behavior	119
Section VI	**Recognition of Patterns of Aggression**	123
Chapter 33	The Nature of Aggression	125
Chapter 34	Why Would Someone Become Aggressive?	133
Chapter 35	What Does Escalation Look Like?	137
Section VII	**De-escalation of Angry Individuals**	145
Chapter 36	Core Principles of Intervention with Angry People	147
Chapter 37	Physical Organization in the Face of Aggression	151
Chapter 38	The Tone and Quality of Your Voice	155
Chapter 39	Preemptive De-escalation	157
Chapter 40	Across the Spectrum of Anger: 20 to 95 Percent	159
Chapter 41	Diamonds in the Rough: Essential Strategies for De-escalating Anger	169
Chapter 42	Paraphrasing: The Gold Standard in De-escalating Anger	175
Chapter 43	Guidelines on Limit Setting	185
Chapter 44	What Doesn't Work (or the Big Mistakes that Seemed Like Such Good Ideas)	187
Section VIII	**Communication with Mentally Ill and Emotionally Disturbed Youth**	193
Chapter 45	Communication with Potentially Aggressive Youthful Family Members	195
Chapter 46	No Brake Pads: A Consideration of the Impulsive Child	201
Chapter 47	Conduct Disorder: Fierce Youth	203
Chapter 48	Dynamite under a Rock: Explosive Kids	205
Chapter 49	"Even if You Force Me, I'll Still Make You Miserable": Opposition-Defiant Kids	207

Chapter 50	PTSD in Young People	209
Chapter 51	Pseudo–Nihilism	211
Section IX	**Control of Rage and a Response to Violence**	**213**
Chapter 52	Preface to Rage	215
Chapter 53	Chaotic Rage: A Consideration of Rage Emerging from Various Disorganized States	217
Chapter 54	Terrified Rage	221
Chapter 55	Hot Rage	225
Chapter 56	Predatory or Cool Rage	239
Chapter 57	De-escalation of Developmentally Disabled Individuals: Special Considerations	243
Chapter 58	When Facing Violence	245
Chapter 59	The Aftermath: What to Do Now?	247
Chapter 60	Conclusion	251
Appendix I	When Monitoring Medication is Part of Your Responsibilities	253
Appendix II	Crisis Intervention Teams for Law Enforcement	255
Endnotes		257
About the Author		259

In Gratitude

This book exists because of my association with Dr. Bea Dixon (www.careinaction.com), who was ahead of her time in pioneering a comprehensive resource to aid families struggling to help mentally ill loved ones.

Introduction

Caring for a loved one suffering from a mental illness is not for the faint of heart. You offer your best – care, attention, and love – but your loved one may not improve. Instead, they may withdraw from the family, require frequent hospitalization or expensive care, and even become hateful or violent.

Even more difficult to bear, you may not be able to ward off darker feelings: a sense of shame at not being up to the task; remorse at having lost your temper or being at your worst when you should be at your best; and, perhaps most painful, a sense of helplessness to make anything better for your loved one – and for yourself.

A diagnosis of severe mental illness is heartbreaking, but it is not only the mentally ill person who suffers. Even in the best circumstances, their illness will affect all those who love them. As a caregiver, you suffer for them, you suffer with them, and sometimes you suffer because of them. Their words may be harsh, even vile, their behaviors unsettling, even frightening, and violence wounds the same whether the perpetrator of that violence is mentally ill or not. Understanding that their behavior is the result of a distortion in perception, an imbalance of neurochemicals, a head injury, or drug abuse may allow you to remain objective and to keep focused on long-range goals, but this understanding is irrelevant when you are not feeling safe.

The first section of this book walks you through core strategies designed to help you maintain greater self-control in your interaction with your ill relative.

The second section shows you how to communicate with your relative when they are experiencing acute symptoms of their illness, offering a "skill map," a range of communication tactics that covers many symptoms, such as the presence of paranoia, mania, hallucinations, and delusions. You will learn new ways to reach to the person behind their illness.

The third section addresses suicide, describing how to discuss this frightening subject with a loved one who may be desperately isolated or angry.

The fourth section addresses threatening behaviors, including aggression, frightening verbal escalations, harsh exchanges, and more. It focuses on your safety and that of your relative during those intense moments, explaining common-sense dos and don'ts in the face of anger, rage, and violence.

EYE OF THE HURRICANE

> Perhaps your worst fear is that you will get hurt or even killed by an aggressor. This guidebook will *not* teach you methods of physical self-defense. If you need training in force-on-force self-defense, which includes evasion, breaking free of holds, or, in the worst cases, fighting back against an attacker, your local police force or sexual assault crisis center may have references to reputable groups.
>
> I will also not teach you how to physically restrain your family member. Those tactics need to be learned firsthand. Any inquiries in this area should be directed to your local mental health agency or psychiatric hospital.

The Undamaged Self

You are walking outside on an icy winter day. You suddenly slip and spin toward the pavement. At the last minute, you thrust out an arm to break your fall. It also breaks your wrist. You go to the hospital, and your arm is put in a cast. For a few weeks or months, your life is different. You cannot write letters or type emails. You have to learn to feed yourself with your left hand, and you must ask a family member to cut your food for you. Life has suddenly become difficult.

Imagine that when you fall, you also strain your knee and, with your broken wrist, are unable to rise again to your feet. The snow turns to sleet, and you become soaking wet. By the time you are found, you get a lung infection that turns into pleurisy. Each breath turns into paroxysms of coughing. You are bedridden for weeks. You are in pain, you are exhausted, and with your injury and illness, you are bored and frustrated as well. You might also get irritable, depressed, or anxious that you will never get back on your feet.

To your family, who has never seen you like this before, you are "like a different person." That is not really true, is it? Despite your miserable days and weeks, you know yourself to be the same. In fact, lying in your bed, there is an aspect of you that simply observes everything: "Wow, am I miserable. I don't think I've ever been so depressed. I am bored to tears. Just look at me, lying here watching stupid TV shows. I should focus and read a book." There is an aspect of you, the deepest, most profoundly *you* part of you, that is not injured or sick. That is your truest identity, your "undamaged self."[1]

Severe mental illness causes mental and emotional disturbances far more severe than the mood of our hypothetical wrist-broken, knee-sprained, pleurisy-ridden invalid. One's ability to think is distorted, and one's reality is skewed. Perceptions may be bizarre, even hallucinatory. Emotions swing from high to low or shift into realms oddly at variance to one's circumstances. A mental illness assaults your family member's worldview—they inescapably perceive a world different from the world the rest of us share. Nonetheless, your loved one is still there. They are not simply a bundle of raw emotions or distorted cognitions. You perceive, like a small light shining in the fog, an essential part of him or her that the illness cannot touch. There is still something intrinsically him, so quintessentially her beyond the illness. It is this that makes your loved ones, so profoundly ill, worth loving.

Speak to the Person within the Illness
Words do not cure severe mental illness. But we can speak to the illness or speak to the person who is ill. We are always talking to the same person, whether we are cruel or kind, insensitive or exquisitely perceptive. When we speak to the person, like throwing a lifeline to someone in the stormy sea, we give them something to hold onto so that the waves do not overwhelm.

Deal with the Behavior, Not the Cause: Symptom-based Response
A proper diagnosis enables a doctor or therapist to determine the proper treatment – the best medication or therapeutic procedures for a person's mental illness. Diagnosis also provides a method of communicating, in general terms, the nature of the person's illness to both professionals and lay people. I must underscore the word "general." Although mental illnesses tend to affect people in much the same manner, ten people with schizophrenia or depression are as diverse as any ten people selected at random.

We cannot depend on diagnosis to learn how to communicate with our ill relatives. Many people can have the same symptoms, but the causes can be very different. Despite these different causes, we end up communicating with such people in much the same manner. On the other hand, many people with the same diagnosis require very different modes of communication if we are going to get through to them. This book, therefore, emphasizes behavior (symptoms) rather than the diagnosis. For example, let us consider hallucinations – perceiving something that is not there. People may hallucinate because they are ill with schizophrenia, bipolar disorder, profound depression, borderline personality disorder, neurological impairment, drug side effects, or severe trauma. Although it is certainly important to determine the cause of the hallucinations to find a helpful treatment, this book focuses on general principles to *communicate with* such a hallucinating person, whatever the cause of the problem.

Beyond these general principles, however, we must remember that we are still communicating with an individual. We are building a relationship with that unique person. Imagine that you and your neighbor have fifteen-year-old sons, both profoundly depressed. Would nothing change if these two boys exchanged homes? After all, they are both depressed. Quite the contrary: almost everything would change!

Getting the Most out of This Book
What follows may seem like techniques or communication strategies, but they are far more than that. Just like in courtship, business, philosophy, and poetry, there is an *art* in speaking with a mentally ill person. The art, however, is not for aesthetic reasons: It is to express care and love, to enable you, the members of a family, to live together in as much peace and joy as possible.

Overlapping Skills
It is unavoidable when you read the chapters in sequence that it will seem that the advice given in an item is *the* procedure to follow. All of the strategies described here overlap. Some are generally applicable and oth-

ers specific to only one type of behavior or symptom. Just because you might be reading about paranoia, for example, doesn't mean that your paranoid relative is not also disorganized, delusional, or manic. What you will be developing is a "skill map" – a range of communication tactics that covers many situations.

SECTION I

Centering: Standing with Strength
and Grace in Crisis Situations

CHAPTER 1

It's Hard to Stay Centered in a Hurricane

Frank and Mary's son has schizophrenia. He believes he will wash off a spiritual shield if he bathes. Therefore, he never lets water touch his skin. He looks terrible and smells bad. Frank is embarrassed to be with him in the presence of other people. Mary can't stand to hug him.

Lisa was diagnosed with bipolar illness. During her manic episodes, she unfairly blames her husband, Greg, for all of her problems, accusing him of terrible things to the point that it becomes harder and harder for him to recall that he ever loved her. He fantasizes about leaving her and then is wracked with guilt. Her words are sometimes so hurtful that he lashes out at her verbally. One day, she says something so awful that he grabs her throat and pins her to the wall. Both of them are so terrified by what happens that they decide to sleep in separate rooms.

Beth is simply tired. She is tired of taking care of her husband, tired of managing his life and the symptoms of his depression. When she looks at him, she no longer sees him as a beloved human being. She sees a living task that never ends, leeching her life away, with virtually no chance of things getting better.

Bob and Brenda talk about how people on the street, in church, or at work react when they see them with their son. Severely autistic, he is a mass of tics and bizarre gestures, mumbling and grunting to himself. Most people appear uncomfortable; some react with fear or even revulsion. Even kinder folks, who offer sympathy, grate on their nerves after awhile.

The symptoms of mental illnesses are particularly taxing on families. If you are like most people, you too might come down on yourself for feeling embarrassed about your relative, for losing feelings of love, for unleashing your temper, or for wishing he or she would disappear out of your life. You too may have reached a point of feeling incompetent and powerless.

It Can Be Different
Do any of the stories above resonate with your own life experience? Have there been times when you became so impatient, embarrassed, angry, or frustrated that you experienced yourself at your worst rather than your best?

You have far more power than you think. Human beings do not exist alone. We are created as human through our first relationships with our caregivers, and we maintain ourselves within this world through relationships. If you want to change the quality of any relationship – and that applies equally to a relationship with a person who has a mental illness – the most powerful way to do so is to change yourself.

Without a sense of centering and calm, it is impossible to help people calm themselves. The strategies in this section revolve around maintaining self-control. For many of us, "control" implies something forceful and rigid. On the contrary, we should aim to develop the ability to adapt to circumstances in a powerful, fluid, and purposeful way. Not only will this enhance your ability to work with your family members on a day-to-day basis, but it will also make you most effective in crisis situations. Sometimes you quietly listen, and other times you quickly intervene. Through centering, you do not become defensive or on your guard. Rather, like a cat walking along a fence, you are agile -- ready for anything that comes.

CHAPTER 2

"I've Got All the Time I Need": Hurrying Slowly

Think back to the days when you learned to drive. Remember how it seemed impossible to look toward the horizon while noting in your periphery children who might run into the street, while using the same foot for the brake and the accelerator, while shifting in proper sequence, while wishing your passenger would *be quiet* so you could concentrate? Now that you are an experienced driver, you can do all these activities at once, and you feel as if you have all the time in the world to carry them out, right?

When your family members are in crisis, they may believe that there is no time and no hope to solve the problem. If you agree, you, too, are in crisis. Instead, you must instill a sense of confidence, first within yourself, and then, within your loved ones, even when you don't (yet) know the best solution. This confidence is exemplified by an attitude that, no matter what, you have all the time you need to find an answer to the problem. Whether the other person agrees or not is not the question. The answer must start with you. This is true regardless of your schedule, the traffic jam, the forgotten doctor's appointment, or your son's belief that the world will end in a few hours. You will act most efficiently and powerfully when operating with a spacious rather than cramped attitude, and this is summed up in that phrase, "I have all the time I need." <u>This is an attitude, not how many seconds are on the clock</u>. It is when we accept the other person's sense of time rather than ours that we lose control of the situation.

This may seem easy to say and hard to accomplish. It is not a mental trick, however. This entire book is meant to help you "slow time down."

- If you can perceive a crisis building, you can intervene earlier, when you actually have more time.
- If you can stabilize your mood – the subject of this entire section of the book – you will function more efficiently and with greater calm.
- If you are familiar with how best to communicate with people in different psychological and emotional states, you will not waste your words. You will say the right thing, rather than anything.
- If you are familiar with the nature of aggression, you will be able to more adequately assess the level of danger your relative is presenting. You will know what is likely to make things worse, and what is likely to make things better.

This set of skills is no different from what is required to cook a complex meal or build a piece of furniture. We can do several things at once when we know what not to do and what we must do at each stage of the process.

You may disagree, thinking of times when the situation was so terrible and happening so fast that it seemed inconceivable that there was enough time. With the proper attitude, however, time "slows down." At the same time, you move both faster and more efficiently.

We cannot make a mentally ill or drug-abusing person "better." It is as if we are standing by the bank of a river at flood, watching someone struggle in the water. If we dive in to save them, they will try to climb on top of us to reach just a little more air. Instead, we remain on the bank, skillfully throwing a rope. We point to it and encourage the drowning person to take hold. Were we to throw too quickly, we'd miss them, or end up with a tangle of cord, elaborate but useless. Instead, "hurrying slowly," we cast it with studied grace. We can only pull them in, however, if they grab the rope. If they refuse, there is nothing we can do. Our best hope that they will take hold is if we are calm and *passionately dispassionate*. When we convey a sense of warm, confident gravity, we pass to the other person the sense that we *both* have all the time we need.

CHAPTER 3

Enhancing Empathy: "I've Got You Under My Skin"

For the quality of your relationship to improve, it is vital that you empathize with your ill relative. A definition is in order here. I can imagine some of you saying, with understandable outrage, "Of course I feel sorry for – concerned about – sad for my relative." These emotions, however, do not exactly show "empathy" but rather *sympathy*, a feeling of caring and concern for another person.

There are two components to empathy: tracking[2] and embodiment. Tracking is the ability to read another person's intentions. This is an observer's stance: for example, you may have nothing in common with a person you are speaking with, but you know that they intend to solicit you for spare change, try to interest you in a second helping of granola, or are really not interested in talking about the history of schisms in the Catholic church in the fourth century, your favorite subject. Embodiment is a felt sense of what it is like to be the other person, or at least, to be in their situation. For example, you see a crying child, lost in a store, looking for her mother. Not only are you concerned *for* her, but you also experience a little of what she must be feeling: terror, grief, and confusion. Without sympathy, we will not care about the other person's distress. Without empathy, we will not know *what* to care about.

Unfortunately, feeling empathy can become difficult when we are dealing with a person who has a brain disorder. How can we comprehend what it is like to believe that the flowers, bobbing in the breeze, are whispering about you? Or that you will become fatally ill if the shadow on the floor touches the bed? Or that, although the room is empty, you can hear three people talking?

When you do not understand another person's world, you can, of course, ask them to tell you about it. This can only take us so far, however, particularly when it comes to understanding the experience of being mentally ill. During the acute phase of your relative's illness, he or she may tell you things that are completely foreign to you. In other cases, he or she may be unwilling to talk at all.

Embodiment
One of the best ways to achieve empathy, to feel a little of what it is like to be another person, is to *move as he does*. Don't do it in that person's presence, for it will surely be upsetting or embarrassing. Instead, go someplace private and begin to sit, stand, and move around the room the way he does.

We cannot easily get into the mind of our ill relative, but by moving like they do, we form a template in our "body-mind" that matches his, and then, at least to a small degree, we begin to experience the world the way he does.

- Perhaps he moves as if his bones are made out of spun glass – they are stiff as well as fragile – and he holds his head cocked over one ear.
- Perhaps she walks stiff-legged, jamming her hipbones up into her pelvis with each stomp, lurching forward.
- Perhaps he pushes his head forward and glowers from under his eyebrows.

Whatever he does, imitate all of it: hands, feet, head, and torso. Move at the same speed and the same rhythm, and breathe in the same pattern. Pick up objects just as he does, and use your eyes to look around you (or not look around you) in the same way. In a short time, even five or ten minutes, you will begin to feel and perceive the world differently in a subtle but real way.

Don't worry. This will not make you ill like your relative. When you are finished with the exercise, just shake your body and breathe deeply. You will return to yourself right away. Your loved ones cannot free themselves from the torment of their world so easily.

CHAPTER 4

The Texture of Relationship: Honing Your Intuition

Intuition is that small voice that you must respect. In intuition, we know something without knowing exactly how we know what we know. Intuition functions best when we are looking a little "sidelong," so to speak, when we are not focusing too hard. It is a wonderful thing when it occurs – it seems like a stroke of luck or random lightning strike. Because intuition is not "hard evidence," we often discount it, even though it may be the *first* sign that we are in a dangerous situation.

- We often minimize such intuitions as they inform others about their concerns, saying, for example, "I know it's nothing, but . . ." In doing so, we inadvertently lead others to minimize the situation.
- Sometimes, we inadvertently cloak our concerns through black humor or jokes: "Watch out, she's going to come back tomorrow and go postal." By saying this in an offhand manner, we try to avoid the sense of fear that we really feel. In joking about it, however, we can easily convince ourselves and others that the concern is not valid.
- We do not voice our hunches at all, feeling awkward or embarrassed because they do not have "hard evidence."
- We are sometimes undermined by "logical" people, either friends or family, or more often, treatment professionals, who minimize our concerns.

Differences among people who are concerned about a mentally ill family member must be discussed respectfully, particularly questions of safety. In many circumstances, each person sees only part of the picture. If one person's idea or intuition is discounted or dismissed out of hand, he or she may cease to speak up – and vital information about everyone's safety is lost.

The Spaces between Us

Intuition is particularly important when communicating with your ill relative, particularly when he or she is becoming agitated. The amount of physical space between the two of you, the positioning of your hands, muscular tension, and the quality of your voice – all those nonverbal expressions – can become more important than what is actually said.

One way to view human relationships is in terms of "space." We describe being close to or distant from another person, complain that someone is "in our face," or worry that we cannot "reach" them. We walk down the street and feel someone examining us from a distance, or lie in bed next to our spouse, feeling like they are a million miles away.

The spaces between human beings have a kind of texture, something that we can feel. The more we can make ourselves aware of the quality of this interpersonal space, the more conscious we will be of what is going on between ourselves and another person.

Think of the boundary between people as a bubble.[3] The space between human beings tends to expand and contract, as well as, metaphorically speaking, change texture, color, and shape, depending on the circumstances. For example, the more relaxed you are, and the warmer you feel toward someone, the less personal space you desire. When you are uncertain or suspicious of someone, you instinctively move to get more distance from them. Even your own mood can shift your bubble: on a good day, you feel open to anything and ready to invite others in; on a bad mood day, your bubble expands to acquire more space to manage your worries. Whatever the quality of your relationship, the bubble is always there.

Exercise A: Four Experiments with Personal Space
Experiment #1: Practice Finding Your Bubble

1. Ask a person (not your ill relative) to stand in front of you much farther away than he or she would ordinarily stand when you engage in a conversation. (**NOTE**: If you practice with your best friend or a loved one, you will not get the sense of space – you will merely want to hug. Work with someone with whom you are not that close.)
2. This volunteer, the "sender," then begins to talk about a lovely experience or something that you are interested in.
3. As the sender talks, have him or her move toward you. (There should not be any body contact between the two of you in this exercise.)
4. You (the "receiver") will become aware of the moment when the sender is too close for comfort – when he or she stepped into your personal space. This sensation is your bubble.
5. When that moment comes, hold up a hand and tell your practice partner to stop.

Let's debrief this step. Ask the sender or other observers whether or not they could tell by your body language that the sender was actually in your bubble before you held up your hand. This is very common. We are socialized to suppress feelings of discomfort when someone moves into our space, particularly if they are not displaying hostility. Have the sender or observers describe what behaviors *you* displayed that informed them that he or she was in your bubble.

Then describe what physical sensation(s) you had that told *you* that the sender was in your space. It is important that you describe your physical sensations: not your emotions. Emotions are a label that we apply to our physical perceptions, and that label can change based on the situation or our own thoughts. This can even be dangerous.

- Let us say that you label a hollow feeling in the pit of your stomach as "anxiety." However, you feel guilty for feeling anxiety when your son approaches you, even when he is aggressive. There-

fore, you suppress the physical sensation, because you do not want to feel such anxiety around a loved one.
- Others use "creative relabeling" – rather than anxiety, you tell yourself that you are worried "for them," or even happy. Once you either suppress your physical reactions, or re-label them so that they are not negative, you have made it impossible to use your body as a means of intuiting what is going on between you and someone else. Rather than relabeling, associate the sensation with a fact, such as, "When someone moves into my personal space, I get a hollow feeling in my stomach." <u>This sensation is your early-warning sign that someone has stepped within your boundary</u>.

Experiment #2: Exploring Your Bubble
Now try the same exercise, but have your partner try to con or convince you to do something you don't want to do. Observe what happens. Do you desire more or less space? Pay particular attention to your physical sensations: In what ways are they the same as your baseline experience (#1) and in what ways are they different?

Experiment #3: Pushing the Edges
Try it one more time with the sender yelling at you. There is no need to make this an overly aggressive or frightening role-play exercise. Your practice partner, for example, could just pretend to be upset because you were late. "You are really thoughtless today! I waited for you out in the rain for one hour. Where were you?"

Study what this interaction did to your desire for more or less space. Take time to reflect on your physical sensations. In what ways are they the same as your baseline experience (#1) and in what ways are they different?

Experiment #4: Reading Your Partner's Bubble
Reverse roles. You become the sender and your partner is the receiver. Repeat the above exercises and watch the other person's nonverbal reactions as you step into his or her personal space.

Are you aware when your partner becomes uncomfortable? What signs did you observe in your partner that made you aware that they were experiencing you as too close? Go into as much detail as you can. This can include body posture, movements or stillness, skin-color changes, eye contact or the lack of, and a host of other behaviors. Having been in the role of the receiver yourself, you will quickly pick up on the subtleties of their nonverbal communication.

Integrating and Using What You've Learned

This kind of practice can increase your intuitive sense of whether the physical space between you makes your mentally ill family member feel comfortable or whether it disturbs, agitates, or frightens him or her. Furthermore, as you note the differences in physical sensations when someone simply steps into your bubble, as opposed to when that person is trying to manipulate you or is aggressive toward you, you will begin to develop an early warning system, which alerts you to a negative interaction developing between you and another person.

Recognizing the texture of your relationship prevents potentially explosive situations from unraveling to the point that either one of you loses control. With practice, you'll be increasingly able to make small, in-the-moment adjustments of spacing that change the quality of your interactions.

Two cautions about personal space

1. *Do not* knowingly step into another's sense of safety or comfort, particularly during stressful times. (Note that this applies to your sense of comfort too.)
2. *Do not* accommodate another person at the expense of your own sense of safety or comfort. It is important to be conscious of your own feelings and able to define limits.

Exercise B: Developing Mindful Intuition

The previous exercise is, admittedly, contrived. Intuitive capabilities can, however, be strengthened with exercise and practice. We can accomplish this by paying closer attention to the *meaning* of the sensations our bodies give us. Unfortunately, many of us have gotten pretty good at tuning out those signals, treating them as a kind of unwanted noise in our systems. Here is an exercise you can try that will help you begin to notice your own intuitive knowledge and responses.

Carry a small notebook with you for at least one week. When someone enters your bubble enough that you have a physical reaction, take some time afterward to note the following:
- Your physical sensation
- How far away or how close did you want them to be?
- What was the intent of their interaction with you?

As for this last item, note down if they were simply trying to communicate with you, if they were trying to con you, or if they were hostile to you. You should also note if they were sad, depressed, angry, manipulative, friendly, or loving, to choose only a few examples. Pay attention to your physical sensations and how much or how little space you desire. Also note more subtle experiences: you might, for example, find that you react differently to a man who is depressed than to a woman with the same symptoms.

After you have disengaged from them, jot those down in your notebook. Use the notebook to gather information so you can recognize patterns.

Here are some hypothetical examples (that may be different from yours in the same circumstances):
- When a person is angry, you feel a tightness in your neck.
- When a person is sad, you feel a desire to pull back from them.
- When you are aware that a person is trying to cheat you, you begin to smile.
- When a person expresses loving feelings toward you, you feel anxious.

There are no rules to these reactions, beyond that they are your own. There is no right way to react, and the only wrong ways would be if you said or did hurtful things to another, or responded in a way that embarrassed you or made you unsafe.

Treasure all of your observations. You will begin to develop a form of conscious intuition that is called *mindfulness*. Mindfulness means that you are:
- Aware of the subtle warning signs within your body that inform you of what is going on between you and another person.
- Able to "track" another's behavior so that you are aware of your effect on them and their effect on you.
- Conscious of your behaviors that, intentionally or not, are destabilizing an already fragile situation.

Think of how being mindful will help you in your relationship with your mentally ill relative. You will readily pick up on his level of discomfort. You will also begin to see the things you do that, despite your good intentions, appear to aggravate or frighten her.

Developing mindfulness requires that you take the time to reflect on given situations, after they have occurred. Over the next couple of weeks, jot down your observations about interactions with various people. What we write down is more easily retained. Do not ignore this step!

CHAPTER 5

It's Not Personal Unless You Make It So

Rule 1: I Don't Have to Agree that We Are in an Argument
A desire to win an argument is associated with primitive mental processes linked to dominance hierarchies. Rather than striving for the truth or for an equitable exchange, we end up striving to overwhelm the other. Unless you are in a struggle for your own or someone else's life, you do not have to win. Your goal should be to establish peace between the two of you.

Rule 2: I Don't Have to Give Back What I Get
The people closest to you can terribly hurt your feelings. Our mentally ill relatives, in particular, can feel so powerless or frustrated that they try to grab a little power for themselves by saying something hurtful. It would be easy to strike back with a cutting remark of your own. You have so much ammunition! This fact, alone, is a tragedy that the intimacies of life provide us with weapons to use against our family members. Let us not take up arms against those we love.

We often believe our counterattacks are justified because they "hurt us first." However justified you my *feel*, striking back is an attempt to wound. When family members hurt your feelings, remember that it is an act of valor not to respond in kind.

Rule 3: It's Not Personal
Realize that although their attack on you might seem personal, it is only so when you make it so. If the attack is untrue, what is there to be upset about? And if the attack is valid, then you are reacting in anger when someone tells you the truth: no matter how ugly the presentation, the truth is something to be faced and accepted rather than fought in anger.

No One Will Own Me
The trouble with the above "rules" is that they work fine until we get our buttons pushed. Then pain and anger clench us inside like a fist. Why does verbal abuse affect us so? Shouldn't we be able to simply brush it off?

The brain is an organ of survival, always ready to respond to threat. We are aware of danger through pattern recognition, a rapid response of the more primitive areas of the brain. A large object moving rapidly toward us, a sudden pain, or a violent grab initiates a cascade of actions – fight/flight/freeze/faint – that are expressed to keep us alive in the worst of circumstances. The curse of being human, however, is that these survival responses are precipitated by noxious stimuli that elicit physiological responses, particu-

15

larly that which shocks or surprises us. When our brain perceives these responses, it responds as if we are in life-threatening danger, even when that is not the case. When our guard is down, and someone verbally assaults us or unexpectedly violates our sense of right and wrong, we physically react in the same way that we do when under life-threatening attack.

In the heat of an argument, people sometimes say things in desperation that they later regret. Other times, they deliberately hone in on a person's weak spot. They say things that feel like a dagger to the gut. We feel beaten or raped by the words that are being said, and we cannot make our attacker stop.

Sometimes your family members will challenge you by offending you or making you explain yourself. Provocative challenges are for the purpose of gaining leverage. By weakening you, the other person feels more personal power. Verbal abuse, however, is not really dangerous to you, except the risk that you will lose control of your own actions, thus fueling further conflict between you.

Bracketing: Naming Your Hot Buttons

Sometimes we can roll with the insults by taking a deep belly breath and speaking in slow and measured tones. This is sometimes not enough, particularly if a family member pushes one of those hot buttons. Beyond knowing what to do or say "in the moment," the real solution comes through a kind of "inoculation" – a tool to make you immune to people trying to get to your hot buttons. This is a technique called *bracketing*: facing your vulnerabilities head on and then taking action so that no one will use them against you.

Bracketing is not easy to do. It takes courage to look closely at yourself and say, "These are my areas of greatest vulnerability." Doing so, however, will give you the greater strength that self-knowledge always brings. *Not* doing so will make you more vulnerable to your family member's attacks.

You might think that talking about your vulnerabilities with a friend could help you to stay truthful and strong. Talking about such difficult issues with another person, however, often results in them trying to reassure or comfort you, reframing the "bad" as "not so bad," or giving you an excuse to explain why you are the way you are. To really identify your vulnerabilities, you must face the worst without the refuge of a comforting friend or witness.

It is important, therefore, to look deeply within yourself and identify your hot buttons. Buttons come in five primary "colors":
1. I can't stand it when someone attacks or demeans <   >, because that's something I love and treasure.
2. I feel outraged when someone demeans <   >, because it is something I believe to be unquestionably right and good.
3. I get defensive when people say or point out <   >, because, to tell the truth, I hate it in myself.
4. I lose it when people say or do <   >, because it's as if they are taking control of me or disrespecting me.
5. They better not say <   >. That's the one word I won't take from anyone.

There is a worksheet on the next page. Feel free to copy it and use to highlight your hot buttons for yourself.

EYE OF THE HURRICANE

Statement	Why does this get to me?
EXAMPLE: When people say or do < >, I lose it because	

Once you are aware of your hot buttons, take inventory. <u>Every morning, upon waking, and even a few more times during the day, run through those vulnerabilities you enumerated above</u>. The idea is the same as checking the gas, mirrors, etc., before leaving your driveway. When (not *if*), a family member – or anyone else – tries to push your buttons, you are not surprised or caught off guard. You expect it without being anxious about it. If you take inventory, you center yourself for another day, ready for the worst without it tearing you down.

People often fool themselves about being centered. It is radically different from merely being relaxed or open. Being centered is a dynamic, active state: like a cat on a fence, not a cow standing in a field. This does not mean that you are at hair-trigger readiness, something closer to paranoia than mindful grace. Rather, you develop a sense of spaciousness, in tune with your surroundings and your emotions. Although not *particularly* expecting an attack, you are not surprised either, because you are used to reminding yourself where you can be hurt. Because you are no longer as vulnerable, you will find it easier to take control of a critical incident. You will also find that you can disengage and walk away from a situation when that's the right thing to do. When you really know your buttons, you will not be blindsided. Your insecurities and weaknesses are still present, but you have control over them.

In essence, you should resolve each day that no one will "drag you down." The only thing that you will take personally is your own dignity.

CHAPTER 6

Circular Breathing: Be the Eye in the Center of the Hurricane

Violence, disputes, and arguments can sweep through one's daily routine with the suddenness and force of a hurricane. Your previously calm day can become chaotic, and worse, you may feel that chaos will overwhelm you too. But, when you can step coolly into the worst of situations, you embody the eye of the hurricane, with all the chaos coalescing and revolving around you.

The root of this skill lies in the breath. When we are upset or agitated and our breathing pattern changes involuntarily, it is as if someone else has taken control of our bodies. When we are breathing slowly and with focused attention, we take back that control. By taking control of our breath, we take control of our lives. We are then in a position to take control of the crisis and do what is best within the given circumstances.

- One simple breathing method is to inhale on a four count, pause on a four count, and exhale on a four count. (**NOTE**: Your natural breathing pattern may conform to a different "count," 4-4-4 is just an example.)[4] Pacing your breath through counting can help keep you cool and focused.
- Take a deep, smooth breath. This helps regulate your breathing and gives you a few seconds to think before you respond.
- A third method for in-the-moment situations is to take a deep breath, let it whoosh out, and then resume normal breathing. (**NOTE**: Don't do this in front of an aggressive person: this breathing method is useful just before you engage with someone – for example, before you walk into your daughter's room to confront her about the food she is hoarding.)

Whenever you feel nervous or agitated, it appears in your behavior and makes the situation worse. The opposite is also true. When you are centered, people tend to feel safe and more peaceful around you. Thus, breathing calmly is one of the most important things you can do. Furthermore, in taking a deep breath, we allow several seconds to go by before responding. In addition to feeling calm when you do speak, your relative is *waiting* for you to respond. You have, implicitly, taken control of the interchange, endowing you with the authority that is necessary to resolve things peacefully.

Two Variations of a Powerful Technique: Circular Breathing

Circular breathing is derived from East Asian martial traditions and was used to keep warriors calm on the battlefield. There are two circular breathing variations. Try both, alternating between them, until you know which one works best for you. Then, exclusively practice the one you prefer. At the initial stages, practice circular breathing sitting in a comfortable position, in a peaceful environment. Once you master this breathing method, it can be used in any environment, with any body posture. <u>If you train regularly, it will kick in automatically, rather than being something you must think about</u>. In essence, your breath itself becomes your center: not your body posture, not the situation in which you find yourself, and not the quality of the relationship you may have with the family member.

> Circular breathing is *not* a "time-out" where you take a few deep breaths and then return to the subject, refreshed. There's no time for that in a crisis. On the contrary, you can be moving very fast while breathing very slowly. You are training your body and mind to go into this breathing as a response to danger and stress, a trained response that should be instantaneous. You are practicing to develop a "pseudo-instinct" – a trained response so bone deep that you do not even have to think about it, anymore than you have to tell yourself to yank your hand from a hot stove.
>
> As someone who has practiced circular breathing for more than thirty years, I can assert that it has become automatic. Unlike in my younger days when the adrenalin would hit and I'd start breathing fast and high in the chest, now my breathing usually slows down in emergency situations.

Circular Breathing Method #1

- Sit comfortably, feet on the floor, hands in your lap.
- Sit relaxed, but upright. Do not slump or twist your posture.
- Keep your eyes open. (*As you practice, so you will do.*) If you practice with your eyes closed, your newly trained nervous system will send an impulse to close your eyes in emergency situations. If you want to use a breathing method for closed-eye guided imagery or relaxation – to get *away* from your problems, so to speak – use another method altogether.
- Breathe in through the nose.
- Imagine the air traveling in a line down the front of your body to a point 2 inches below the navel.
- Momentarily pause, letting the breath remain in a dynamic equilibrium.
- Without straining or holding the breath, exhale through your nose.
- As you exhale, imagine the air looping around your lower body, between your legs, and up through the base of your spine.
- As you continue to exhale, imagine the air going up your spine and around your head and then out of your nose.

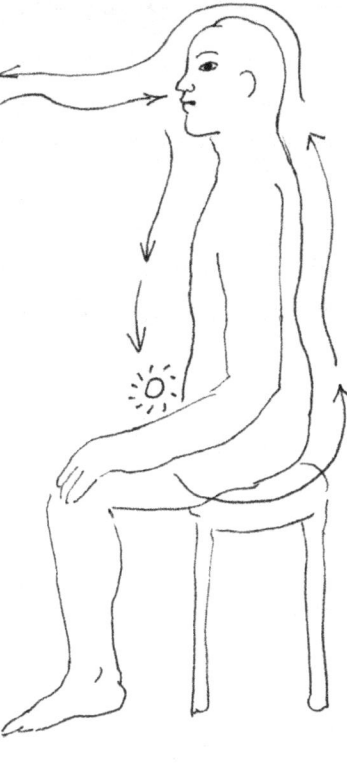

Circular Breathing Method #2

- Sit comfortably, feet on the floor, hands in your lap.
- Sit relaxed, but upright. Do not slump or twist your posture.
- Keep your eyes open. (*As you practice, so you will do.*) If you practice with your eyes closed, your newly trained nervous system will send an impulse to close your eyes in emergency situations. If you want to use a breathing method for closed-eye guided imagery or relaxation – to get *away* from your problems, so to speak – use another method altogether.
- Breathe in through the nose.
- Imagine the air around the head, looping down the back, falling down each vertebrae, continuing down past the base of the spine to the perineum, and looping again, this time up the front of the body to a point 2 inches below the navel.
- Momentarily pause, letting the breath remain in a dynamic equilibrium.
- Without straining or holding the breath, exhale through your nose.
- As you exhale, imagine the air ascending up the centerline of your body and out your nose.

How to Practice Circular Breathing

Some people find it helpful to imagine that their breath has light or color. Others take a finger or object to trace a line down and around the centerline of the body to help focus their attention. Choose the variation that works better for you.

When you first practice, sit and get balanced. Begin to practice the method you have chosen in calm situations: while driving, for example, or reading the newspaper. Don't regard this as a huge task, like getting in shape or memorizing long passages in a book – simply do it several minutes at a time.

Once you develop some skill, try circular breathing while standing, leaning, or even walking. You will soon be able to use this breathing in any posture and under any circumstance. Most people find that after a short time they do not need to visualize the circulation of the breath. You literally will feel it, a ring of energy running through your body. You begin to feel balanced and ready for anything.

Once you are comfortable with your chosen breathing pattern, experiment with it in slightly stressful circumstances, like being caught in traffic or stuck in the supermarket check-out line, with the person in front of you painstakingly counting out change and coupons. Try it also when afflicted with anxiety: stage fright, a meeting with your boss, or a discussion with a family member who always seems to put you off balance. When you can better manage yourself in these slightly aggravating or anxiety-provoking situations, you are ready to use it in a crisis situation. If you have practiced enough, you will shift into this mode of breathing when you find yourself in a crisis, without even thinking about it. You will no longer need to tell yourself to "do" circular breathing. It will become reflexive, automatic, replacing old patterns of breathing that actually increased anxiety or anger within you.

Remember, this is a skill to use during emergencies, not for relaxation or meditative purposes. Instead, you are trying to develop an "omni-directional potential energy." You are ready to fight, to dodge, to leave, to think gracefully and intelligently -- whatever is required for the situation at hand.

When Should You Use Circular Breathing?

The way you physically organize affects your thinking. For example, if you maintain the posture and breathing of a depressed person (slumped body, shallow breathing, sighing), you actually start to feel depressed. Similarly, if you clench your fists and glare around you with tension in your body, you start to feel angry. (You have probably observed people work themselves up in just this way). Circular breathing is used to create an adaptable mind-set in which you are equally prepared for an easy conversation or for an emergency, yet fixed on neither.

This breathing method is helpful when you are *anticipating* a crisis situation, perhaps when you are expecting a troublesome conversation with your family member. This breathing activates the entire nervous system in a way that enhances both creativity and the ability to survive.

Even in the middle of a confrontation, particularly a verbal one, there are many times when this breathing will have a very powerful effect. Not only do we get more stressed or upset in the presence of an upset person, but we also become more peaceful in the presence of a calm one. Using this breathing method is a vital tool in making you the latter type, a man or woman of quiet power.

You should use this breathing method after the crisis is resolved as well. Circular breathing will bring you back to a calm and relaxed state -- prepared to handle the next crisis, should one occur -- and enable you to go on with your day <u>without carrying the crisis with you</u>.

Breathing for Healing from Trauma or Warding off Traumatic Reactions

Circular breathing, along with a particular method of imagery work, is an effective method of warding off the effects of potentially traumatic event.

Post-traumatic stress is not defined by how horrible the event sounds in description, but by the victim's response to the event. PTSD is not exactly a problem of memory: it is a problem because the event has not fully *become* a memory. The event is still primarily experienced as if it were happening right now.

Or think of a trauma as a scar: It may not be pretty, and it certainly is a signpost that something significant happened, but it no longer hurts. A trauma, on the other hand, is an open wound. In PTSD, the person's nervous system is set to react as if there were an emergency whenever the trauma is recalled. This can be anything from an explicit memory to a small reminder: For example, although you do not consciously know why, you get anxious every time someone coughs, because your daughter was having an asthma attack right before another family member attempted suicide. Unconsciously, you react to each cough as if they are about to make another suicide attempt.

Because trauma affects the brain at the deepest, most primitive levels, those associated with survival, logical interventions (anything from reassurance to cognitive therapy) offer only equivocal success in helping people emerge from trauma. Image-associated breathing techniques, which affect the brain as a whole, can assist people in realizing that the event is over, no longer a part of present experience.

How to Do Imagery-associated Breath Work

- Let us imagine that something upsetting has happened to you. Perhaps you even recall an old trauma that still plagues your mind.
- Whenever you think about it (or it intrudes into your consciousness), your body tenses or twists. Your breathing pattern often changes.
- If this is your situation, go someplace where you will not be disturbed for a while. Make the mental image of that trauma as vivid as you can tolerate. This takes some courage, because most of us simultaneously "avoid-as-we-remember." Rather, if only for a moment, meet it head on. Notice, in fine detail, how you physically and emotionally react. As difficult as this may be, it is important to clearly establish what it "does" to you.

- Now take a couple of deep sighs. Sighing breaks up patterns of muscular tension and respiration. This is like rebooting your computer when the program is corrupt.
- Mentally say to the ugly experience, "Hush. You move right over there to my right (or left). I'll get to you in a minute." For some people, it is even helpful to make a physical gesture, "guiding" or "pushing" the experience off to the side. We cannot *force* ourselves to stop thinking about an experience if it has psychological power. Instead, we move it aside, as if we are guiding a wounded person to a waiting room while we organize ourselves to properly deal with them.
- Now initiate your preferred method of circular breathing.
- As the memory creeps back in (and it will), just breathe and center yourself, again placing the memory off to the side. Once again say, "Hush, I'll get to you in a minute." Just ease it aside until you are ready to deal with it.
- When your breathing is smooth and your body is centered, you will be relaxed like an athlete, ready to move but with no wasted effort.
- Deliberately bring that ugly memory or trauma into your thoughts and imagination. As you find yourself reacting, continue circular breathing, trying to bring yourself back to physical balance *while* you focus on the traumatic memory.

> **If facing the trauma is overwhelming:**
> - Focus on one sense at a time: what you heard, smelled, saw, or felt.
> - Focus on the trauma very briefly, and then breathe through the momentary flash of emotion and re-experiencing of the trauma. Do this several times, as if dipping your toe in very cold water, gradually getting acclimated to it, rather than plunging in headfirst.

- Bit by bit, in either one session or a few, you will notice that you are increasingly able to hold the image with a relaxed body and a balanced posture. You are now able to re-experience the memory without the same painful, tense, or distorted response you used in the past. You are, metaphorically speaking, turning the open wound into scar tissue.

Think of how you hold babies so that they are safe: you do not drop or squeeze them so tightly that they are frightened or uncomfortable. To be strong in the face of trauma is very similar in that you internally hold the memory with all the gentle strength with which you hold babies so that they are safe, whether asleep or struggling to see over your shoulder. You are not wiping the slate of memory clean. Rather, you are placing it in a proper context: it is something that happened to you, but it does not define you.

A particular value of circular breathing imagery work: doing for yourself
You can use this method to "inoculate" yourself against stressful, even potentially traumatic, experiences so that life will continue to be enjoyable or will become enjoyable once again, even as you continue to live in a highly stressful family environment. You will begin to develop what author David Grossman calls a "bulletproof mind." The goal is not to restore some kind of mythic "innocence" that you had "pre-trauma." The goal is to relegate the experience to its proper place – something ugly that happened in the past that in no way controls the present.

CHAPTER 7

The Intoxication and Joy of Righteous Anger

Most people consider anger to be a harmful emotion, one that upsets the angry person as well as the recipient. But this is not true for everyone. There are people who, although neither cruel nor hurtful, do not mind fighting, particularly when they believe their cause is just. Such individuals go off center in an interesting way: they get calm, even happy, when someone offends them. Perhaps they may smile and mentally say, "If you want trouble, you came to the right place."

With family, such people have an especially difficult task: they must recognize that when they feel *good*, they are in danger of becoming part of the problem. Instead of imposing calm on a situation, they escalate it. They define the person they are dealing with as the aggressor, and such a "happy warrior" feels completely righteous in responding in kind.

The procedures described here are actually difficult for people who go into righteous rage, because they do not *feel* that there is a problem. Circular breathing (Chapter 6), for example, provides a real sense of peace and relief for those who are anxious, stressed, or frightened. If confrontation feels good to you, however, such calming breathing seems like the last thing you would like to do. You think, "Center myself? Hell, no. I'm right where I want to be."

The righteously angry person may be known for this type of reaction, but he or she is the one most likely to *not* recognize this, and *not* believe they need to do any breathing or calming. If this is you, recognize it! If this is another family member, alert them to this flaw in their skills, because this type of attitude puts other family members at severe risk.

This is not about becoming some sort of Zen sage, never angered, never off-balance. Of course, you will at times be angry. In many situations you *should* be angry. It may even keep you alive. The problem is when anger justifies anything from treating aggravating or troublesome family members with contempt to actions that are either overly harsh or truly not in anyone's best interest.

CHAPTER 8

A Fair Witness

Feelings of helplessness, guilt, or shame isolate us terribly; it is as if we are exiled from the human family. Caring for someone with a chronic illness is hard in the best of times. It is far more painful when your loved one refuses to listen to you, and acts in ways that makes their symptoms even more severe. Even worse, they may become aggressive or even violent toward you.

During such stressful times, you sometimes need to be able to rely on someone who can give you good advice. You may have a problem for which no advice can help. In these times, you need a "fair witness."

Fair witnesses are people who know you, who care for you, and who simply can hear you out. They are not people upon whom you vent. They are people to whom you can speak, who don't offer gratuitous advice, criticism, or judgment. Instead, they simply stay with you in the presence of your pain. They ensure that you are not alone.

It may be necessary for you to educate people close to you how to be a fair witness. Here is an example of what you might say to someone whom you wish would fulfill the role of fair witness:

Example: Talking with someone about being a fair witness
"I've been having a hard time these last few months. I need your help, but not necessarily in the way you may think. What is most difficult for me is having no one I can simply talk with about what it's like caring for Anna. Everybody thinks I'm asking for advice. If I want advice, I *will* ask for it. I'll say something like, 'Hey, let me bounce some ideas off of you. I don't know what to do about this problem – would you give me some feedback?' But that's not what I need most of the time. I need not to feel so alone. I need someone I care about to just hear me out. Sometimes I get so angry, so frustrated, or so damn sad, and I just need to say it to someone without worrying what that person thinks of me. I promise I'm not going to dump my problems on you. I just need someone to be truly with me sometimes, maybe to let me know that there's nothing to do but keep on doing what I'm doing. Maybe you can help me see the absurdity, the humor when I've forgotten how. Will you be that for me, my friend? If I ever get out of line or ask too much, I trust you to let me know. I don't want a counselor. I just want you to help me stay standing by hearing me out."

SECTION II

Communication with People with Unusual, Intense, or Eccentric Styles

CHAPTER 9

Tell It Like It Is: Communication with Concrete Thinkers

Concrete thinkers have a lot of difficulty, or even a complete inability, to understand metaphors, slang, or imagery. Instead, they take everything you say literally. Here are some examples:

- "Way to go!" an expression meant as praise. The concrete individual thinks, "I'm not going anywhere." Or "Where?" Or, "Do they want me to leave now?"
- "Don't give me any attitude," an expression that means that the person shouldn't be oppositional or aggressive. The concrete individual thinks, "I'm not giving them anything," or "My attitudes are mine. How do I give them?"
- "What a beautiful evening. With that sunset, the sea was like a burning pool of molten gold!" The concrete individual is worried that the sea is made of fiery liquid metal.
- "OK. So you don't have to worry any more. The nurse will be here shortly. I want you to hold the cloth on your arm and press it really firmly so that you don't bleed. Just look in my eyes. Listen to what I'm saying. The nurse will be here in just a minute."

Consider this last example: The potential that you may add to their confusion is huge! It would be far more effective to break your communication up into single items. Your tone of voice should be firm, calm, reassuring. Repeat phrases when they have not registered it the first time. <u>Shouting to "get through" to the person will only make things worse</u>.

Example: Communication with someone who is a concrete thinker
- The nurse is coming.
- Hold the cloth hard on your arm.
- Yes, really hard.
- I know you are bleeding. I'm holding the cloth on your leg, and you hold the one on your arm.
- Good. Hold the cloth on your arm.
- Hold the cloth on your arm.
- Hold the cloth on your arm.
- I know it's scary. The nurse will be here in a little while. She's going to help you.

Concrete thinkers

You will recognize *concrete thinkers* because they take what you say literally. Therefore, be sure to do the following:
- Use clear, short sentences, with a firm, calm voice.
- Give directions using simple, easy-to-understand words.
- Show a minimum of emotion. Don't get irritated when they don't immediately understand you. They respond much more to your *tone* of voice than to *what* you say.

CHAPTER 10

Rigid Personality (Asperger's Syndrome, "High Functioning Autism," and Other Similar Disorders)

Individuals with a "rigid personality" are frequently socially withdrawn, often very intelligent outcasts, who may live their lives mostly in their own home, even their own room. Many are socially active in an online environment. They may have tremendous difficulty negotiating social interactions. They find other people to be incomprehensible, confusing, or threatening. They can have tremendous difficulty understanding what others are thinking or feeling from their facial expressions, body posture, and vocal tone.

Other people, particularly some individuals with schizophrenia, often show a similar combination of "cluelessness" and rigidity in communication with others. Such rigid personalities can become fixated on their own preoccupations and imagine that everyone else shares them.

> **Example: A child with a rigid personality, fixated on his own preoccupations**
> When asked what he thought the bully, who was beating him up, was thinking, a child with Asperger's syndrome said, "Oh, he was thinking of Lewis and Clark." When asked why the bully would be thinking of that, the child replied, "What else could he be thinking about? Lewis and Clark took the greatest journey." It was a good ten minutes before the caregiver could direct him to a new subject.

They can also be very literal or concrete (Chapter 9) and they can get obsessive, stuck on thoughts and behaviors (Chapter 13). Some are simply not interested in or aware of other's feelings. This can lead them to be very blunt, or painfully honest. When you do not understand right away what they are talking about, they might call you stupid, not out of malice, but in their way of thinking, it is something that anyone would understand. A famous mathematician who clearly had this personality type was well known for saying of rival theories, "That's so stupid it's not even wrong."

Examples: Socially clueless, unintentionally hurtful communication
- "What is that on your face? Rosacea, I'm guessing, unless it's some kind of rash. You better hope it is a rash because there's no cure for rosacea and it just gets worse and worse. Many people end up with deformed faces because of it."
- "You've gained a lot of weight in the last year. I don't mind, but many men think that is disgusting."

When attempting to calm a person who displays a rigid personality, stating and reiterating the rules is the first method of intervention. State each rule in a matter-of-fact way, as if simply providing information. Follow up with a logical sequence of steps to resolve their problem. Rules are reassuring to someone who finds human interactions chaotic or confusing. Think of the lights imbedded in the floor of an airplane that show the way in an emergency. Rules serve the same function for the rigid person. <u>When you set such limits, do not scold! Keep your voice calm and matter-of-fact.</u>

Example: Explaining the rules
"Carl, the rule when we are eating is that you turn off the computer. I understand that you also are concerned about sunspot activity and its effect on the weather. But we have a rule in the house to stop other activities until after dinner. Carl, I understand you think that sunspots are dangerous, but the rule is to eat first and do research afterward."

Example: Sequence of de-escalation for a person who demonstrates a rigid personality
Pavel: "Someone has taken my book! No one is allowed to touch my book or any of my things! Someone is going to get socked right now!"

Family caregiver: "Pavel, I want to hear about this, but the rule is no yelling in our house. Stop yelling, and tell me about your book."

Pavel: "But I want to yell. I am very angry."

Family caregiver: "But you must not yell. It is against the rules here."

Pavel: "I think that is a stupid rule! I am angry and want to yell."

Family caregiver: "It is still the rule. Stop shouting and we will talk."

> Pavel *(in a quiet voice, but clenching his fists and pounding them together)*: "I'm really mad about my book. Someone took it."
>
> Family caregiver: "Pavel, I really want to hear about this, but you must remember that we have another rule. No pounding your fists together."
>
> Pavel: "That is another stupid rule."
>
> (Eventually, Pavel sits and talks quietly.)
>
> Family caregiver: "You are really upset about not knowing where your book is. You are also upset that someone may have borrowed it or touched it. Let's go to your room and look for it."

- Be prepared for nit-picking arguments about exceptions to the rules, special conditions, and so on. The person is *not* trying to play games here: he or she is just trying to be as specific as possible so that they can figure out exactly how to act. At times, you will feel like you are having a discussion with a very obsessive lawyer.
- Give them detailed concrete instructions when they are confused or upset.
- Do not try to validate their feelings. Even more so, do not talk about your own feelings. As described above, other people – and particularly their feelings – are the most incomprehensible thing in the universe to people on the autistic spectrum.
- Stay very logical – give just the facts!

> Do your best to avoid physical contact, particularly in heated moments. Many folks with rigid personalities detest even the lightest touch and can react violently.

Some people with rigid personalities who do not want to hurt or hit anyone still need a way to discharge tension. Without such an option, they feel like they are going to explode. They can go to a safe room and yell for a while, or pound a heavy bag or pillow, and then return to solve the problem. However, please refer to the discussion on venting in Chapter 44. It is only through careful work together and a long-term relationship that you will learn if such a strong expression of emotions is actually calming or if it is stimulating – leading to dangerous escalation.

> **Review: Communication with rigid personalities**
>
> You will recognize the family member with a rigid personality because they get stuck on subjects that seem rather odd in relation to the current circumstances. Furthermore, they seem out-of-sync with society and unconscious of their effect on others. When calming or de-escalating these family members, you should follow these steps:
> 1. State the rules in a matter-of-fact way, as if providing information.
> 2. Follow up with a logical sequence of steps to solve their problem.
> 3. Caution: validating their feelings will very likely confuse and distress them, as will talking about *your* feelings.

CHAPTER 11

Information Processing and Retention: Consolidating Gains

Being mentally ill requires considerable survival skills. Imagine trying to stand upright in a windstorm, or trying to have all your conversations in noisy restaurants, no matter how important the subject. One skill that many mentally ill people develop is the art of "faking normal." People around them may do things that the mentally ill person perceives as frightening, but they don't show their fear. Other people may anger them, but they smile and pretend everything is all right. Conversations and ideas may be too complex, too fast, too metaphoric or irrelevant to them, but they have learned to pick up the rhythm of the other person's speech, nod at the right moments, smile or laugh when needed, and agree with the tag lines that invite such agreement.

Therefore, it is important when you are trying to pass on information to your loved ones to never assume that they understand just because they have either said that they do or nodded at the right moment. You need to check to see that you do, in fact, understand one another. There are several ways to do this:

The least effective method is to repeat yourself, using other words. If they have either tuned you out or didn't understand you the first time, they may merely fake understanding again. You *will* know if this is a good approach with your family member if you get the desired response.

> This is different from the repetition you must do with the latent (Chapter 22) or concrete thinker (Chapter 9), when you *should* repeat yourself when giving instructions. In those cases, you are repeating yourself to help the person track what you are saying. But when trying to check if the person *did* understand what you said, simply repeating yourself and assuming the other person understood is often a mistake.

Have your family member repeat back your instructions. This, too, can be problematic, because some people may simply echo what you are saying without any comprehension.

Ask open-ended questions,, which is more helpful than asking questions that contain the answer. If you say, "So, you will call your doctor tomorrow, won't you?" they may agree with you, hoping to please you. Instead ask, "What are you going to do tomorrow?"

Use open sentences.. "So, Diane, if I've got it right, I will call your doctor tomorrow and explain the problem. And you will . . ." Of course, you hope that she will fill in the rest of the sentence. If not, you have some more explaining to do.

Write down the most important points. Many people do not assimilate a lot of information that they hear, no matter how hard they listen. In these situations, you may find that writing the most important points of your conversation on a 3 x 5 card is beneficial to their understanding. You give them the card, review the points, and tell them to check the card if they have difficulty remembering what to do.

Review: How to consolidate gains
- Although sometimes useful, the least effective way is to simply repeat yourself, hoping that their replies really mean that they understand.
- Have the family member repeat back your instructions.
- Use open sentences and questions, allowing the family member to fill in the blanks.
- Write down on a card the most important points of understanding as a reference.

CHAPTER 12

Coping with Stubborn Refusals

There may be something that your family member should do – either by himself or with you – but he stubbornly refuses. It would not be surprising if you started bossing him around, but this often makes things worse. All people, mentally ill or not, have pride, and they don't like another person talking down to them or controlling their lives. Most people will "fight back" when they think they are being oppressed, and being bossed around feels like one is living in a dictatorship in one's own home.

Nonetheless, there are many occasions when, despite treating your family member with respect and understanding, they refuse to comply with requests and rules. For example, a family member won't take her medications, respect others' right to speak during a family meeting, fill out paperwork, or comply with treatment recommendations.

Once you are clear that your approach is not creating the problem, how can you elicit compliance?

Focus on the task at hand and do not take the impasse personally. Taking things personally makes the situation much more difficult to solve.

Clarify the message. Be clear about what you each need to do now. Do not bring in previous examples of their noncompliance, such as "the last time this happened," or "you always," or "remember when you . . ." Focus on the immediate problem.

Stay on topic. Do not allow the person to divert your attention to unrelated issues. Simply say, "We can talk about that later, but right now . . ."

Use a strong and calm voice. Make your tone of voice strong but not forceful or aggressive.

Depersonalize your role in the interactions. Rather than saying, "Josiah, I expect you to . . ." try saying, "Josiah, you know you are expected to . . ." or "The rules of the house are . . ."

State the consequences. Consequences are *not* punishment designed to break the other person's will or *make* him do what you want. Consequences should be provided as "information," rather than threat, the same way you inform someone on a cold winter day, "If you stick your tongue on that metal pole, you are going to get stuck." Or, in a situation more specific to problems you may have with your loved one, you might state, "If you do not take your medications, you will have to talk about that today with your case manager."

Place the power in their hands. Without handing over your authority, allow your family member to be the decision maker, clarifying their role in complying or not complying with your request or directive. After summing up the situation, say something like, "It looks like you've got something to decide. You are absolutely correct. You don't have to do it. You can attend the parenting class, which the court will look favorably upon, and you will learn something in the process, or you can continue to refuse to go, which is something you are free to do. You will surely be asked to explain that to the judge during your next court hearing in June." If, at this point, you simply stand and look at him, it can be interpreted as a challenge. <u>Instead, ease back, ease away, and give him some time to think</u>. Perhaps you can say, "Let me know when you've made up your mind about what you want to do." Be sure to thank the person if he does comply.

Be careful: If you have found your relative's resistance to be frustrating, your "thank you" can easily sound sarcastic.

Review: Coping with stubborn refusals
- Observe your behavior: Make sure you are not being domineering or authoritarian.
- Do not take the impasse personally.
- Clarify the message.
- Stay on topic.
- Use a calm and strong voice.
- De-personalize your role.
- State the consequences.
- Place the power in their hands.
- Thank your relative when the task is finished.

CHAPTER 13

Stuck: Coping with Repetitive Demands, Questions, and Obsessions

Your family member may make repetitive demands for information that you have already answered or explained in exhaustive detail. There can be a variety of reasons for this, and each should be dealt with in a different manner:

They become "stuck" in an obsessive thought or idea. No matter how many times you answer their question, they have to ask it again. This is often a sign of obsessive-compulsive disorder (OCD), a condition frequently missed by evaluators because, due to the embarrassing nature of this affliction, people can become skilled at covering it up. It is important to help them get professional assistance specific to this disorder. In some cases, you will contact the proper mental health service provider yourself if they are unable to do so on their own.[5]

Others obsess as part of a disorder like schizophrenia, developmental disability, or other serious impairments of cognition. These individuals are not playing games; they have cognitive deficits that cripple their ability to understand and/or retain information. If they ask the questions because they either forgot or didn't understand the answer, it is most reasonable to answer them again. Do this in a matter-of-fact tone and not sarcastically. It can get very wearing to answer the same questions over and over, and sometimes that weariness can show up in our voice and facial expression if we are not careful. If they are not able to retain the information, please refer to the information in Chapter 11.

Some people repeat a question *intending* to be irritating or challenging. In a bland tone of voice, simply say, "You already know the answer to that," or otherwise calmly point out that they already have the information, and *move on*, either physically or by changing the subject. If you linger after you respond, particularly while holding eye contact, it can be seen as a challenge, as if to say, "So how do you like my answer, huh?" By disengaging, you are saying, "I'm not participating in the game."

Sometimes the person is genuinely pleading for information, but what they really want to know is "behind" the question they are asking. For example, your family member may have already asked five times, "Is my case manager coming to visit today?" You answer, "You are really worried about this, even though I've told you he's coming at four o'clock. What's different about Jack coming today?" Then, and not before, she reveals that yesterday she picked up his glasses to try them on, and she broke them. She is worried that Jack will be mad when he arrives.

Sometimes, people *perseverate*, meaning they get stuck on a subject and feel like they have to talk about it. If your loved one has a topic about which they regularly obsess, you might say this: "I know this is very important to you, and you want to talk about this and ask me questions. But you also know I have a lot of things to do. I will make you an agreement. We will talk about this for ten minutes every day, right after breakfast. But it will be ten minutes only. I will listen carefully and answer your questions, but you have to think hard to decide exactly what you want to talk about each day, because at the end of ten minutes, I'll say 'time,' and that's it for that day." What is most important is that at the end of the imposed time limit, you firmly end the conversation or questioning for that day. With some people, you can agree upon two or three time periods a day. What is most important, though, is to hold exactly to the time.

> **Summary: Helping someone with obsessive concerns**
> - If they are showing symptoms of obsessive-compulsive disorder, arrange a professional assessment for them, as this disorder requires specific treatment.
> - If they are repeating themselves due to cognitive impairments, do whatever you can to help them understand or remember.
> - If they are using such an interaction as a control tactic to make you repeat what they already know, refuse to participate.
> - Listen for the meaning behind the question and address their *real* concern.

CHAPTER 14

The Need for Reassurance

Many mentally ill people are quite anxious. Suffering from anxiety is living as if something that you are afraid might occur *is happening right now,* or living with feelings of imminent doom. For example, your family member reads about an earthquake in Japan and imagines what it might be like if that happened in their home town, and suddenly, they feel as horrible as if the ground has started shaking right beneath their feet.

You must draw a graceful line with your loved one. Despite what may be considerable sympathy that you feel, do not coddle them. If you treat them like they are too weak or fragile for this world, they will very likely believe you. They may think that something awful is going to happen and that is why you are talking in such careful tones. If you are too dismissive of their fears, however, you will alienate them, making them feel that much more abandoned. Part of true reassurance is *assurance* that you take your relative seriously, but do not indulge in what is weakest in them.

> **Helping someone afflicted with anxiety**
> - Do not treat them like they are fragile.
> - Do not make your voice "overconfident," or "jovial," or in any other manner be dismissive of their concerns.
> - Talk with them about their worries, using a confident voice that makes the person feel stronger for listening.

CHAPTER 15

Dealing with Individuals with Pronounced Mood Swings

These individuals, whose behavior is sometimes referred to as labile, are angry one minute, sad the next, and happy the next. Those diagnosed with borderline personality disorder, bipolar disorder, or neurological damage, be it from traumatic brain injury or traumatic levels of drug abuse, often display labile modes.

Such people can be hard to communicate with because as you try to deal with one mood, they may have already switched to another one. Just when you think you have achieved a moment of success, your family member may shift to anger, panic, or any other extreme emotion.

They often try to gain control over us even when they have no control over themselves, through verbal abuse, provocative statements, complaining, passive aggression, blaming, apologies that are quickly retracted or denied, and ingratiation – all interspersed with periods when they are friendly or loving.

Coping with Mood Swings

Rather than responding to the family member's momentary moods, either verbally or with body language that suggests your own anger or frustration, you must remain balanced and emotionally nonreactive (Section I). The more you are unaffected by their emotional storms, the more likely it is that they will calm down. Remember the teachers you had in grade school who, when they walked into the room, calmed the children just by their presence? The children didn't even know *why* they calmed down. This is an "active" calm that provides a sense of safety and stability within the people around you.

> **Review: Mood swings**
> - Do not mirror their emotional state or allow them to elicit from you an inappropriate emotional response.
> - Remain powerfully calm.
> - Speak in a firm, yet calm and controlled manner.
> - Use de-escalation tactics as presented in later sections of this book to deal with expressions of aggression.

CHAPTER 16

Moving Past the Past

Some people store up grievances, particularly about old issues within the family. This is even more difficult with mentally ill people, because their memories may be distorted or even delusional. Frequent complaints about the past can become a significant source of conflict within the family. There are a variety of approaches to take:

Acknowledge their concerns. Family members often merely need to express their frustrations or feelings of helplessness, and they view you as the only available outlet to do so. Allowing them to express their feelings (in an appropriate manner) and acknowledging their viewpoint may be enough to alleviate their anger. Do not agree or disagree with them, or otherwise reinforce their feelings of persecution, just recognize their complaints and then move forward.

Apologize. When your family member complains, yet again, about something directly concerning you, think about it carefully. Perhaps, in this instance, you *were* wrong. If so, apologize sincerely and fully. In some situations, this is enough. However, <u>you should be wary of apologizing to a family member merely as a means of moving them off a specific subject or grievance</u>. An apology may lead the family member to believe they are now in control of the relationship, and that you will act cautiously so you don't upset them in the future.

What if an apology is not enough? Some people *perseverate* – they continue to bring up a complaint over and over again.
- You may say to the family member, "You are still upset about this. You want to talk about it again, don't you?" Notice that you don't ask the family member – you merely state your understanding. This is empowering because they have the opportunity to correct or adjust your understanding. At the same time, you are probably right, and thereby, you demonstrate that you understand them. This, alone, is very powerful.
- If you are aware that the family member has a legitimate, unresolved complaint, firmly and kindly say, "Tomas, I said I am sorry and I meant it. I will never do anything like that again. You don't have to worry about that." From this point, you have a number of alternatives. One option is *paraphrasing* (see Chapter 42) to try to ascertain if there is more that is disturbing your family member, because logically speaking, the proper response to an individual's complaint or grievance *is* an apology.

Complaints are their own reward. Certain people are never satisfied because the complaint becomes a "rewarding" activity in itself. Others bear a pervasive resentment toward you, an institution, or even life itself. In these cases, simply take the issue off the table, permanently. Remind them that you have already addressed this complaint, so there is nothing more to discuss. However, other folks are simply not satisfied: the complaint becomes a rewarding activity in itself. In this case, firmly and kindly say, "I really do not have anything more I can say. I am sorry but I won't talk about it any more. I hope one day you will accept my apology."

One complaint after another. Some people bear a general resentment toward a family member, and even sincere apologies fuel more complaints. For that reason, apologize only for that which you are sorry for – not for things you think you are right about or things that are beyond your control. .For example, your relative might say, "OK, so you apologized about not letting me go to the prom. You really didn't want me ever to have a boyfriend. Remember the time you said Billy was no good for me just because he'd been arrested?" You may offer a response like this:

"Jenny, I am sorry for hurting your feelings before the prom. I spoke very harshly. I'm sorry for that. I'm not sorry, however, that I wouldn't let you go out with Billy because of his criminal record. I'm also not sorry that I didn't let him into the house; he was drunk and I don't let drunken people into the house. Even so, I am sad that you missed the prom: you looked forward to that. Given the circumstances, I did the best I could at the time, and that is what I am doing right now too." In other words, an apology should not compromise your standards.

> **Review: Moving past the past**
> 1. Acknowledge their concerns.
> 2. If you were wrong, sincerely apologize.
> 3. When family members are stuck on an issue
>   - Validate the family member's continued distress.
>   - Reiterate a necessary apology, emphatically, with reassurance.
> 4. When complaints are their own reward, set a firm limit and take the issue "off the table."
> 5. If complaining becomes a "rewarding" activity in itself, firmly and kindly set limits. When one complaint follows another, give a "specific" apology, without compromising your own standards.

CHAPTER 17

"Would You Just Get off Your Rear End?"
Coping with Lack of Motivation

You've surely been in situations where you ask or even tell your family member to do something, particularly something that is necessary for their well-being, and they stare vacantly at you, voice a million questions, express misgivings or anxiety, or drift into a monologue about something completely different. Other mentally ill family members seem to lack motivation; they just won't do what *we* think is good for them.

In such cases, you must first ask is if the family member is truly capable of doing what you think they should do, or if they even understand what you are asking. You may want them to participate in a group meeting at the mental health center, but they suffer from terrible social anxiety and being so close to other people makes them miserable. They may be happier alone, and, in fact, will be far more likely to comply with the rest of their treatment if they are allowed to do maintain their solitude. This may not be the life you desire for your family member, but this is who they are.

You must also ask yourself if what you want them to do is really important. For example, your family member would look so much nicer if he wore different clothes, but he doesn't see it that way.
- Perhaps he hates the feel of certain material on his hypersensitive skin.
- Maybe he doesn't want to look well dressed. He reveals that he is afraid that if he looks handsome, strange women will bother or sexually harass him.
- Perhaps he feels terribly unsafe when he goes out of the home – yet he bravely does that every day so that he can go to his place of employment. Added attention might make him feel so uneasy that he will quit his job.

On the other hand, if you do for your mentally ill loved one what he could do for himself, he may become quite comfortable in his dependency. It is an easy life when someone takes care of you.

Finally, you should note how you attempt to motivate your family member. Do you like the sound of your voice? Are you pleading, whining, nagging, yelling, or making other unattractive sounds? Offer advice in a firm tone of voice, and neither hover nor sound like a "cheerleader" to get him to comply. When you are dignified, your family member will respect you more, sometimes in spite of himself. People are far more likely accept advice from a person they respect.

> **Review: Coping with a family member's lack of motivation**
> - Ascertain if they are capable of complying with your request or directive.
> - Is it really important?
> - Do not do for others what they can do for themselves.
> - Have you lost your dignity in the way that you are trying to get them to comply? Act in a manner that merits respect.

CHAPTER 18

"If There Is a Problem, that Would Be Your Fault": Useful Tactics for Dealing with Symptoms of Paranoia and Persecutory Delusions

> This chapter focuses on tactics specific to paranoia. Rather than the delusional state (Chapter 24), this discussion will focus on an attitude: a sense of being persecuted, blaming others for problems, and a hair-trigger sensitivity to being vulnerable. The delusional paranoid individual has this attitude complicated by fixed false beliefs and even hallucinations.

Understanding Paranoia and Persecution

It can be terribly difficult to live with someone who is experiencing paranoia. A sense of persecution is only part of the paranoid dilemma. The paranoid world is a contradiction of dominance and submission. The paranoid individual often tries to dominate other people in their lives, and all the while they are terrified or enraged at the thought of being forced to submit to anyone else. This is a primitive defense mechanism that can be summed up in a phrase: "If there is a problem here, that would be your fault."

Paranoia refers not only to a psychotic or delusional state, but also to the far more common paranoid character, in which the person has a consistent attitude of blame, resentment of authority, fear of vulnerability, and expectations of betrayal. <u>Stimulant users, notably those addicted to methamphetamine and cocaine, frequently display these behaviors.</u>

People experiencing paranoia are, at core level, very frightened, but they cover this up with suspicion and aggression. Paranoid people are "counter-phobic"; they are aggressive toward what they are afraid of. Imagine your family member like a big, angry porcupine. They feel excruciatingly vulnerable, having no quills on their underside, so to speak, so they try to keep their backs to you all the time, hunched over and ready to strike in hair-trigger reaction. On the other hand, some paranoid people may be very ingratiating, perceiving you as possessing a kind of power they want to ally themselves with, so that they can better defeat their enemies or "control you from below." In the latter case, the paranoid person tells you that you are the boss, so that you *think* you have control, but when you let your attention slip, the paranoid person can do what he wants.

When healthy people care for another person, they feel both vulnerable and powerful. Paranoid people, however, experience love, evoking feelings of vulnerability, as an attack. For this reason, paranoid people are particularly volatile within their families. Paranoid family members are torn. When they feel comfortable, they also recoil, because those loving feelings of affection or trust might make them vulnerable. Assuming that you might be "out to get them," they figure they might as well get it over with, so they start to use provocative, ugly language, so that you, in response, show your "true colors."

You should, therefore, be prepared for the family member to suddenly act out with suspicion or accusations during times that are uneventful or even friendly. It is as if their quills, the paranoid defenses that they believe keep them safe, are softening as they relax.

Being mistaken is another form of vulnerability. Often not admitting to wrongdoing or error, they automatically *project* negative feelings onto others. If, for example, they feel hate, they believe, "You hate me." If they have difficulty in understanding an application for public assistance, they might say, "I wouldn't have messed it up if it hadn't been for you. I shouldn't have trusted you." If you don't understand what they are saying, paranoid people assume you are pretending, denying that you are ignorant or wrong.

Individuals experiencing paranoia live in their own world like detectives, searching for clues and evidence to prove what they already know is true. They may have *ideas of reference*, in which they believe that others' conversations, glances, or actions are directed at them, and no amount of arguing will dissuade them. They assume that others are probably conspiring against them, talking about them, and laughing at them; their actions, in response to this belief, often evoke the behavior they fear.

When people in paranoid states are afraid, they often attack, either verbally or physically. Even without an overt attack, they frequently make other people uncomfortable because of their aggressive or standoffish behavior. If they sense fear in you, however, due to the emotions they have evoked by their own behavior, they expect you to attack, and they will then "attack you back first." It is important, therefore, to master your anxiety and fear so that you do not betray your feelings with trembling hands, a shaking voice, or an inability to hold eye contact. Circular breathing, described in Chapter 6, is invaluable to this end.

Try to Let Them Know What Is Going On

Because these family members are suspicious, they will often question your actions and instructions. Whenever you can, tell them what you are doing. Better yet, show them:

> "Arnie, I was writing the grocery list. See. Milk, eggs, and butter. I was just about to write the vegetables I'm going to buy."

USEFUL TACTICS FOR DEALING WITH SYMPTOMS OF PARANOIA AND PERSECUTORY DELUSIONS

At the same time, you should not accept incessant quizzing. You are not required to explain every action. You will have to learn to strike a balance. Sometimes it is quite right to simply say, "Kent, I've answered enough questions today." Or "Amy, I've told you everything I know."

Personal Space – Physical and Psychological – with the Paranoid Individual

Paranoid individuals feel safest when you differentiate yourself from them, so that you are not interwoven in their delusional fears. A more distant, impersonal relationship is preferable to a warm and friendly one. Essentially, you imagine yourself in a dance – like a waltz, without contact – three arm's lengths apart. The "proper" distance is one that does not unnecessarily trigger fear and anger. Remember that the paranoid person can get lonely, just like anyone else. It is your responsibility, however, to maintain the "space," stepping back, metaphorically or actually, when they get too close. This is better, in the long run, than trying to seize an opportunity when they let their guard down to make your relationship "closer."

> **Example: "Feeling too close" for a paranoid person**
> Imagine a nice day, a barbecue perhaps, with everyone in the family relaxed, laughing, and telling stories. Elizabeth, who is afflicted with many paranoid delusions, is also having a good time. She is sitting in a chair in the sun, laughing. You haven't seen her like this in months – her face open, the light gleaming on her hair. You feel like she has returned to you, as she was before her illness. You feel close to her, and she seems relaxed among the family. Warning! You watch and sense that she realizes she's let down her guard and feels vulnerable. Suddenly, her face snaps into a familiar glare. When a five-year-old grandchild bumps her leg, she yells: "Theo is the worst child I've ever seen. He tried to stomp on my leg. You've raised him like a hoodlum and soon he'll be smoking crack with the other hoodlums!" Not surprisingly, Theo's mother and father rise to the child's defense, and the party is ruined.

Many individuals with paranoia are preoccupied, even obsessed, with fears that they will be invaded, violated, or controlled. Some find most physical contact, particularly that which is unsolicited, to be noxious. Because of these fears, personal spacing issues are important, particularly for the safety of other family members.

- **Maintain the angle**. Particularly when sitting, turn your body at a slight angle, so that physical "confrontation" is a choice rather than a requirement. If you face a paranoid individual directly, you *force* them to turn away if they don't want to face you. This is true whether you are standing or sitting.
- **Never let your guard down**. This does not require *you* to be at hair-trigger readiness. However, never "take your ease" with a paranoid family member. You live, sadly, in an avalanche zone, and anything could set off another landslide. Rather, be calm and alert.
- **Too close is as dangerous as a threat**. Try to be aware when things are getting too relaxed. You may not be able to stop the family member's sudden anger, but it should not be unexpected. Per-

haps, as in the party described above, it might be time to take the children home, maybe sooner than you would like, but at least it might head off another explosion in front of them.
- **Distance = peace**. There may be situations that activate the person's paranoia: notable are those that either bring up old resentments or are too stimulating. Alcohol can make things worse as well. It may be necessary to have a party without alcohol, and they need to know this before the party. Or, sad to say, perhaps you can no longer have parties with them there.

Paranoid Aggression

There is not a specific "paranoid rage." Instead, paranoia is an engine that drives rage in all its various forms. Paranoid family members can exhibit fear, frustration, intimidation, and manipulation. When such an individual gets in a state of rage (Section IX) you will de-escalate them using tactics specific to the mode of rage they are exhibiting rather than de-escalate paranoia itself.

Some disorganized people can experience an *omni-directional dread*, an inchoate terror that is inescapable. In this case, you will de-escalate them using the principles in Chapter 21 regarding the disorganized family member.

Review: Paranoia and persecution

The paranoid person has an attitude that whatever is wrong is another person's fault. Whether delusional or not, they see others as conspiring against them or persecuting them. They perceive any sense of vulnerability – even the ease of friendship or rapport – as dangerous.
- Use all the standard methods of communication we use for delusional people when speaking with *paranoid* delusional family members.
- Let them know what's going on.
- Avoid emotional and emotive language.
- Be aware of both physical and emotional spacing. Maintain a correct distancing: not too close or too far.
- Maintain your center. The paranoid person is usually assaultive when they feel under attack, perceive you as controlling them, or sense that you are afraid.

SECTION III

A Consideration of People Who Behave
in Ways that Cause Strife Between
Themselves and Other Family Members

CHAPTER 19

Borderline Personality Disorder and Splitting

Borderline personality disorder, like any pathological character trait, is a spectrum disorder, an accentuation of qualities common to all humanity. Any of us can be swept by feelings that seem beyond our control. Any of us can act on feelings that result in our making decisions that are not in our best interest, that may even be damaging to ourselves and others. Sometimes we are impulsive, and sometimes we get angry, even enraged.

The particular dilemma of individuals with borderline personality disorder is that they live in an existential universe: whatever they feel right now is their only reality. What for us are remarkable episodes in a usually calm and focused life are everyday occurrences for the person with borderline personality. Those on the mild end of the spectrum will be quite emotional, overreacting to events that others could take in stride. For those whose disorder is more severe, it is as if their nervous system – at least that which modulates emotion – lacks protective sheathing. Imagine trying to live your daily life with two layers of skin peeled off. Any mundane experience could bring agony.

When life is felt with such exquisite force, one's current emotions are inescapable. The person who has such character traits lives with the passion, but also with the lack of emotional resilience, like that of a toddler. There is considerable evidence that the development of borderline personality disorder is due to a combination of emotional sensitivity (basic disposition) and an abusive/chaotic upbringing. Many have experienced sexual and/or physical abuse as children. It is unknown if the abuse is a precipitant of the development of borderline character traits, or if the prevalence of abuse histories is due to predatory individuals seeking out emotionally sensitive children so that they are abused in greater numbers. However, many people who struggle with borderline symptoms do not have an abuse history or a chaotic family background.

> **If a family member reveals that they have been abused**
> Victims of abuse, particularly those with borderline traits, may frequently raise the subject of their abuse history. Some abuse victims may have learned to use it as a tragic strategy to gain power in interpersonal relationships, because people will "back off" when the subject is raised. For example, a family member who is trying to set a limit feels she is being abusive when the family member cries and accuses her of being just like her father.

> Most people, however, are not manipulative, even unconsciously. They may have been taught in therapy to speak about what is distressing them – and, in particular, what they have learned is the cause of their psychological distress. Many people rush to comfort the person when they raise their history of abuse, particularly if they do so with strong emotions. This indicates that their abuse history has become a means of eliciting comfort. The problem, however, is that nothing is healed: their "wound" is merely reopened, and later, once the comforting person has left to attend to other tasks, the person may feel raw and exposed, or worry that their family member holds them in contempt or will reveal their information. They may then go into a crisis, perhaps even become suicidal.
>
> For this reason, the issue of abuse requires sensitivity:
> - If a family member reveals current abuse, ensure their safety and report the situation to the proper authorities as necessary.
> - If a family member decides that you are trustworthy and reveals, for the first time, a history of physical or sexual abuse, listen with care and respect. Tell the person that you have the utmost respect for the courage it must have taken to reveal this information. Then help them arrange an appointment with a therapist properly trained in abuse issues.

Another aspect of their psyche is an "allergy to ambiguity." They see the world and the people in it as good or bad, perfect or foul. Just like a toddler, there are few grey areas in their lives.

Because of this combination of character traits, individuals with borderline personality disorder often find themselves in crises, including suicide attempts; parasuicidal acts (self-mutilating behaviors or repeat suicide "attempts" that were either gestures for effect or staged in a manner that despite the seriousness of the act, are found out (Chapter 32); impulsive assaultive acts, particularly those involving family or other close relationships; and brief psychotic episodes. In essence, such a person believes that whatever feeling they are having right now is the only possible reality. For example, road rage is a borderline reaction: they get cut off on the freeway, it makes them mad, and instead of cooling down, they chase after them and smash into their car. On the flip side, they may meet someone attractive in a bar, and within five seconds, they know that this is the love of their life.

What Is Splitting?

In reaction to the dramatic and emergent events that so often occur in such individual's lives, many of the people associated with them, including family members, disagree about what is best for them, even to the point of arguing about who is at fault for the current crisis. Those who have tried to educate themselves about borderline personality disorder and abuse tend to explain away or excuse aggressive or manipulative behaviors, especially when their loved one has a previous history of trauma or abuse. When the individuals associated with a borderline person get tangled up in intense disputes about what is best for them, this type of conflict is called *splitting*.

Splitting is a method of defense in which an individual presents a different picture to each person with whom they interact. This "divide and confuse" strategy sets people against each other, keeping the "heat" off the individual in question. The person who uses splitting tries, thereby, to present a "face" that fits each person with whom they are in relationship. This is not a conscious process: think of a television nature show where an octopus swims to a rock and instantaneously creates the rock pattern on his skin, and then, swimming into a bed of kelp, takes on a pattern of wavy green lines.

Splitting, however, is not as straightforward as the octopus' defenses. Splitting is triggered by strong (and usually negative or immature) emotions. People experiencing these strong emotions do not make well-reasoned decisions. Therefore, the behaviors they enact are often a *reaction*. Their reaction can be remarkably inaccurate: for example, a young woman returns home from a date, discouraged because her boyfriend yelled at her. As she enters the home she doesn't realize she's tracking mud on the just-cleaned floor, causing her dad to yell at her to take off her shoes; she reacts that her dad is abusive, just like her boyfriend. They are both men and they both yell! So she screams at her father that he's hated her throughout her life, and she's sick of being so mistreated.

Returning to the example from nature, not all animals use protective coloring to hide. Others are flamboyantly colored to indicate that they are poisonous or taste really bad. Similarly, another way to split people, and thereby to be left alone, is to be so irritating or obnoxious that people stay away.

Splitting is a defense that is often the best a frightened child or an emotionally fragile adult can do to survive in chaotic circumstances. It is ineffective, however, for functioning in normal society. Such a person never learns how to relate to others: they know merely how to react. And, not surprisingly, they are frequently "off base":
- They misinterpret others' intentions.
- They often have a poor grasp of their effect on other people and how to actually speak to them.
- They do not know how to get what they truly desire. Expecting a refusal, the emotionally fragile person will not ask politely for something. Instead, they might try to get it through a guilt trip, a demand, blame, or trickery. They may resent the person who hasn't given them what they want, even though they haven't asked.

Such people are not necessarily resistant to help. In fact, they may have gone tried all kinds of therapy or other treatments, from orthodox to "new age." However, it is as if they have a "nourishment barrier"[6] – even when help is offered, they cannot accept it or perceive accurately that it is there for the taking. Your family member may frequently call 9-1-1 and other crisis lines, and also may often use hospital, mental health, police, and other emergency medical services. Each of the responders may think that they have the best idea about how to deal with your loved one, and this can result in backbiting or out-and-out arguments between individuals or agencies. And all of them may disagree with you.

Example: Splitting

Joanna is insecure about her weight. She is sure that her father is critical as well, although he has never said anything. She complains to her mother about her father's attitude toward her weight. Her mother comforts her. Unfortunately, this pattern, frequently repeated, has taught Joanna to solicit comfort by complaining about being hurt by others. When she finds her fifteen-year-old brother surfing the Internet for risqué photographs, she tells her father, but he doesn't react as she expects. So she exaggerates the nature of the photos, describing them as raw pornography. This angers her father, who snaps at her, "Why didn't you tell me that in the first place?" Her dad stomps off to confront her brother, and she complains to her mother about her father yelling at her. Her mother, rather fed up with Joanna lately, says, "Stop making mountains out of molehills." Joanna, distraught at receiving comfort from neither parent, goes to her room, takes an Exacto knife, and cuts deeply into her arm, as she has done before. Emerging from the bedroom, with blood dripping onto the floor, she stops everything. Her father, berating her brother for the "pornography," is speechless, her brother is terrified, and her mother runs and calls 9-1-1.

People who play out the borderline pattern also "split themselves." They either feel wonderful or terrible, sometimes in rapid successful. They fall in love easily, idealizing as perfect the object of their affections, and fall out of love just as quickly. Once out of infatuation, they often hate their previous lover and can do anything from assault to slander to a suicide attempt. They are passionately happy or passionately miserable.

Splitting is a process, not an act. Other family members and professionals are also *participants* in splitting, and, quite frankly, sometimes the actions of some of these people *create* the splitting process. Not surprisingly, a family member with borderline personality disorder will appear quite different to a mother trying to build a supportive, non-confrontational relationship, than to a father responsible for their financial well-being, and a brother, who is sick of having family vacations cancelled due to his sister's crises. Needless to say, each of these individuals responds to the family member with borderline traits differently, and each may believe that they have the best idea on how to deal with them. Unfortunately, these varying opinions can lead to arguments about the best course of action.

In cases such as these, one or another party may decide to unilaterally make a decision based on what they believe is best for their loved one. However, if all members of the family remain at odds, the "victory" by the person who made the unilateral decision will be short lived. They will most likely continue to be "at odds together." Thus, whenever a family gets intensely at odds regarding a single member, suggest the possibility of splitting and see if you can, by comparing observations, ascertain if the family member with borderline traits interacts differently with various people, this behavior creating the adversarial situation.

A Solution

Intervention with family members who suffer from borderline personality disorder requires several components.

- Stay on task. The information in Section I is absolutely essential for your emotional survival. Your relative will try to get *you* to react by using anger outbursts, accusations, and playing different family members against one another.
- As this is a disorder of emotions, the intervention must focus on these areas. If a child receives attention for negative behavior, he or she will increase such behaviors. So, too, for the individual with borderline character traits. Whenever the individual is disruptive and "acting out," interactions should be matter-of-fact and brief.
- Given that borderline family members are quite reactive to other people's emotions, be like the perfect uncle or aunt. If you maintain a degree of emotional distance, you don't get worked up.
- When the family member begins to show calm, graceful, mature behavior, your emotional interactions with them should be exemplified by more warmth and approval.
- Be prepared for some family members to "flare" when they are treated differently than they desire ("I'm upset and you are not comforting me!" is one example). They may escalate their behaviors, sometimes in very dangerous ways. Like a child who is used to getting what he wants through tantrums, borderline family members must be treated, consistently, with matter-of-fact calm. Although the family member, in the middle of his or her emotional storm, may not agree, kindness and ethics are both best served when you act in a way that will, in the long run, help the family member manage those storms.
- Dialectical-Behavioral Therapy (DBT), pioneered by Dr. Marsha Linehan of the University of Washington, is increasingly regarded as best-practice therapy for those with borderline personality disorder. If you live with someone who is struggling with borderline personality disorder, you would do well to consult with Dr. Linehan or another professional (or psychiatric agency) fully trained in DBT methods.
- When family members are involved in frequent disagreements about another family member, compare notes. He or she may be presenting a different "face" to each person in the family.
- Agree on common responses to behavior. Your family member is reactive -- you all must *not* be.

Review: Dealing with splitting
- Stay focused on whether or not there is really an emergent issue.
- Do not react to complaints or side issues. Reward positive behaviors and deal with negative behaviors with an absolute minimum of emotion (thereby offering no reward).
- When abuse issues are raised, be comforting. Paradoxically, a little emotional distance is not only better for you but also better for your loved one. From your side, your emotional interaction should exemplify "warm distance."
- Pool resources to arrive at a common viewpoint and a plan.

CHAPTER 20

Bad Intentions: Recognizing the Strategies of Opportunistic and Manipulative Family Members

It is a heartbreaking reality that some people, even people we love, do not mean us well. If they love us, it is only in conditional ways: their love is based on what we do for them. Even worse, we may live with someone who delights in conning or taking advantage of others. They may view us as opportunities to gain something they want, or animated toys to play with for their own amusement.

Others do not *intend* to do harm; they are merely trying to survive. Based on a lifetime of negative experience, however, the best survival strategy they can come up with entails lying and manipulating so that they aren't "caught." They use splitting (Chapter 19), a "divide and disappear" strategy, to keep family members arguing about them instead of focusing on their negative behavior.

The most difficult people to live with – and to help – are those who are like a wolf in sheep's clothing. If they have done a "good job" of manipulating us, we do not even realize that their attitude toward us is predatory. Eventually, we realize that the more we try to help them, the more they break our hearts.

A Compendium of Manipulative Strategies

Manipulative strategies are as varied as malevolence, desperation, and/or human creativity can devise. Let us consider the following:

Reframing: making something bad acceptable. It is heartbreaking recognize that a loved one is acting in hurtful or cruel ways. Because bond you feel toward your loved one, you tend to give them the benefit of the doubt. Sadly, the manipulative family member assesses you, tracking your reactions to figure out how to evoke the most sympathy or protective reaction.

Example: Reframing

"I know he threatened to kill the nurse. He didn't know what else to do. He was frightened by another patient at the clinic and he thought if he pulled the knife on her, he would be hospitalized and would be able to get away from the guy he was afraid of. He'd never hurt anyone!"

Putting you on the spot. Manipulative people put you on the spot by asking for a decision in front of others where your refusal will cause disappointment or distress.

> **Example: Putting you on the spot**
> While holding her son's hand, a woman says to her mother, who is responsible for supervising her court-mandated visits to the child: "You know, I promised him that we'd celebrate his birthday party here. It's his seventh birthday. It won't hurt if he sees me, his mother, for just few extra hours. Please, you are his grandmother!"

Telling lies of omission. Often dishonesty is manifested as a "lie of omission." They will tell you reassuring aspects of a situation but not include their intention to harm. For example, your son promises that he didn't bring any drugs into the house. However, he considers marijuana and raw opium to be "herbs." Technically, he hasn't lied, has he?

Quid pro quo. If people do us a favor, we humans feel like we owe them. By deliberately making it hard to get information or work with them, and then offering information that was long awaited, they may be trying to get you to let down your guard, because he "came around."

> **Example: Quid pro quo**
> "OK Dad, you gotta stop grilling me. How long has this conversation been going on, anyway? Forty-five minutes. You just won't let up. OK, I'll tell you the truth. I did drink some alcohol last week. But it was just one time. I'll tell you the truth. I didn't like it. I hope you feel better now. I didn't like lying to you – I just was embarrassed. I feel good about telling you the truth." If he plays this gambit well, you won't ask *what else* he's been up to – you are, instead, grateful to him for finally coming around.

Making reassuring promises. One sign of coercion is a reassuring promise when none was asked for. For example: "I know you might be concerned because of last week. But you don't have to worry. I only need to talk with you for five minutes, I promise."

Giving too much information. One way to manage the perceptions of others is to talk too much, too elaborately.

Example: Too much information

"Mom, I was going to go the interview. I was! What happened was that I pulled up at the employment office and there was this lady, she was crying. I mean, I couldn't walk right past her. So I asked if she was OK. She just opened her heart up to me, Mom. She lost her job, and she had to pull her kids out of school. Well, I couldn't just leave her there, desperate like that. So I sat down and we talked. She's a good woman, Mom. I really should be a counselor; I've got a real talent for this. So after we finished our conversation, I decided to come home and research being a counselor. What? You should be happy. I've got a direction now."

Things just happen. The person is somehow "accident prone" in ways that undermine tasks or responsibilities.

Examples: Things happening
- "Gee, it broke. I am *so* sorry!"
- "I don't know what happened. I must have misplaced the documents. No, I didn't try to do that. I tried to do exactly what you told me to!"
- "I did try to get to the doctor's office. You don't think I wanted to have my car break down, do you? Now I have to wait six weeks for another appointment! I cannot believe you are blaming me for a mechanical failure, like I knew I'd get a flat."

Gaining leverage points. The manipulator will attack you not only through your weak points, but also through your best points. The manipulator scans his or her victim looking for leverage – anything, strong or weak, that they can use.

Examples: Leverage points
- If you are religious, you likely have a faith in the redemption of people. A family member's showing contrition, even in a nonreligious context, may lead you to let down your guard.
- Let us say that one of your proudest attributes is your willingness to help the underdog or the oppressed. The manipulator will "become" a victim of oppression, and then, when other people have caught him doing something out of line, you will, believing what you were set up to believe, defend the person who is, once again, being unfairly "victimized."
- "I watch the way you care for Kane every morning. Seriously, dude, I am modeling myself on you. If I have kids, I'm going to be a dad just like you."

Grooming behavior. The manipulative person may set up a situation where he creates in you a little anxiety and then relieves it *while making a request you would have granted anyway*.

> **Examples: Grooming behavior**
> - He stands a little too close to you, and then, pulling back, makes a request that you would have granted anyway. He is training you to feel good when you give him something.
> - Realizing that you feel good about yourself when you give advice, he frequently asks for your opinion. Then, when he gets caught at something, he immediately expresses contrition and asks you how to make things better.

Rumor-mongering and conscious splitting. Splitting (Chapter 19) is a defense based on emotional reactivity. Classic splitting is an "automatic process." Manipulators, on the other hand, *deliberately* split by spreading rumors or stories about other family members or caregivers.

Disturbing the equilibrium. These are strategies to make you uncomfortable, off-centered, or uneasy.
- They might say something over the line, and then when confronted, laugh and say they were just joking.
- Manipulators stare, intimidate, mumble, and so on, to elicit a negative response, which then justifies their aggression.
- They make sudden movements such as a mock attack, then smile and say, "Just kidding."

Playing a victim role. Manipulators will often use a victim's role – even a real history – as leverage, trying to elicit "privileged guilt." This is a powerful gambit for foster or adoptive children. It is also common in people who have lived in a chaotic or violent home. Their non-abusive or reformed caregiver is separated from the abuser, but the manipulative person has ample ammunition to make the caregiver feel guilty for staying as long as they did, for not better protecting them, or for any number of other "sins."

Blaming. The more responsibility is theirs, the more they blame others. Sometimes such people will blame or attack, and then when confronted, will straight-facedly deny it *or* ask a question like, "Why are you are so sensitive?" If manipulators don't get what they want, they may complain bitterly about how they trusted you, and this is what happened.

Examples: Blaming
- "I cannot believe this. I finally get away from dad and you said you would help me. But you are all over my case. I thought, knowing what I'm going through, you'd lighten up. I mean, you just left me there."
- "So I tell you I'm having a little problem with drugs – nothing major – and you go all 'intervention' on me. Just because you had to go to AA to get clean doesn't mean I have to."

Using manipulative language, including the following:
- Denying direct responsibility: "I got caught up in something."
- Denying personal responsibility: "Nobody told me."
- Minimizing: "I made a mistake."
- Colluding/excluding: "You know what I mean." (Or you would if you were smart.)
- Obsequious noncompliance: "I don't know." (The manipulative person says this so the wise parent will explain what they already know, thereby enabling them to control them because they are speaking at their beck and call.)
- Defining something as true, so it must be true: "Honestly," or "I'll tell you the truth," or "I wouldn't lie to you."
- You are like all the rest: "I should have known you wouldn't understand."

What to Do when a Family Member Is Controlling and Manipulative
- Consult and consult again. Do not discount the observations of family, friends, and professionals involved in your loved one's care. Try to ascertain if you are "split": at odds due to the manipulative strategies of your family member.
- Recognize that the family member whom you consider your star, the one to whom you devote the most energy or attention, may in fact have successfully groomed you.
- You must create a strong, comprehensive plan to hold a family member to the highest standard of behavior. Whatever they may have suffered, there is no legitimate excuse for making you or others suffer.
- Some manipulative people "rise above themselves" when they are held to high standards. Others do everything in their power to make things worse for you. They will try to undermine the rules and boundaries you set, make you doubt yourself, or simply take over the power within the family. If they are committed to manipulation and violation, the best thing to do is make sure that they cannot hurt you. Call the police when they engage in criminal actions. If they are a client of the mental health system, a substance abuse treatment program, or a private practitioner, make it clear to all of their treatment providers and to the manipulative person that if certain limits are violated, they will no longer be allowed to live in your home, receive support from you, or even contact you. Follow through if you make such a decision. (Make sure it is not a threat, which is just forceful air blown out your mouth. A decision is something you clearly know is the right thing to do, one that you will not go back on.)

SECTION IV

Communication with Those with Severe Mental Illness or Other Conditions that Can Cause Severe Disability

CHAPTER 21

Struggling in a Fog: Dealing with Symptoms of Disorganization

> Disorganization is a general term to describe what it is like when individuals cannot adequately organize their cognitions, perceptions, and/or feelings so that they can function in the real world. Please note that, as elsewhere in this book, I am referring to behavioral manifestations, not the inner experience of the disorganized person, because, as you will see below, there are different types of individuals within the disorganized rubric.
>
> Among the many causes of disorganization and delirium are metabolic or infectious disorders. For this reason, severe disorganization should always be regarded, first and foremost, as a medical emergency until such causes have been ruled out. If not immediately attended to, such disorders can cause permanent, even life-threatening, damage.

Disorganized people may, perhaps, be *autistic*, overwhelmed by the incomprehensible emotional communications of people and the overly rich and complex sensory impressions that they receive. When colors have sounds and music creates odors and swathes of light, autistic individuals may become rapt or lost in the experience. The most incomprehensible thing to the autistic person is interaction with other human beings, so they may become overwhelmed in social interactions.

Developmentally delayed individuals often lack the maturity to manage complex or frustrating situations. In addition, due to their cognitive limitations, they are not skilled at problem solving.

Profoundly psychotic people (Chapters 24 and 25) also become disorganized, where even their delusions break down into chaos. Oddly enough, delusions, despite the myriad problems they cause, are an organizing principle. If you believe yourself to be surrounded by enemies, or are on a mission to save the world, you have to focus on what to do next, delusional though your thoughts might be.

Severe intoxication, withdrawal, and long-term damage from intoxicating substances can create disorganized, even delirious states.

All of these problems can also apply to someone who is demented due to a head injury, Alzheimer's disease, or other forms of senility. Finally, severely traumatized individuals can become so overwhelmed that they shift into a chaotic, disorganized state.

> You will know you are dealing with a disorganized person because they are nearly incoherent, or it is otherwise impossible to communicate with them. They may seem to shift from one emotion to another, and it is very hard, if not impossible, to hold their attention.

Small Bits at a Time

Do not ask disorganized family members to do things that are beyond their ability to comprehend or organize. For example, it may be unreasonable to expect disorganized individuals to, unattended, do something as complex as cleaning up their room, which can include picking up, folding, and putting away clothes; making the bed; and other tasks. Some disorganized people may get distracted by the texture of the towel they are folding, for example, or the play of light on the floor. Others, confused, aimlessly move things around. Therefore, make sure to give specific instructions. There is no point in being irritable. That just makes things harder for these individuals because they usually do not know why you are upset. This becomes an added disorganizing factor for them.

Not only should your instructions be specific, but they should also be simple and divided in small, manageable bits. Your sentences should be short. Each sentence should contain only one important message, and it is likely that even in the best circumstances, you will have to repeat this message several times before it sinks in. Rather than saying, "Pick up your clothes," you may have to say, "Pick up your red blouse. Put it on the bed. Pick up your plaid dress. Put that on the bed, too. Now fold your red blouse." If you really want your disorganized family member to accomplish a task, you may have to firmly but kindly supervise them every step of the way.

Of course, you should hold your family member to a high standard: just don't make it an impossible one.

Let Me Repeat Myself

When we are not understood, our usual impulse is to elaborate: we use different words and expressive hand and facial gestures, or we intensify the emotional tone of our communication. With disorganized people, it is often better to simply repeat the same statement or question word-for-word, sometimes four, five, or more times. Do not browbeat them. You should not increase your volume, shouting at them to get through to them. Your repetition becomes a touchstone of stability. It is the one consistent point at that moment. If you change your vocal tone or get irritated, you will defeat the purpose of your repetition. If you keep your nonverbal communication stable and calm, the disorganized individual will become more, rather than less, under control.

Examples: Here is an example of the wrong way and then the right way to communicate with a disorganized family member:
Wrong:

"You've left your chores long enough. This room is a mess, and you've just put it off too long. Now there is mold on the carpet, and it smells terrible. I don't know where we can even begin. This place is horrible!"

Rather than venting your feelings, your tone of voice should be firm, calm, and with little emotion other than, possibly, some warmth.

Better:

"Jiro, it is time to do your chores."

"Put down the book, Jiro. Jiro, put down the book. Jiro, put down the book." (**NOTE:** Do not use a nagging tone. Slowly repeat each sentence, with pauses between them, to give Jiro time to act.)

"Good. Stand up."

"Stand up, Jiro. Good."

"Pick up your clothes and put them on the bed."

"Pick up your clothes and put them on the bed."

Imagine that this is too "big" a task. He seems overwhelmed. So you re-adjust:

"Jiro, pick up the red sweater and put it on the bed. Good."

"Jiro, pick up the blue jeans and put them on the bed."

It may make you uncomfortable to be so direct. Naturally, you will have to figure out a style that works best for you and your family member. "Please" might be a good idea, or it may not. Remember that "please" and "thank you" are added information, and <u>with a concrete or disorganized individual, more information does not help</u>. It is far kinder to be clear than to be polite.

Creating Room for Success

Your family member should have daily tasks that are necessary, but are also failure-free. Life should not be a perpetual struggle; one needs to be successful at something, no matter how small. While positive reinforcement is usually rewarding to anyone, it can mean a great deal to mentally ill and disorganized individuals. Indeed, for some people, this may be the only positive feedback they ever receive.

Behavioral Charts

Behavioral charts can be helpful for some people. First of all, this divides tasks into small bits. This also provides your family member with a check-off chart where everyone can see what needs to be done and how much has been accomplished.

Be Aware of and Attend to Sensory Needs

Consider what environment would make your family members feel most comfortable, safe, and stable. Loud noises may be distracting or overwhelming. Lights may be too bright and glaring. The music you play may be irritating or disturbing. Although there is certainly a limit on how closely you can approach this ideal, your relationship with your family members will be much more positive if the environment is one in which they feel comfortable.

Magical Thinking

This is a term that overlaps with delusions (Chapter 24). Magical thinking is telling stories, which you then believe. It is most common among small children, senile and demented adults, and developmentally delayed individuals. Unlike psychotic delusions, magical thinking does not have the same enclosed quality, where a fundamental truth is revealed and then locked into place within the person's mind. Rather, the fantasies that arise within the disorganized person are repeated, proclaimed, and then believed.

Magical thinking sometimes emerges out of a confused state, where the mind latches onto a detail of what is perceived and constructs a story around it. John, for example, notices that his home health care provider is physically round and wear glasses, like his grandmother, so he honestly believes that John is his grandmother. In other cases, it can also be fable making – the kinds of stories very young people tell.

> ### Example: Fable making – a form of magical thinking
> A developmentally disabled teenager, with a long history of aggression, confided to me that he could heal knife wounds. "You just peel off the skin of a salmon and put it over the wound. It'll be totally healed in one night. There won't even be a scar."

Once you've established that a claim or statement is not true, there is little to be gained by arguing about it. Sometimes, just let it go. Other times, you can say, even with a little tiredness in your voice, "I've heard that story before. You don't have to tell me again." Or, "Let's not talk about that anymore. What do you want to have for dinner tonight?" Then, simply move on to another topic, shifting your family member's focus toward issues of immediate concern.

> **Review: Dealing with symptoms of disorganization**
> You will know you are dealing with a disorganized family member when you notice the following:
> - The family member is nearly incoherent, and it may be impossible to communicate with them.
> - The family member seems to shift from one emotion to another, with no logical reason or explanation.
> - Focusing their attention is very hard, if not impossible.
> - They may offer fantasy statements – magical thinking – that, unlike delusions, have the naïve character of a child's fantasy.
>
> **Remember to:**
> - Divide tasks into small bits.
> - Give simple, specific instructions.
> - Be realistic about what the family member can and cannot do.
> - Repeat your instructions rather than elaborate on them. Do not change your vocal tone.
> - Do not argue with magical thinking; redirect the family member to the task and issues at hand.
> - Use a dramatic voice with children or those who seem to be childlike

CHAPTER 22

Dropping Stones in a Well: Latency

Latency, a behavior that is often an aspect of disorganization, is observed when people respond to communication in a v-e-r-y s-l-o-w manner. When you ask a question, they quietly talk to themselves as they puzzle out what you might be saying, or they may engage in odd stereotypical movements, which might either have a meaning important only to them or be a self-soothing behavior. Some latent individuals may simply stare away, a vacuous look on their face.

> You will recognize latency when the person to whom you are speaking not only delays his or her answers, but also replies with somewhat odd and disjointed answers that aren't related to your questions. This is different from being silent or defiant. You get the sense that they are not "there" – that it is about something going on inside of them, and not about you at all.

Some people who are manifesting latency may be confused: you might say, "Take care," meaning, "Good-bye, I hope all goes well for you," and they, being very concrete (Chapter 9), wonder, "Take care of what?" Others may hear voices or be overwhelmed by outside stimuli – the glitter of light on the varnish of the piano and the white keys that look like teeth: in these cases, your words seem very far away. Others may be cognitively impaired, and they simply do not understand what you are saying.

Were you to drop a stone in a well, you would expect to hear a splash as the stone hits the water at the bottom. Imagine the latent mind like a very old well, with bricks sticking out and a tangle of tree roots halfway down. The stone hits the roots and bounces off a brick, then another and another. You don't hear a splash this time: you hear nothing. So you throw more stones, one after another. You now have many stones bouncing around, colliding into each other, adding to your frustration, without the first stone ever reaching the bottom of the well. In other words, adding more words doesn't enhance communication with latent individuals.

Coping with Latency: Keep It Simple

Be patient. Although communicating with such a person can be frustrating and often time consuming, you must remain calm if you hope to succeed in communicating with them. Indeed, any frustration or anger you display will only further confuse the family member.

Keep your sentences and instructions short and direct. Minimize all the qualifiers – such as "you might", "maybe," or "kind of" – that you ordinarily put in your sentences.

Don't dance when you talk. Try to minimize your changeable hand gestures and facial expressions. This does not mean you should speak robotically, but simplicity is best.

Repeat. Latent people usually do *not* need things explained in further detail; they just didn't get it the first time. So, say the same thing again. <u>Make sure you use the same tone of voice when your repeat yourself. Adding other emotions is overloading the communication with new data that they have to try to understand</u>. Repetition is like somehow throwing the *same* pebble down the well, reinforcing the original. Rather than adding a new stone, you are doubling, tripling weight to the one already there. Now the stone can get through the roots and bricks and hit bottom.

Repeat back. When you think your communication has been successful, try to get the family member to repeat the instructions back to you in their own words.

Review: Communication with the latent family member
- Be patient.
- Keep your sentences short and direct.
- Minimize hand gestures and changeable facial expressions.
- Repeat the instructions, using the same words and the same tone of voice.
- Try to get the latent individual to repeat back your instructions.

CHAPTER 23

Withdrawal from Intoxicating Substances

Some mental disabilities are caused by drug use. Sometimes primary mental illness is made worse by drug abuse. This is referred to as a *dual diagnosis*. Because this book focuses on dealing with behaviors, not specific diagnoses, I have not tried to distinguish the effects of each and every drug and compared them to each and every mental disorder. We must, however, consider the topic of drug withdrawal.

First and foremost, alcohol and drug withdrawal are medical emergencies. If your relative is undergoing drug withdrawal, your responsibility is to keep them calm until emergency medical personnel and/or police arrive. Why would the police be called in addition to emergency medical personnel? Many people withdrawing from drugs can be very aggressive, due to their discomfort or due to their frustration at you for not providing them with more money or drugs. The presence of police may be necessary to keep everyone safe.

People in withdrawal are often in pain or feel quite ill. They may also be frightened or irritable and focused, in a completely self-centered way, on getting their needs met. Paradoxically, they may display a high level of resistance to accepting proper medical attention, or insist that they are well enough to be left alone. The signs of withdrawal (and proper responses) can include the following:
- Unstable coordination. Try to get them to sit or lie down for their safety.
- Restlessness and agitation. Try to reduce stimulating input.
- Unpredictable and sudden actions. Keep your movements calm and slow so that you do not elicit their startle reflex, which can easily provoke them to attack.
- Slurred or incoherent speech. Speak in a calm, quiet voice and make an extra effort to understand what they are saying. Provide short explanations.
- Abnormally rigid muscles.
- Being argumentative and demanding. Try to redirect or de-escalate them, depending on the mode of anger or rage they exhibit.

Calming Individuals in Withdrawal
Be calm and firm. Redirect them when they get very demanding, and reassure them that help is on the way. To reiterate, this is a medical emergency. You are simply trying to calm them until help arrives.

For the purposes of de-escalation, there is no specific state of withdrawal anger or rage. The individual in withdrawal, if enraged, will shift into one of the modes of anger or rage outlined in the later sections of this book. You will, therefore, control and de-escalate them based on what mode of rage they are exhibiting.

CHAPTER 24

Psychosis: Delusions and Hallucinations

> Psychosis is a general term to denote people who are suffering from either delusions or hallucinations. This can be caused by a number of mental illnesses and other syndromes: schizophrenia; bipolar disorder; intoxication, withdrawal, side effects, or neurological damage from drugs or medications; head injuries; trauma; or extreme agitation. As I noted in the forward, this book will address behaviors, not the diagnoses. This chapter will apply to anyone who is showing psychotic symptoms, whatever the cause may be.

What Is a Delusion?

A delusion is a belief that does not fit reality – sort of. Actually, it's a lot more than that. There are a lot of people who have strange beliefs: unconventional religious ideas; dietary and health habits that range from fruit and water to high protein and fat; or beliefs in aliens, crop circles, and telepathy. It's possible that some of those are *your* beliefs – they are eccentric to me, but not to you. Unique ideas and beliefs are not, however, delusional.

A delusional belief does not even have to be unusual. I may state that the FBI is following me. The FBI does follow people! I may believe that I am getting special wisdom every time I read the Bible. That puts me in a group with hundreds of millions of people.

The hallmark of a delusional belief is its "locked-in" quality. It has the same relation to an ordinary belief as a cult has to a religion. Religions may be strict or relaxed, but most churches have open doors. People leave churches all the time and find new ones to attend, or chose not to go to church at all. A cult, however, is far more difficult to leave, because people become locked into the cult doctrine. Delusions are like cults with one member.

When people become delusional, it is as if they had a revelation. All the confusing thoughts they have had, all the worries, prayers, fantasies, or ideas suddenly coalesce into the *belief.* Such beliefs are unshakable, unarguable, and unalterable by conflicting evidence.

Types of Delusions

Grandiose delusions. People believe that they have been appointed on a special mission; have extraordinary or unusual powers; or are special, remarkable beings.

Religious delusions. Often linked with grandiose delusions, such people may become religiously preoccupied, focusing all their attention on their beliefs, which may be self-made or associated with mainstream doctrines.

Jealous delusions. The person may believe, against all evidence, that their partner is unfaithful to them. To be sure, many rational people experience jealousy. Jealous delusions, however, are far more severe than insecure emotions. The delusional jealous person concocts infidelity out of the slightest glance, a change in clothing, or a five-minute delay in returning home. Perpetrators of domestic violence, particularly those with a paranoid or borderline character structure (Chapters 18 and 19) often manifest this type of delusional psychosis in periods of stress.

Delusional stalking.[7] People believe that another person is in love with them, is married to them, or has been, somehow, designated as theirs, whether they know it or not. Delusional stalking is called erotomania.

Persecutory delusions (paranoia). Such people may believe that they have enemies: people, institutions, or other powers have hostile intentions toward them or may be committing evil actions against. The paranoid individual is a grandiose victim. They believe that others are sending energy toward them, thinking about them, talking about them, or looking at them with malevolent intent. The paranoid attitude has already been discussed (Chapter 18). Delusional paranoia is far more than a severe attitude, however: it is an unshakable belief, bolstered by false hallucinations and false interpretations of other's actions.

What Is a Hallucination?

A hallucination is a disturbance in perception. One perceives things in a way that does not conform to reality. Hallucinations are often, but not always, accompanied by delusions.

Types of Hallucinations

One can experience hallucinations with any of one of the senses:

Auditory hallucinations. There are two levels of auditory hallucinations. The first level is *auditory distortion*. One mishears what is said. People with persecutory delusions often display a "listening attitude." They enter a situation that evokes their paranoia and expect to be victimized, accused, talked about, or assaulted. They either mishear people based on what they expect to hear, or in more severe cases, they truly hear hallucinatory voices uttering just what they expected or feared. For example, a person experiencing paranoia is in the middle of a restaurant and they hear someone say, "Say, do you want the chicken or the ribs?" They hear, "Let's say we get this chicken in the ribs."[8]

The second level is true *auditory hallucination*. Close your eyes when someone speaks to you. Do you still hear their voice? When people have an auditory hallucination, it is *that* vivid. It is not imagination – it is an experience. That is why you cannot simply say, "The voice isn't real." That makes as much sense to them as someone telling you that the lightening and thunder that just shorted out your electricity and shook your house didn't happen.

Visual hallucinations. People may experience *visual distortions*. The distorted visual image appears to move, melt, emerge toward you, or even speak. Think of a Salvador Dali painting in which the objects melt and flow. Look at your carpet and imagine tiny eyes appearing in the rough surface, or little fingers emerging from the cracks in the walls.

The second level is true *visual hallucination,* in which objects or beings appear that no one else can see. They can be inanimate or alive. Perhaps there are flowers blooming from the floor, or an angel hovering overhead – in either case, only the hallucinating person can see them.

Olfactory hallucinations refer to smells. This is sometimes a sign of brain injury, as the part of the brain that detects odors is at the front of the head, a frequent target of blows. Other people, without head injuries, and purely psychotic, may get focused on their own body smells, and believe, for example, that they are rotting away. Some people claim they that they can smell poison gas seeping through the walls. If your relative suddenly begins complaining of olfactory hallucinations, they should get a medical exam as soon as possible. Head injury, stroke, or other traumatic insults to the brain must be ruled out before olfactory hallucinations can be considered part of a mental illness. Furthermore, the longer you wait, the more severe any damage will be. This is true even if your relative already *has* a mental illness.

Tactile hallucinations are sensations within the body. A sensation of bugs crawling in the limbs is a frequent side effect of drugs such as methamphetamine or cocaine. It can also be a side effect of the person's psychiatric medication. Other people have complained of experiencing sexual invasion or snakes crawling into their bodies. A medical doctor should always check this symptom, particularly if your loved one is using medications or has a history of drug abuse.

The Torment of Hallucinations
Hallucinations torment their victims in a variety of ways:
- For unknown reasons, hallucinated voices are almost always cruel. People can be ordered to do awful or degrading things, or they may simply hear ugly sounds and demeaning words. Visual hallucinations can be as haunting as ghosts. Olfactory hallucinations are often foul odors, and tactile hallucinations are almost always very unpleasant sensations.

- People try to tell others what they perceive, but their experience is denied over and over again. They can be teased or laughed at. Ironically, the people they tell often torment them in ways similar to the torment of the hallucinations.
- Psychotic people find that their worldview is called into question every day. They don't know what is real and what is not. Imagine reaching to pick up your tea and not knowing if the liquid will disappear or if the handle of the cup will suddenly twine around your finger like a little snake. Imagine this is true of every object in your life. In such circumstances, the person finds it difficult to trust anything at all.

Hallucinations can be horrible
Most people who experience hallucinations describe them as negative, cruel, or frightening. I have interviewed people who have watched their bodies rotting, seen people on the street turn into deformed monsters, and witnessed wounds open up on their bodies. Beasts emerge from wall hangings, satanic claws edge around doorframes. All too often, the hallucinations are nightmarish.

Hallucinations are not *necessarily* horrible
Some people have benign hallucinations, like guardian angels that warn them to not cross the street against the light, for example, or to lower their voice in a public place.

CHAPTER 25

Communication with Someone Who is Experiencing Delusions or Hallucinations

> **NOTE**: A central strategy in communication with all people, but particularly useful with psychotic individuals, is paraphrasing (Chapter 42).

Disengage

Communicating with a psychotic person can be very draining, even maddening. Like cultists trying to convert you to their group, they may insist that you accept their beliefs, or even more problematic, insist that you *do* believe, but simply won't admit it. If you try to argue with them, they may become more focused on debating your resistance, or furious that you deny what is, to them, absolutely true.

There is often no good reason to continue such a discussion. Delusions are not like some sort of backed-up fluid that you vent and drain away.

It is terribly lonely to be delusional – locked up in one's own inner world, as if nothing in the world outside offers any alternative. But discussion and argument seem to cement the delusions even further – the more one talks about it, the more one believes it to be true, locking them even further into their lonely delusional world.

> **Rule #1: Disengage**
> There are many occasions when nothing at all can be accomplished by talking about delusions or hallucinations. In such cases, disengage, especially if more discussion tends to elicit an angry or irrational response.

Islands of Sanity

Imagine being dropped overboard into the ocean, with its cold and buffeting waves, not to mention everything from sharks to jellyfish. This is like the delusional world: there seems to be no way out, and it is so overwhelming that you cannot take your mind off of it. Even in the ocean, however, there are small patches of land – islands. If you can only get to them, you can put your feet on solid ground.

For the psychotic individual, there are "islands of sanity," areas of their lives where they are not delusional. They may be convinced, for example, that someone is poisoning their food and only canned goods are safe to eat, or that someone is beaming messages directly into their brain. Imagine, however, that you begin talking about football, and as you begin discussing the Steelers' next opponent, the family member, without even realizing it, takes his mind off his delusions. For a brief moment, he has a moment of respite. If you steer conversations toward these islands of sanity, they may begin to associate you with a sense of stability, someone with whom they can have moments of clarity and peace.

> **Rule #2: Move toward the islands of sanity**
> Pay attention to areas of thought and subjects where your family member is not delusional, and talk about those subjects whenever possible. Link one island of sanity with other islands – think of yourself as expanding the size of the landmass, creating an area where life is predictable and safe. If the family member gets stuck within his or her delusions, you may find that changing the subject requires real finesse. Nonetheless, do so whenever you can, because talking about the delusion often makes things worse for the family member. Talking about "healthy" subjects brings peace.

When *Should* You Talk About the Delusions?

Let us imagine that your family member is sure that he is the Archangel Michael. If you recall this biblical story, Michael casts Satan out of heaven. Michael is power incarnate, the righteous sword of the Lord God. Further, imagine that your family member sometimes believes he perceives Satan's work in the behavior of people around him. On one occasion, he was arrested after hammering on his neighbor's door, armed with a sword, yelling that he was going to cut Satan out of the hearts of the children to save them for the Lord. Based on this past history of violence, you *should* ask direct questions about his delusions, whenever he begins to talk about God, angels, Satan, or anything else that is connected to these dangerous thoughts. For instance, you may ask:

- "John, are you telling me that you think you have seen Satan? Where?"
- "Why do you think that this is Satan's work?"
- "Do you think you should do anything about this?"
- "What do you think you should do?"

If John's answers are bland and not aggressive, then you can change the subject at the appropriate time. If, however, his answers sound potentially dangerous, then you must act. For example, were he to say, "Don't call me John! I'm Michael, the Lord's most beloved angel. Satan will have no place on this earth when I take my righteous sword in my strong right arm!" This would obviously be a potential crisis.

Dangerous answers are an alarm call to get help – alerting his doctor, his care team, and in some cases, the police. He may need his medications adjusted or more frequent contact with his treatment team. But whatever the appropriate response, you must act when he is dangerous again.

COMMUNICATION WITH SOMEONE WHO IS EXPERIENCING DELUSIONS OR HALLUCINATIONS

> **Rule #3: Talk about the delusions to assess risk**
> Talk about the delusions as a means of threat assessment. Ask direct questions, particularly about their intention to hurt themselves or others. If they do not bring such subjects up for discussion, but their delusions have been a problem in the past, occasionally bring the subject up yourself, just to see if they have become decompensated again.

Don't Agree – At Least Most of the Time

Although agreement may seem like the path of least resistance, doing so can present problems. When you agree with delusions and/or hallucinations, you will entrench them even more deeply into the family member's belief system.

Example: The mistake of agreeing with delusions

Nadia claims that she gave birth to a child who was stolen. Yet she has no memory of giving birth. She is, at times, quite belligerent and demanding about her belief, but in her heart, she doubts that it is true. One day her brother, tired of hearing about it and hoping for a little peace, says, "Nadia, it's true. I saw the baby before they took her away. But they didn't steal her. There is this organization called 'The Guardians of Light.' When they find a special child, one who will someday help the world, they take that child, adopt her, and teach her how to be a world leader. Adrienne is one of those children. That's why they took her. So you don't have to worry any more." This does not ease Nadia's mind. Instead, it locks in her beliefs. She no longer doubts – and when she introduces the subject again and again, she becomes more aggressive because no one is doing anything to help, even though she knows it has to be true.

When you agree with delusions or hallucinations, you can be incorporated into the delusional system. Sometimes this can be ostensibly benign, but wearying. All that happens is that the person incessantly wants to talk about the delusions with the only person who seems to share that point of view. <u>It can be much more dangerous, however.</u>

Example: Incorporation within a delusional system

James plays the guitar. James began to believe that his cousin Richard and he were part of the same rock band. One day, he was convinced that Richard had stolen a song that they had co-written and sold it to a major record label. He heard it on the radio every day, but he had not been paid for it. Calling his cousin a thief, he attacked him with a chair.

Just because one is mentally ill does not mean the person is gullible or stupid.

> **Example: The delusional person is not necessarily gullible**
> Alcee began agreeing with his son's delusions because he was tired of arguing with him. Now, every time Hugh mentioned his fears about the church down the street, his dad agreed. Hugh realized, however, that he was being brushed off; that his father was patronizing him. He felt like a small child running to his father with a fantasy, only to be patted on the head and sent on his way. He was furious and decided that the best way to show his father how upset he'd become was to destroy his father's prized stamp collection, worth thousands of dollars.

Don't Disagree – At Least Most of the Time

Common sense seems to demand that you speak for reality. When people see something that isn't there, shouldn't you tell them so? If they have an irrational belief, why not argue them out of it, or at least, diplomatically point out where they are wrong? This is problematic, however, because you are arguing *reality* with someone.

Look around your room. What color are your walls? If I go to your home and tell you they are red when they are pale green, will you ever believe me, no matter how many times I repeat myself, no matter how much intensity I direct at you? Of course not! If you are having a conversation with your daughter, will you believe me if I tell you that she is an iguana?

The fundamental problem with arguing with delusional or hallucinating people is that you are telling them that their senses and their brains are lying to them. If they had any trust in you before, it is unlikely that telling them that the world as they see it is not real will improve that rapport. Individuals experiencing psychosis find everyday life to be very stressful and sometimes quite frightening. It is very important that you have as few arguments as possible.

Sometimes, however, a delusional family member may ask, or even plead with you, for disagreement because they do not want to believe what their delusions tell them. At other times, a hallucinating person can make a tenuous distinction between real perceptions and hallucinations, and will ask you if you think something hallucinated are real. In these cases, *when you have been invited*, it is acceptable to state that not only do you not perceive or believe the hallucination or delusion, but you *also* do not think it is real.

> **Rule #5: Don't disagree, at least most of the time**
> Do not engage in arguments about whether the psychotic person's perceptions are real. You can make an exception, in which you state that you do not believe that the delusional belief is correct or that the hallucination is not real *when* they doubt it themselves, and request a "reality check." Even here, do not simply state, "That's not real." Discuss the situation with the family member for a few minutes, so you are clear what they are truly concerned about and what they are asking from you.

An Important Exception to the "Don't Disagree" Rule: Erotomania, Stalking, and Pathological Jealousy

Stalking delusions are particularly dangerous because another person is the focus of the delusions. The stalker selfishly believes that he or she has a right to approach or harass the victim. This is a crime. Above all else, the victim needs to be protected. This often requires you to call the police to report your relative. In many other situations, you are morally obligated to call the victim to warn them of your relative's focused interest. In situations where your relative is fixated, but has not yet begun stalking the object of their desire, you must very calmly, but directly, say that it is not true that the victim is destined for, in love with, or otherwise involved with your family member. Do not engage in long discussions, much less arguments. Simply state that it is not true. Otherwise, your "conditional" demurrals may be taken as agreement.

Similar to stalking delusions, you must not validate, even through silence, your family member when they are expressing pathological jealous delusions. <u>If it would be unsafe to disagree with your family member in these circumstances, you need help, from either or both the police and the mental health system.</u>

> **Rule #6: Disagree! The exception of erotomania**
> In any case where your relative has a fixed delusion about another person that leads them to stalk or harass them, you must call the police and, in many cases, you must also call and warn the object of your relative's delusions. Even when their delusions are "low-level," and it does not appear necessary to call for outside intervention, do not agree with or be noncommittal about their delusions. Firmly and directly disagree with the person's delusional belief that they are in a relationship with a person or that the person is destined for them.

Differentiation: A Respectful Way to Distinguish Between Your World and Theirs

Psychosis can affect every aspect of a person's existence. It becomes impossible to escape oneself. Your delusional beliefs can so preoccupy you that there is almost no moment that they are not part of your thoughts. Just when you think you are at peace, an ugly voice suddenly rises inside your head, and accuses you of something obscene, or as you gaze at the leaves outside your window, you see beings beckoning to you to jump from your window. Worse, much of this is something you cannot share or talk about. People disbelieve you, or minimize your concerns, telling you to stop imagining things. Even the people you love are tainted by the psychotic experience; the psychotic person may become terrified or enraged toward those who could, otherwise, protect and care for them. <u>It is like seeing yourself in a world of distorted mirrors: wherever you look is just a twisted aspect of yourself</u>.

When your family member voices a delusion or talks about a hallucination, the surest way to make that vital distinction between your world and theirs is to *differentiate*: to perceive or express a difference. You should acknowledge the family member's perceptions and beliefs, while also informing them that, although you do not share their perceptions, you are not arguing that theirs are invalid. You are, however, attempting to have the family member also become aware that other viewpoints do exist.

Remember the image of the psychotic person's world being like one of mirrors? Now, imagine standing behind a one-way mirror that you can see through when you turn on a light. When you differentiate, it can give them the best chance to look through the "mirror" of their psychosis, able to see you as an independent being.[9] Paradoxically, it is when we are different from someone else that we actually can be in relationship with that person.

Examples: Differentiation
- Alice, I see the table and chairs, the pictures on the wall, and the books on the floor. There is, however, something that you see that I don't. I do not see a bowl of boiling oil in the corner of the room. No, I'm not saying you don't see it. I believe you do. I'm simply saying that it is something you see that I don't. I don't know why that is.
- Umberto, I only hear two voices in this room – yours and mine. I don't hear a woman's voice at all. What do you hear her say?
- I know that you believe the United Nations has been sending black helicopters over the farm. But honestly, I don't believe that. We've talked about it before, and we just have to agree that we have different views. I don't want to talk about it anymore this week. Your mind is free to have your beliefs, and mine is free to have mine, and it is no fun at all to argue about this.

Differentiation keeps the lines of communication open. Think of two people from different cultures, or even two beings from different planets, trying to explain what it is like to live in their respective worlds. By maintaining a way to continue to talk, despite your differences, the family member is more likely to be open with you in other areas. If mentally ill people feel shut down or discounted when they try to talk about their perceptions or beliefs, it is very unlikely that they will be open about any other area of concern.

COMMUNICATION WITH SOMEONE WHO IS EXPERIENCING DELUSIONS OR HALLUCINATIONS

In some circumstances, you can act in concert with their belief without endorsing it: "I can't see the laser beams, but I know lasers don't pass through solid objects. Maybe you will feel safer sitting in that room over there."[10]

> **Rule #7: Differentiate**
> You give the person the "right" to their own perceptions and beliefs. Inform them that you do not perceive what they do, but you are not arguing that *they* do not see it. In some cases, you can take their delusions into account without agreeing with them.

Steam Valve: When the Pressure is Too Great

Some people, either with symptoms of psychosis or mania (Chapter 26) are so full of things to say, think, or feel that they seem like they are going to explode from the pressure. Words cascade out of them in floods of thought, in flights of ideas. Even when they make sense, they totally dominate the "air time" in the room, without allowing you to speak or to change the subject. At other times, they do not make sense at all. Their words may sound like poetry – "clang associations" – as they link words by sound, not by inherent meaning. They may jump from idea to idea, in what are called loose associations, or tangential thinking.

Sometimes you simply have to say, with utmost kindness, "You have talked enough for awhile. It's time to be quiet. Hush." For some people, this works quite well for both sides. It is honest, it is direct, and it sets a limit.

At other times, one needs to let a little pressure off, like opening a valve in a steam pipe. Then you create space to say a bit of what you have to say. First, put out a hand, palm down, fingers curved at waist level – use this to interrupt. If they don't perceive it, put up both hands, using a little drama in your facial expression to get their attention, and interrupt them. You let out a little pressure, so to speak, ask or say something, get a bit of information in return and let them return to their cascade of ideas. You let out a little more pressure, and then once again, gently interrupt. Each time you speak, you first show that you were listening – tracking what they say – but summing it up a little, and then you ask your question or make your statement.

Example: Steam valving

Raymond: "I was looking outside my window at the birdfeeder, and it was covered with goldfinches. The lemony yellow just burned my eyes so badly I closed the curtains. My eyes were burned by the fiery birds."

Caregiver *(interrupting firmly)*: "Raymond, I want to hear more about those birds. I haven't seen any goldfinches this year. But before you tell me more, I have a question. Did you call your doctor for an appointment?"

Raymond: "Yes, I did, behind the closed drapes, where the birds couldn't burn my eyes out. I called and talked to a very nice nurse. They have a sound that is piercing to the brain, and a single glance can burn your eyes to a crisp. The birds, not the nurses."

Caregiver: "I can see you are worried about your eyes. That's why you have the sunglasses, huh? I want you to tell me how the sunglasses are working, but first, what day is your appointment?"

Raymond: "It's on a Thursday, but I don't know when, or what time. I'm burning among the birds, you see, with their lemony scalding flame."

As you see, *steam valving* is for the purpose of letting the person tell enough of what is pressuring him internally so that he does not fight you for the conversational floor. If you simply insist he stop talking about his delusions, and then demand to know where the medications are, he may simply go silent (complying with your command), or become more irrational as he perceives your frustration, which he may find frightening.

Rule #8: Steam valve

This is useful for people whose speech is a cascade of words and ideas, often tangential or delusional. You listen, and then, tactfully but firmly, interrupt. Sum up what the person says, tell them you want to hear more, but first you have a question to ask. On other occasions, you have an instruction to give, or something to tell the family member, and after they listen or comply, you let them return to their cascade of words. Listen a bit, then, interrupt again. Remember, you must show in your response/interruption that you have been listening.

Structure and Predictability

Some people experiencing psychosis live in a world that seems about to fall into complete chaos, something frightening and unpredictable. One of the kindest things you can do is to help establish a sense

COMMUNICATION WITH SOMEONE WHO IS EXPERIENCING DELUSIONS OR HALLUCINATIONS

of order. This can include creating a comfortable home environment for your mentally ill loved one, where, as much as possible, life follows certain routines. I am not suggesting that you make a clockwork environment in which every minute and every activity is timed. Nonetheless, try to make the world a familiar place, with few surprises. Whenever possible, prepare your family member well in advance when something new is going to happen, such as visiting a new doctor, buying new clothes, or establishing a new routine. For many people with psychosis, surprise and change are shocking. If there's no time for advance notice, use a low-key approach to introducing novelty, an approach that minimizes the "shock of the new.".

When introducing a change, make your voice matter-of-fact. If you are too tentative and solicitous, they may think that something awful is going to happen and that is why you are talking in such careful tones. At the same time, do not affect a cheerful, aren't-we-having-fun tone of voice. Remember, the family member is anxious, even frightened. When you portray in your voice that it is "no big thing," you are, in effect, trivializing their very real concerns. Patronizing or belittling a family member will compromise their opportunity to make progress with their illness and may upset them enough that they react with more volatility when the fearful change occurs.

> **Rule #9: Structure and predictability**
> The more predictable and organized the environment around the person with psychosis, the safer they will feel.

Physical Space, Physical Contact, and Eye Contact with Family Members Experiencing Psychotic Symptoms

Be acutely aware when you are inadvertently pressuring the psychotic person by standing or sitting too close to them. Consider this *your* responsibility: do not expect the person to tell you of their discomfort. Indeed, the first sign that you are too close may be an assault. You can sometimes teach them either to speak up for themselves, or simply move away. You should not add to their difficulties, however, by looming over them or blocking them in such a way that they feel they cannot escape.

Other individuals who experience psychotic symptoms are not aware of personal space, and they may stand or sit too close to you. Firmly, without any harshness in your tone, tell them to move back: "Monty, I really want to hear what you are saying, but you are standing too close to me. I'd like you to take three steps back and then we can continue." Similarly, if a family member moves behind you, turn, make direct eye contact, and firmly tell them that if they wish to talk with you, they should approach from the front.

> Limit setting is a marvelous means of assessment. Consider the different responses a family member might make to your statement that they should not come up behind you:
> - A blank, bewildered stare: they don't understand what you are talking about.
> - Apologies: they are worried that you are mad at them because they did "something wrong."
> - A sneer: "What's the matter. Are you paranoid or something? I just wanted to see the picture."
> - A confrontation: "I can do what I want. You can't tell me how to live my life!"

For many individuals with psychosis, direct, sustained eye contact is the equivalent of physical contact or an intrusion into their personal space (Chapter 4). Mentally ill family members can misinterpret direct eye contact as aggressive, threatening, or seductive. Be aware of how your family members wish to be treated "visually." If they are uncomfortable with being looked at directly, occasionally "touch base" by making brief eye contact, then ease your eyes away, and then back again. <u>If, however, a family member is becoming aggressive, whether psychotic or not, direct eye contact is absolutely imperative</u>.

Physical contact presents the same dilemma as eye contact. For some, physical contact is obnoxious, confusing, overexciting, or invasive – the possibilities are endless. <u>You must be clear that the physical contact you offer (a hug, a pat on the shoulder, a kiss, for example, is welcome by your psychotic family member, and also something that they understand)</u>. Even when it clearly *could be* the right thing to do (for example, putting an arm around the shoulder of a distraught teenager who just got word that her dog died), that is still predicated upon whether your family member agrees. Some people, however, are too inarticulate, anxious, shy, or confused to express what they feel. Pay attention to the subtle information they often give you, sometimes in spite of themselves. You will often be quite able to tell if your family member welcomes or rejects a hand on the shoulder: by muscular tension, stiffening, pulling away, or other clear physical signs. Other people, however, are so lost inside themselves that these reactions are hidden. Don't assume, then, that a lack of reaction means acceptance.

> **Rule #10: Body spacing, body contact, and eye contact**
> - Be aware of physical spacing: do not stand too close. If your family member stands too close to you, tactfully but firmly tell them to move back. Similarly, firmly tell people not to walk up close behind you. If nothing else, this can get the person in a lot of trouble out in the community.
> - Limit eye contact: many people with psychosis become anxious by too direct eye contact, experiencing it as either a threat or a challenge.
> - Any physical contact is contingent on your family member's wishes and what is right for both of you. Be absolutely sure that body contact – essentially a firm hand momentarily on the shoulder -- is welcome.

CHAPTER 26

Welcome to The Rollercoaster: Tactics for Dealing with Symptoms of Mania

Mania is a state of high energy. Manic individuals usually require little sleep and are often excited, grandiose, agitated, or irritable. They may have flights of ideas, which can be either creative or irrational, or both at the same time. Their speech is often pressured: not only is it rapid, but there is also a sense that they have more to say than they can get out, like water forcing through a too-narrow aperture. They are usually overconfident, and this confidence is often accompanied by a sense of invulnerability.

Manic people can also be extremely selfish. They feel wonderful, and their own needs and desires become the only thing that matters. They often use poor judgment, and they engage in behaviors that can put them or others at risk.

The manic state is most commonly associated with bipolar disorder (manic-depressive disorder), in which periods of mania are interspersed with periods of depression. Some drugs can also cause manic episodes (particularly stimulant drugs such as methamphetamine or cocaine), and mania can be a side effect of psychiatric medications. People with traumatic brain injuries may exhibit periods of agitation that look very much like mania, but these episodes are usually more extreme and disorganized than the classic manic state. On the other hand, manic people can get so agitated (manic excitement) that they shift into a delirium state. Whatever the cause, delirious individuals are de-escalated using the strategies for chaotic rage (Chapter 53).

Manic people are particularly vulnerable because they are most in danger when they feel wonderful. Imagine a beautiful spring day: the sky is blue, birds are singing, and a gentle breeze is blowing. You wake up and leap out of bed, happy to be alive. You have so much energy that it is difficult to contain. When you think about the work you have to do today, it seems so easy: you will be finished in no time at all! You just know you will make some new friends today, maybe hook up with an attractive person and everything will click and you'll be in love or at least lust -- so you are going to the park, the club, the bar, wherever, and enjoy life. Imagine that feeling day after day, multiplied by ten- or twenty fold. Can you see how easy it would be to make unwise choices? How your overconfidence and explosive energy could lead you to take the day off work, seven days running; or pick up a woman just because she has a smile like a girl you remember from grade school; or take out a consolidation loan, without reading the paperwork, because the man at the bank is so nice, and nice people in banks never lie?

When you feel this good, it seems like a good idea to feel *even better*. Thus, manic individuals often turn to drugs and alcohol in order to "keep the good times rolling." Conversely, manic family members may also try to calm themselves with depressant drugs, such as barbiturates, heroin, and alcohol. Alcohol can have a paradoxical effect on some manic individuals, however, further exciting rather than sedating them.

Manic people often talk in rapid cascades of words, a waterfall of ideas leaping from one area to another. Sometimes you can follow their thoughts, although they are speaking very rapidly, but at other times, they leap and zigzag, making connections that have little or no meaning to you.

Manic energy often turns sexual, and the person may get involved with people who may be inappropriate for them or even dangerous.

They may spend money on anything and everything, running their credit cards to the max.

Some family members with mania become very irritable, with a hair-trigger temper. They may also become provocative, teasing and taunting other people. Think of the dynamic between the Warner Brother cartoon characters of the Roadrunner and the Coyote. Everything seems all in good fun at first, but it goes way too far. Others may try to start fights. Because some manic people so easily become angry or even violent, it is important for you to familiarize yourself with strategies for de-escalating anger and rage (see Section VII).

Finally, in extreme manic states, people can become psychotic, with all the symptoms of grandiosity, persecutory, paranoid, and religious delusions that any other psychotic individual might.

Brittle Grandiosity

Manic people can act or describe themselves as if they do not have a care in the world. They spin ideas, one after another, and expect both agreement and admiration. They seem utterly self-confident. Think of manic grandiosity, however, as a fragile structure, like a tower made of spun sugar. It glitters, it glows, and it's huge, but tap the wrong strut or beam, and the entire tower falls down in shards.

A healthy, self-confident individual is the kind of person who can handle criticism or teasing easily; they are resilient. Unfair criticisms are met with a gracious laugh or a dignified response. The manic person, on the other hand, if teased for their somewhat irrational ideas, can misinterpret this as an attack, thinking they are being mocked. Criticism or perceived teasing may be met with sudden aggression or rage. In other words, consider the manic flight of words to be a kind of hysteria. Even when these family members appear happy, it is as if they were on a giddy flight hanging onto a helium balloon. Miscalculated teasing or criticism is experienced as if you poked at the balloon with a needle.

Humor can occasionally be a useful form of communication with such family members. But you need to be calm and centered (Section I). Even if you say something funny, <u>your purpose must be to catch their attention and slow things down, not have fun with them</u>. Trying to *match* wits with them is like trying to catch a dragonfly in flight. Help them slow down instead.

Watch Out! Mania Can Be Infectious

Being with these family members can be exciting, particularly if they are at low or moderate levels of elevation. They can be brilliant conversationalists: witty, sexy, provocative, and entertaining. It can be like having your own comedian, fast on their feet, bawdy, and full of fun. We can easily catch their mood, beginning to feel grandiose and overconfident ourselves.

Family members with mania assume that you are in absolute agreement with them when you "hitch a ride" on their energy. They have a sense of union with you and think that what they want is what you want. They assume that their actions and behaviors, no matter how noncompliant, are acceptable. However, when you subsequently set a limit on those behaviors, the manic family member may suddenly turn on you in betrayed anger.

The expression "he's a drag" refers to someone who slows the party down and that is not a bad idea with these family members.
- Stay centered.
- Do not get swept away or swept up in their energy.
- Focus on slowing things down. Speak slowly and take things step-by-step.

The Medication Struggle: It's *Not* Like Diabetes

Mania is a unique state in that one feels wonderful, healthy, confident, and effective, even when one is actually not doing well at all. If the mania is due to drug abuse, of course people must stop using if they are going to heal. If mania is due to a medication side effect, then they must see a doctor.

When the problem is caused by bipolar disorder, medication can usually control the symptoms. Some bipolar folks believe, in some ways correctly, that they will feel worse when they take the medications. Yes, perhaps they will be calm, more organized, sleep more hours, and not get in as much trouble. They may also avoid crushing periods of depression. However, life will lose a wonderful glow, and the hours of each day will be more like lead than gold. <u>Unlike almost any other condition, "ill" manic people often feel right with themselves, in a state of mystic transport, ecstasy, or just plain fun</u>. Unlike almost any other condition, profoundly "ill" family members often feel best when they are most ill. People with bipolar illness will resist taking medication unless their life on medication is rich and interesting, so much so that they are willing to spurn the dangerous wonders that the manic state seems to offer.

When encouraging a bipolar person to take medications, many professionals and family members say, "It's a condition like diabetes. You need to take it every day to maintain yourself. It's not like medicine for a sore throat that you take until you are cured, and then never have to take again." Although this is true, there is a very profound difference between diabetes and bipolar disorder. If you do not take your medicine for diabetes, you very quickly become seriously ill, and you feel awful, too. If people with bipolar disorder discontinue medications, they often feel much better than when they were taking them. Therefore, it is far better to focus your discussion on the important aspects of these family members' lives *while* on medication. In short, ordinary medicated life should be tangibly better *to them* than the un-medicated carnival of the manic state. If not, it is very unlikely that your family member will be med-compliant.

> **Review: Interacting with the manic individual**
>
> You will recognize the manic person because they will display super-high energy. They will often talk very fast, and their ideas will zigzag from one to another. They often act like comedians with a rapid-fire delivery. Their behavior may also be either sexualized or hair-trigger aggressive. In either case, they will also be provocative.
>
> - Remain calm and centered.
> - Be conscious of the family member's brittle grandiosity, a fragile state of mind, in spite of his or her claims to the contrary. Grandiose does not mean strong!
> - Do not bluntly criticize.
> - Do not tease or joke around. If you use humor, it is for slowing them down, not having fun.
> - Try to assist them in complying with doctor's orders regarding their medications. At the same time, the metaphor linking diabetes and other chronic illnesses with bipolar disorder is often useless. Develop individualized strategies that resonate with the family member, highlighting the wonders of the medicated, well-ordered, and productive life. If the family member does not desire this life, they will usually be noncompliant with medication regimens.

CHAPTER 27

Communication and De-escalation with Elderly Family Members

Getting old is not an illness. Furthermore, older adults are not a monolithic category. They are people, like us, simply older. Everything in this book -- every character type, every mode of aggression, every syndrome, and every de-escalation strategy -- applies to older adults as well. However, there are issues specific to communication with mentally ill or cognitively impaired elderly folks.

Despite their age, elderly people do assault others, particularly caregivers. Their rage can emerge from confusion, medical conditions, pain, adverse drug reactions, mental illness, pure meanness or hate, or any number of stressors. The following, which have both human and tactical value, should be considered:

- Be aware that elderly people may resist help. This may be due to disorganization, confusion brought on by dementia, a combination of severe depression and fear, or pride ("At least I still have the strength to refuse someone.").
- Don't assume that they are stupid or mentally infirm just because they are elderly. Do not talk to your family member like he or she is a child or is feebleminded. The best way to help your family member stay young is, paradoxically, to speak to them as an adult, not a child.
- Speak respectfully, befitting the age and seniority of the person. Too many people speak to the elderly in a patronizing, demeaning tone.
- You may become frustrated at their leaden stubbornness; "they won't do what is good for them." Remember that what appears to be stubbornness may be a profound expression of fear. The most proximate change that many elderly people are concerned with is death, and in their confusion or fear, any situation provoking anxiety evokes the fear of death. <u>You may think they are defiant – but they simply may be scared out of their wits</u>.
- Do not talk around or about the elderly person to others as if they are not there.
- Do not barrage them with choices, decisions, or too much information.
- Some elderly folks can be subject to episodes of rage, and despite their age, can be very strong. Paranoia (Chapter 18), whatever the cause, is one of the frequent triggers of rage in elderly people, particularly those with dementia or adverse drug reactions. As your elderly family member becomes paranoid, you can often change the subject, so that the object of their suspicion recedes from their awareness.
- The rage and violence that emerges with elderly people is frequently chaotic (Chapter 53) or terrified (Chapter 54).

SECTION V

Suicide

CHAPTER 28

Why Would You Suspect that Your Family Member Is Suicidal?

You are not a counselor, yet the question of suicide cannot be avoided if you live with a mentally ill or drug-abusing family member.

For those who are not suicidal, it is an apocalyptic action: literally self-annihilation. For the suicidal person, however, it is an attempt to solve a problem. They find themselves in an intolerable situation, and nothing they can come up with lessens their pain. They feel trapped, unable to conceive of an end to their torment, whether it is due to the actions of other people or something generated from within.

Suicide is also the killing of a human being. That it is done by one's own hand does not make it less murderous. Given that there is murderous intent and often a weapon, you must also consider the safety of other family members or professionals who might have any connection – even mere proximity – to the suicidal person. The difference between murder and suicide is sometimes no more than what direction the weapon is pointing.

Warning Signs

Given that few people announce that they are suicidal, what triggers might drive someone toward suicide?

Significant negative changes: divorce or a romantic break-up; conflict at the worksite; a humiliating incident; a large disappointment such as getting fired, economic reversals, or the like.

Warning signs that suggest negative changes: a radical change in appearance, particularly styles that set them apart from the group of which they were previously a member; hostility toward friends, coworkers, or family; social withdrawal and isolation; giving away prized possessions; writing or drawing with morbid or despairing themes; a depressed demeanor; allusions to a lack of a future or to the pointlessness of it all, and so on.

The intangibles: Sometimes, without knowing why, you have a sense of foreboding. On other occasions, you think something "ridiculous," such as, "I don't think he will live out the year," or "I wonder if this is the last time I will see my son." Such thoughts are often an intuitive sense that something is profoundly wrong. Approaching someone when your "evidence" is so vague requires some tact or delicacy, but approach you must.

> **Warning: Do not discount "intangible thoughts regarding suicide"**
> Such thoughts are often immediately followed by a second thought: "I'm being ridiculous," or "I wonder where *that* came from?" That discounting "second thought" proves nothing – that we rarely think that way about anyone is evidence that an apparently idle thought about a loved one's possible death is never ridiculous, never accidental, and never idle.

CHAPTER 29

The Essentials of Intervention with Someone You Believe Might Be Suicidal: Who Should Ask the Questions and What Should You Say?

Just because you share DNA with someone does not make you the proper person to ask if they are suicidal. Do you *know* that he or she respects you? If not, you are probably not the person to speak with them. To be sure, there are people who are isolated and alienated, and it is *only* through asking such questions that respect between you will be born, but you must at least have a sense that he or she does not hold you in contempt or mistrust you. If you are not the right person, your task is to tell others (family members or professionals) why you are worried so they will take your concerns seriously. If, however, you are the right person, what must you do?

Where should you speak? Choose a setting where you will have no interruptions.

Demeanor. Avoid too much direct eye contact or close physical proximity, which may cause your loved one to shut down. Sit at an angle, occasionally glancing toward them. Eye contact, when it happens, will then seem significant, rather than intrusive.

Meander. If your family member is wary, "wander around," so to speak, talking about this and that. Take time to build up some rapport.

Do not be too nondirective, however. If you try to talk like a counselor, only mirroring what he or she says, your relative may find you maddening. They might feel as if you are treating them like spun glass or playing games with them. Suicide is too important for tiptoeing around: you can only help when you are courageous enough to speak the truth.

Ask direct questions. When you have a real concern that your loved one is considering or planning suicide, you must speak directly with them. Vague statements leave them an "out."
- You: "You aren't thinking of hurting yourself, are you?"
- Loved one: "No, I'm not." (*Soon I'll be feeling no pain, and anyway, you don't really want to hear the real answer, do you?*)

When a true concern about suicide arises, the *correct* question is, "Are you thinking of killing yourself?" Most suicidal people will be relieved to know someone is strong enough to ask direct questions and listen to what is really going on inside them. If your family member is not suicidal, they will let you know. If they are outraged that you asked such a question, explain why you were worried. They should be able to clearly explain why you do not need to be concerned. One final point: Directly questioning them about suicide will *not* put the idea in their head if it was not there to begin with.

Speak in a calm, matter-of-fact tone of voice. If you sound nervous, you'll appear unreliable. If you're joking or off-hand, your loved one will feel that you are not taking them seriously. If you are too tentative, they will not trust you enough to be honest; tentative people act like they don't want to hear the truth. Conversely, if you present yourself as too "together," they may experience this as a slap in the face, their lack of ease contrasting so negatively with your confidence. If you are *overly* warm or "sensitive," you'll sound like a hovering counselor, that soft-voiced, gentle soul who cannot be trusted to stand up and fight, but seeks refuge in being "nice." A calm, matter-of-fact tone shows that you are not panicked by the situation, and that you can accept anything they say. Remember your responsibility is not to save them, but rather to offer them a hand so they can save themselves.

Act as if you have all the time you need to help them. If you act like there is little time, your loved one will believe you, and they'll think they must rush to a decision or conclusion.

Don't give advice too soon without really understanding what's going on. It's easy to say something glib that doesn't help at all. For example, if you say, "Think of us," they might think, "Yeah, your tears dropping on my grave are the best payback I can think of!"

Never dare them to do it. That kind of stupidity only works in the movies. The classically stupid sentence is, "Cutting? If you were serious, you would cut your wrists lengthwise, not crosswise." Or, as some harsh parents have said to a teen, "You don't have the guts to do it." The intention may be to "scare the person straight," but the result, in some cases, may be that they take your advice and make a serious attempt to kill themselves.

Don't get in a debate, particularly a religious debate. Some people use suicidal behavior as a way to feel some personal power in a world over which they have little control. Debates about the meaning of life, the nature of heaven, or the immorality of suicide will break rapport and will aggravate one or both of you. You can win the argument – they, too, feel terrible about breaking the values of your religion – but this simply makes them feel *more* suicidal.

CHAPTER 30

The Four Questions

The following are the standard questions to ask when you are worried about a family member. As you can see, there is a progression in which greater specificity indicates greater danger. You are trying to determine if your loved one is a) in immediate danger, or b) in potential, more long-term danger. You must then decide if you need to contact mental heath services or the police.

Do not use the following questions as a checklist. Instead, use them in the natural flow of conversation, understanding that your family member may wander off on all sorts of tangents before being ready to answer the next question.

If you arrive at an impasse or do not know what to say or do, call your local crisis line,. You can also call the local mental health center, or in cases of serious risk, call 9-1-1.

The Four Questions
(Your loved one's possible answers are in CAPITAL letters.)

1. "Are you planning to kill yourself?"
- "NO." If they answer no, explain why you are concerned about them. If they cannot satisfactorily counter your suspicions, call emergency response personnel to assure their safety, despite their denials.

Example: Confrontation after denial of suicidal intentions
"Your boyfriend called me and said that you told him that your motto was 'live fast, die young, and leave a beautiful corpse.' And then you said, 'If anything happens to me, make sure I'm wearing the green velvet mini-dress and my pearl earrings.' That sounds like a suicidal statement to me. I'm worried about you. What did you mean by that?"

- "I DON'T WANT TO KILL MYSELF, BUT I PRAY I WON'T WAKE UP IN THE MORNING." This could be termed soft suicidal ideation. Do not minimize this – their pain is very real. People in this situation can usually be linked with a mental health outreach worker, a counselor, an employee assistance program at work, or an appointment with their doctor the next day.

- "I'M NOT TELLING YOU." If you have collateral evidence that they *might* be suicidal, call the local crisis line for more advice (laws regarding suicide intervention and the services available differ from state to state). If there is no crisis line, call 9-1-1.
- "YES I AM." This is your first clear red flag. Continue talking!

2. "How would you do it?"
- "I DON'T KNOW." This, too, means you have time. You should be able to negotiate an agreement with them to seek or accept treatment after further supportive discussion. Find out if there are any impediments to seeking treatment: "I'm not going to see a counselor. All they do is look at you and repeat what you say." Or, "The only counselor in town goes to our church. I'm not going to see her."
- "I'M NOT TELLING YOU!" Same as above (under question #1).
- "I COULD DO IT ALL SORTS OF WAYS." (They give you a list in a rather defiant or bored tone.) This is manipulation – it doesn't mean they won't make a suicide attempt, but it usually comes from an "I'll show you!" attitude. At this point, you must make it clear that you take suicidal threats very seriously, and you are not going to allow yourself to be placed in a position where you have to guess how suicidal they are. Call the crisis line and ask what to do. If there is no crisis line, call 9-1-1.
- "YEAH, I'M GOING TO CUT MY WRISTS." If they have a clear method in mind, this is the second red flag. Keep talking!
- "I'VE THOUGHT OF JUMPING OFF A BRIDGE, BUT IF I DON'T HAVE THE GUTS, I'LL USE PILLS." If they respond with a method and a backup plan, this is another clear red flag. Keep talking!

3. "Do you have the means to do it?"
(**NOTE:** This is not *how* you would ask the question – it is the subject matter of the question. Questions, depending on the circumstances, might be, "How would you get to the bridge?" Or "Do you have the pills?")
- "NO." Once again, that gives you some time. You may be able to negotiate with them to follow up with treatment, or agree to have a mental health outreach team or even police come to speak with them.
- "YES." If they are talking about guns or knives, find out if they have the weapon – and where. This is *very* dangerous. Be sure to alert emergency response personnel of the potential threat: "Can the police come out to see my son? He says he wants to kill himself. He says he has a gun. He's really mad at me and won't tell me where the gun is." In some circumstances, particularly when your loved one is angry or distraught, leave the location for your own safety and *then* call 9-1-1.
- "I'M NOT TELLING YOU." See the response after question #1 above.

4. "When do you plan on killing yourself?"
This question helps you gauge immediacy. How established is the plan, and is anyone else "timed" to suffer? (For example, "ON MOM'S BIRTHDAY.")

The more "positive" answers you get to these four questions, the greater the risk of a lethal outcome.

CHAPTER 31

Further Discussion with Your Loved One When They are Suicidal

In most cases, you will have fully accomplished all that you need to do. You know if your loved one is suicidal, and, if so, how close they are to the act. In many cases, however, the conversation is far from over: they trust you and want to talk more, or you are on a phone with them and you are trying to keep them talking. You don't have to ask every one of the following questions. You may already know some of the answers.

> As they continue to talk, on their own they'll often pull back from the intent to kill themselves, or they'll become more amenable to de-escalation because they feel that "at last, someone is willing to listen to me." If you do not have the right answer, continue to dialogue: caring human contact brings people back from the edge.

Questions Designed to Get More Information and to Keep Them Talking
"Have you tried to kill yourself before?"

"**Have you ever tried to do it another way?**" Desperate people become very concrete and literal, only thinking of their chosen method. They may have made several attempts before, by other means, but that often doesn't even come into their mind.

"**Have you been drinking? Using any drugs?**" Don't push this one if you have a sense that they will be more worried about getting arrested for use or possession, or if this is a sore spot, causing them to argue with you about their right to get high.

"What's happened that things are so bad that suicide makes sense today?"

"**What else have you tried to get yourself out of this situation?**" Be careful: a prickly person could respond by thinking or saying, "Oh, so you think I'm stupid?" Or "Now I have to explain myself again."

Other Suggestions for Communicating with Suicidal People
Remember that if anybody in your family or someone they cared about has ever attempted suicide, this serves as an example of <u>"successful" problem solving</u>. It is worthwhile to open up the subject of another loved one's suicide and discover what it meant to your relative.

Talk with them about their recent stresses: what they have lost, what has hurt them, and all the things in their life that are so distressing that they want to stop their life right now – forever.

Don't make guarantees of how wonderful life will be or how much better they will feel if only they . . . Instead, explain the difficulties they face. This may sound "negative," but it is heard as honesty, rather than sugar coating the problem.

> **Example: No guarantees**
> "No, I'm not guaranteeing counseling will help. And you will have to work to find a <u>good</u> counselor. Even then, it won't be easy. It might be the hardest thing you've ever done. But it's something you haven't tried."

Don't be a cheerleader. If you are too "positive," it is as if you are "in it together." If you act as if things are *too* important to you, the suicidal person, paradoxically, begins to feel that they are doing things for you rather than for themselves.

Don't try to bolster their "self esteem." You may know that they've got a talent, are attractive, or have a wonderful family. If you point this out to them – "You have so many reasons to live!" – you will break rapport entirely. It is very likely that they know these things about themselves. They look in the mirror and they see the beautiful face, but inside, they feel corrupt and foul. They look at their mom and dad, whom they deeply love, and think, "They would be so happy without me." They may think that their existence is an assault on their family. You can sometimes ask them *why* it isn't enough, if you have sufficient rapport, but do not *tell* them it *should* be enough.

Frame things with negatives. Sometimes it is best to acknowledge how difficult life has been for the person. If they do not realize that you grasp what a terrible time they have had, as well as comprehending what an effort it has been to stay alive, they will shut you out.

> **Example: Framing things with negatives**
> "You've had a bad time – there is no doubt about that. Yet, somehow, you held it together all these days. What's different about today?"

Identify the intended "victims." Try to ascertain whom the suicide is intended to hurt. You will be able, thus, to get a better sense if the person is also homicidal, or on the cusp between self-harm and an intention to take others along. We can tell if there are others intended to suffer when we ask, "Who will find your body?" Or "Who will identify your body?" Some people are utterly shocked at the question, so preoccupied with their own pain that they didn't even think that their husband, for example, would be the one to find them upon returning home from work. Others describe that same scene with happiness: hoping, thereby, that their family member will never have a good night's sleep again.

Don't wear your heart on your sleeve. The story your loved one tells may be heart-rending. I am not trying to encourage cynicism, but you must not allow yourself to become so emotionally involved that you feel betrayed, or simply burned out, if the family member rejects or minimizes your efforts to help. Ironically, contempt, irritation, or frustration are exactly what many suicidal people expect from their family, yet that is what their behavior elicits.

> **Internal questions that sidetrack us**
> - "I don't know if I would want to live in such a miserable situation." It's not about you! The fact that they are talking with you means they still have some hope for another answer. Remember, dialogue is what's important here. Sometimes all they are asking for is a fair witness (Chapter 8).
> - "Why is it important that they live?" Or "I know I should care, but I don't." In cases like these, make death itself your enemy. Your family member contacted you, asked you for help, so your attitude should be that you will do your level best to speak for life. When you simply speak in strong, calm tones, you are, in effect, a voice from the land of the living to one trying to cross over into the land of the dead.

CHAPTER 32

Self-Mutilation and Parasuicidal Behavior

One of the most confusing actions that a person can do – at least to those outside the situation – is self-mutilation. When it is an enactment of something that looks like a suicide attempt, but somehow has survival "built in," it is referred to as "parasuicidal behavior." These are examples of self-mutilating behaviors, without suicidal intent:
- Rubbing an eraser on the wrist until all the skin is peeled away and a weeping lesion in the flesh remains.
- Repetitively stubbing out a burning cigarette on one's face and genitals.
- Running a needle in and out of the flesh of one's belly.
- Hacking open one's wrists on the corner of a table, and then, after being stitched up by a doctor, tearing out the stitches again.
- Compulsively adorning the body, particularly that which is transgressive and outside of social norms.
- Slicing open the abdominal wall all the way to the fascia that hold the organs.

The hallmark of these shocking actions is that the person does not intend to die. Even in the last horrifying example, the woman in question, a former nurse who used a scalpel with the skill of a surgeon, calls for help after she makes the cut.

There are a number of reasons why someone would commit such acts:

Self-hatred. The person punishes himself or herself through self-torture and disfiguration.

Attention seeking. These cases usually, but not always, are typified by more superficial wounds. Such individuals "require" others to pay attention to them, particularly family members or loved ones who become afraid that they will be responsible for their death if they do not act. In the case of the young man who threaded a needle in-and-out of the folds of his belly (cited above), he was an unpopular, socially inept boy who craved attention. By this action, he received some; in fact, at least once a day, other students at his school would dare him to do it again.

"Primitive medicine." These people are metaphorically "draining out" the poisons in their bodies by bleeding themselves, similar to the historical European and American medical practice of bloodletting to "cure" a variety of physical and mental health illnesses.

A struggle to feel something. Some people, in the throes of deep depression or trauma, literally feel numb. Absent any apparent emotions, they use these torturous acts to help them feel alive.

Stress reduction. Physical wounding results in the release of endorphins, neurochemicals that have a pain-relieving effect similar to opiates such as morphine and heroin. A common example is the "runner's high" experienced after a particularly vigorous workout. People can become habituated to endorphin release, and activities that stimulate it can become addictive. One cuts to feel a sense of well-being.

> **Example: Cutting to relieve stress**
> A young woman told me that, after years of verbal and emotional abuse by her father, "I felt like I was walking on egg shells all the time. Then, when my mom and I finally left, it was like I couldn't stand any emotions at all. Even when I was happy, I would still feel like I was going to explode." She described one day cutting herself on the forearm with an Exacto knife, and to her shock, feeling a sense of warmth and peace. Not psychological warmth alone, but a warm floating sensation as well. Several weeks later she tried it again, and soon it became a compulsive behavior.

Rehearsal. Some family members want to commit suicide, or profess to do so, but their underlying fears make them hesitant, resulting in numerous "failed" attempts at suicide.

We must also recognize that the line of self-mutilation has "moved." We see individuals who have tattoos over much of their body; multiple piercings, including their tongue or sexual organs; branding; and metal implants placed under the skin. Most of these people talk about endorphin release. Many refer to themselves as "modern primitives," stating that they are making their own bodies into works of art. If your family member is doing any of these things, it is quite understandable that you are concerned. As far as a manifestation of truly psychologically disturbed behaviors, we should be concerned about the following:

- One who manifests emotional stress or depression, or otherwise displays some of the warning signs of suicide. This is, by definition, an emergency.
- Self-mutilation that is a sign of severe psychopathology, either due to a psychotic process or a terrible abuse of oneself. We must ask: Is it a life-threatening situation? Do they need to be placed in a hospital because their psychosis may lead them to do irrevocable harm to themselves? Is this a manifestation of a severe character disorder, so that the person would benefit from a referral to a particular type of therapy best suited to help them with their situation?
- It is simply a medical emergency, where the person had no intention of harming him- or herself, at least as far as they are concerned. Imagine a person who has undertaken do-it-herself splitting of her tongue in emulation of a snake, something this author has seen. However, in this case, the bleeding doesn't stop and the wound is septic. Triage is based on risk, not aesthetics.

The best way to answer these questions is to ask some. Ask your relative the questions described in previous chapters to find out if they are suicidal. Beyond that, establish a respectful and clear dialogue with your loved one; go into enough depth so that you understand their intention in their self-mutilation.

Crying Wolf: Identifying and Helping Parasuicidal Individuals
Many apparently suicidal people make suicidal threats – and even attempts – over and over again. In many cases, these attempts are with overdoses of drugs or medications or self-mutilating behaviors, usually cutting on their body with a sharp blade.

Whether or not it is their intent, they have as much power over your family as a perpetrator of domestic violence. You may become profoundly self-conscious, afraid that you will say or do the wrong thing, thereby precipitating the violence.

Such individuals need long-term psychotherapeutic treatment, a subject that is beyond the scope of this book. The most important thing for you, while you are living with or caring for such a person, and while you are trying to get them into treatment, is to use the centering tactics in Section I. The only way your family member will not be able to control you is if you can control yourself.
- Overly panicky or sympathetic behavior is rewarding, resulting in more and more suicidal threats.
- Overly distant behavior will result in the parasuicidal person escalating, because they think that you are not taking them seriously.
- Overly angry behavior will result in the parasuicidal person taking a kind of revenge upon you by further self-harm.

By calming yourself, and keeping a clear perspective on what you can and cannot do, their actions will not control you.

SECTION VI

Recognition of Patterns of Aggression

CHAPTER 33

The Nature of Aggression

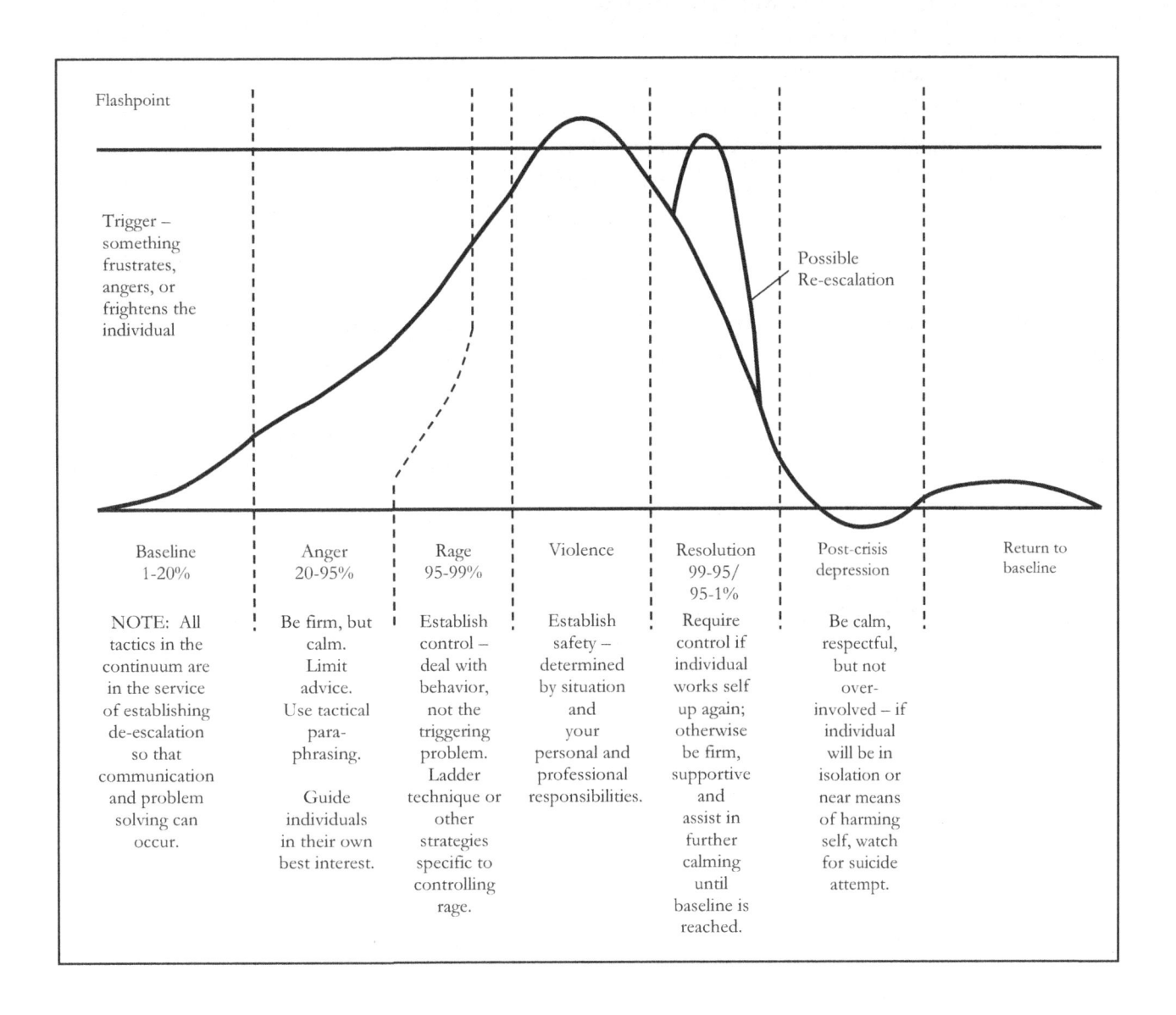

Flashpoint						
Trigger – something frustrates, angers, or frightens the individual				Possible Re-escalation		
Baseline 1-20%	Anger 20-95%	Rage 95-99%	Violence	Resolution 99-95/ 95-1%	Post-crisis depression	Return to baseline
NOTE: All tactics in the continuum are in the service of establishing de-escalation so that communication and problem solving can occur.	Be firm, but calm. Limit advice. Use tactical para-phrasing. Guide individuals in their own best interest.	Establish control – deal with behavior, not the triggering problem. Ladder technique or other strategies specific to controlling rage.	Establish safety – determined by situation and your personal and professional responsibilities.	Require control if individual works self up again; otherwise be firm, supportive and assist in further calming until baseline is reached.	Be calm, respectful, but not over-involved – if individual will be in isolation or near means of harming self, watch for suicide attempt.	

Begin by Looking Back

First, take some time to reflect on the aggressive and/or violent incidents that have occurred with your relative. Looking over past incidents is a helpful and necessary first step in learning to manage crises more effectively. In a notebook jot down your memories of the experiences you've had trying to manage your loved one's anger or rage.

Talk about Anger

During a calm period, ask your loved one some questions about anger. If they get uncomfortable, end the subject but come back to it another time. The questions help determine your relative's patterns of aggression, so that he or she can calm down and become more self-aware, , as well as give you information so that you can help them back to a peaceful state:

- What kinds of things make you mad?
- Are there any things that make you mad here, in this home?
- What kinds of things make you feel easy inside?
- What kinds of things make you feel peaceful?
- When you do get mad, what can we do to help you feel peaceful?
- When you are mad, is it better to talk to you or to leave you alone?
- What do you think we should do when you want to argue and we don't want to argue with you?

If she asks you why you are questioning her, explain that you are trying to learn as much as possible so that you can live together happily and peacefully. Tell her that she can ask you questions, too.

Remember that, in many ways, you are already the expert on communicating with your family member. You have been doing this longer than anyone else. So consider the above questions to be examples: Formulate your own questions based on your relationship.

> **Example: Your relative tells you about her pattern of escalation**
>
> "When I get upset, I want to leave the room. Sometimes I want to take a walk. But you expect me to talk about things right away! This really upsets me, and then I want to hit you because you won't leave me alone to think."

The Cycle of Aggression

An outburst of aggression usually occurs in a cycle that starts with relative calm and ends with relative calm. The aggressive cycle usually appears to start with an apparent *triggering event*, though, in fact, the crisis may have been fulminating for some time. The reader may recognize the term "trigger," being familiar with it in terms of substance-abuse relapse. The same concept applies with acts of violence. Just as addicts have certain triggers that elicit the urge to use drugs, aggressive people have triggers that cue them to become violent.

Baseline: From 0 to 20

When we are calm, we are at *baseline*, which is represented as 0 to 20 on the accompanying chart. At baseline, we use the parts of the brain most responsible for our finest human characteristics: thinking, creating, and forming social relationships. The rating scale goes up to 20, underscoring that one can have a little heat and energy and still be fully rational.

Anger: From 20 to 95

A triggering event elicits a change in both thinking and feeling. It can be something that threatens an individual's sense of safety, frustrates him because he hasn't gotten what he wanted , or is simply cues that he is now justified in using a skill (aggression) with which he is confident. Once aggression is triggered, the person becomes first irritable, then *angry*.

If baseline is presented as being 0 to 20 on the scale of aggression, with actual violence being 100, anger represents the numbers 20 through 95. If the person at baseline is eminently human, the angry person is the quintessential mammal, concerned above all else about dominance hierarchies.

Regardless of the numeric value, the angry person is still trying to communicate with you. However, because we perceive their attempts to communicate as obnoxious, domineering, frightening, or irrational, we often do not construe their actions as communication. They, on the other hand, experience an increasing sense of frustration or even desperation at their inability to make themselves understood, further fueling their anger. There are several reasons such people grow angrier as the perceived conflict continues:
- Some people simply cannot accept anyone disagreeing with them, especially when they believe they are right.
- When you do not seem to grasp what they are saying, they see you as being disinterested, or too stupid to understand.
- Your lack of comprehension implicitly accuses *them* of stupidity or unreasonableness, as if to say, "You are too stupid to make any sense."
- When you do not agree or comply with them, you are frustrating them in achieving something they desire.
- They have a sense of being wronged, experiencing a direct threat to their "position." Dominance hierarchy, for humans, includes not only one's position vis-à-vis others, but one's self-image.
- Many males have a misconstrued and hypersensitive sense of "respect," especially in the social context of our nation's inner-cities.[11] Resistance, disagreement, or perceived slights are often seen as being disrespectful toward the person, causing them to lash out in anger or violence in an effort to regain their "street cred."

As people become more agitated, the areas of the brain that mediate basic emotions take over. At this point, equity, negotiation, or compromise become less and less attractive. In their increasing frustration, angry people attempt to dominate you: to *make* you either see things their way or comply with them, whether you agree or not. Their domineering behavior is, as much as anything else, an attempt to "get through" to you.

Think of arguments you have had when, frustrated, you said such things as, "No, that's not what I'm saying! Do I have to explain it again?" or "Let me put it another way!" or "You just don't get it! What do I have to say to make you understand?" We become progressively more intense, often raising our voices (as if that will help the other person understand) because we desperately want the other person to grasp what we are saying. This type of escalation is counter-productive, despite our intentions, because we tend to make less sense when we are angry.

Anger is accompanied by physical arousal that functions as a feedback loop, driving us toward further arousal. At this point, we no longer care about the truth: we care about being "right" and proving the other "wrong." The disagreement has become a win or lose situation. We interrupt more frequently, cutting other people off, and we only listen to pick out the flaws in their argument.

To de-escalate and control your angry family member, you should attempt to *line up* with them, demonstrating that you comprehend what they are so intensely trying to say, thereby proving that their concerns are important to you too. (Line-up tactics will be the subject of Section VII.) This in itself is powerfully disarming, not only calming them down, but also helping you to work together to actually solve the problem.

Rage: From 95 to 99

How can we tell the difference between anger and rage? When someone is angry, you too may become angry. You might also become concerned, upset, hurt, confused, or frustrated. Usually, however, you are not afraid. Why? Although angry people may *later* become violent if they become further agitated, that is not their aim. Instead, their intention is to communicate with you, albeit dramatically, loudly, or forcefully. At worst they are trying to dominate or intimidate you so that you will do what they want. As abhorrent as this may be, it is still communication.

When people are enraged, however, they are, in effect, trying to "switch themselves on" to becoming violent. Many people slowly work themselves up, while others lash out violently with seemingly no prior warning, verbal or otherwise. Usually however, even non-communicative family members will signal their anger or intentions through their body language and other nonverbal forms of communication.

Most of the time, anger does not result in violence. One reason for this is that people possess a number of self-inhibitors that work to control their behaviors and prevent them from acting out their baser instincts. Within a state of rage, however, the person is *trying* to overcome those inhibitors, so that they can do what they actually desire: violence. What are some of the prime inhibitors?

- **A fear of consequences**. The fear of counterattack, legal consequences, social disapproval, financial costs, and many other possible negative outcomes serve to inhibit one's resorting to violence. This includes inhibitors that are innate to healthy neurological organization, as well as acquired inhibitors (for example, worrying about a loved one's disapproval).
- **Morality**. Most individuals possess a core set of moral principles that prevent them from harming others. It seems to be innate among most humans that, faced with the vulnerability of another human being, we find in their defenselessness a "demand" to treat them without violence.[12]
- **Self-image**. A man may see himself, for example, as the kind of person who does not hit women, make a public display of aggression or lose control of himself. A woman may see herself as caring,

nurturing, and empathetic to the plight of the less fortunate. A positive self-image, and fears of tarnishing that image, will often preclude an individual from committing a violent act.
- **The relationship**. A feeling of responsibility toward the other person, e.g. friendship, love, family relations, and so on, may hold an individual back from violence.
- **Learned helplessness**. Some people -- survivors of abuse, for example -- have tried to defend themselves in the past and have failed repeatedly. They may believe that fighting back is a futile effort, only leading to more pain and abuse. Their rage, however, is there: inside. There are phrases like, "a cornered rat," or "the worm turns," which describe a person who has suppressed their rage, sometimes for years, because fighting back always meant failure, pain, even destruction to them. Given enough frustration or threat, such people sometimes explode.

The enraged person, therefore, simultaneously strives to overcome their self-inhibitors while another part of them struggles to maintain them. As their rage increases, they are no longer trying to communicate: they are working themselves up to an attack. Enraged people are like dinosaurs or lizards. Their rage is almost instinctive; they desire to destroy, not merely to dominate.

What is the difference, then, between rage and violence? Rage is like a rocket ship on the launching pad, right before liftoff. The rocket has not yet moved, but there are flames and steam billowing out, with a roar so loud the ground shakes, a roiling moment of explosive, tenuous equilibrium. Fuel could still be cut to the rocket engines so that it will sit silent on the launching pad, but there are only a few moments to act before liftoff. In keeping with this metaphor, liftoff is the equivalent of the initiation of violence.

What you *should* experience in the face of rage is fear. This is not a bad thing. Fear tells us that we are in danger and that we must do something – *now*! We will most likely be able to handle the situation, but we had better devote every power we have to survival. Fear demands attention, but it should not paralyze you into non-action, mentally or physically, in the face of anger and rage. Fear switches us on so that our internal emergency response systems are activated. A sense of powerlessness is a *conclusion* that some people reach when they are afraid, limiting their ability to control the situation or to defend themselves.[13] Fear demands attention. Imagine two people about to be hit with a fist. One feels a sense of helplessness, a crumbling inward. The other feels a sense of outrage and instantaneously knows that they will somehow win. They have an internal sense that even if their body is wounded, their spirit will never be overcome. Fear can and should be a call to arms, not a sign of defeat.

To work with the enraged person, you must establish *control*, especially if the person's behavior presents an immediate threat to you or others. Control tactics, whether verbal or physical, are geared to establish the conditions that make the aggressive person no longer dangerous. (Recognition of specific rage states and controls tactics will be described in Section IX)

The difference between anger and rage

Imagine someone hands you a huge plastic container. Through its translucent sides, you can see a dark, hairy shape: a goliath bird-eater, the world's biggest spider. As it rustles around, its weight shifts the container in your hands as if it were filled with mercury. Is it creepy? Sure it is. Is there any reason to be afraid? Not really. As long as the lid is firmly on the container, you are absolutely safe.

This is the equivalent of anger – internally, you say, "I hope the lid stays on that thing. I'd better be careful how I hold this."

Now, imagine your friend takes the container, bends down, and to your surprise and horror, takes off the lid. The spider emerges onto the floor right next to your leg. It raises its front legs in threat display and opens and closes its ¾ inch fangs. There is something poisonous, hairy, and mean in the room, and it is not enclosed in a container! The spider is out of the box. This, metaphorically, is rage.

However, the fear that now arises within you does not make you helpless. You can still step on the spider or jump up on a table. Believing that you are helpless near the spider is an interpretation, not a fact. Fear is simply the warning cry – the drums at the brink of battle – that demand that you *must* act right now.

Violence: 100 on the Scale

Violence does not begin when someone is hit or injured. It can be perpetrated simply through the infliction of fear of imminent danger and attack. Some of the legal terms for this are terroristic threats, harassment, stalking, and menacing. In short, a violent act occurs whenever there is good reason to believe that you or someone else is about to be hurt. If the person does not have a weapon, we are talking about someone who is at about three arm's length distance, approaching in a menacing way.[14] If the person is violent and has a gun, all the person has to do is point it toward you at any distance. Even if the weapon is not pointing at you, it is still violence if the person verbally or even implicitly threatens you. In short, violence starts when you have good reason to believe that you or someone else is about to be hurt.

Your guiding principle is *safety:* You do whatever is most effective to protect yourself and the people around you. Whenever you can, escape and get help. However, if you are responsible for the protection of others, such as small children or disabled family members who are under your care, or you are otherwise unable to leave, escape may be either not possible or endurable. <u>Safety is defined by what you must protect</u>. This includes yourself, other vulnerable people, and, as delineated in our laws defining permissible self-defense, even the aggressive family member – as best you can in the circumstances you are facing.

The right to defend yourself

In the event of an actual assault when escape is impossible, it is an absolute human right to fight back to protect yourself and other potential victims. That the aggressor may also be a suffering individual, maybe even a member of your family, does not abrogate this right. I hope that you will never face such a horrible situation. At the same time, it is necessary to be clear with yourself, on a mental and spiritual basis, that you are willing to act to defend yourself and others. You must do this now. Trying to discover this within yourself once the assault is occurring is far too late. Remember that protecting yourself is not only a personal matter. You are protecting everyone who cares for you from the harm that they will suffer if you are maimed or killed.

Self-defense tactics are well beyond the scope of this book. Those interested should consult with recognized experts in the field to find a self-defense program suitable for your needs.

The essential principle of self-defense, however, is simple:

Imagine a door with seven locks and no keys. You are locked behind the door, and all that is good in life – your family, your love, your dreams, your values, even your integrity and dignity – is secured on the other side of the door. How will you go through the door? The answer, of course, is any way you can – with tooth and nail, and any implement you can reach. A violent aggressor is that "door." You have a perfect right to be on the other side.

CHAPTER 34

Why Would Someone Become Aggressive?

As you know from your own experience, there are many reasons to become angry, or even enraged. Without a capacity for aggression, humanity would never have survived. Yet most aggression seems far apart from the basic activities of hunting or self-defense. Much of it is irrational, destructive, vicious, or cruel. Why would someone be swept by rage when it causes so much harm? Why would people be prepared to throw away a future, even a life, driven by emotions that they themselves might be horrified to have expressed even a few moments later?

We can better establish safety with an aggressive family member when we understand what has driven them to anger or rage.

Anger and rage can develop because people are confused or disorganized. They can't understand what is going on around them or "inside" them due to cognitive distortions or a chaotic situation (too much information for them to sort out). People who experience this confusion are those who are profoundly mentally ill, autistic, developmentally disabled, intoxicated, or simply overwhelmed by emotion or the incomprehensible situation in which they find themselves. Imagine walking in a forest and suddenly a huge spider web drops on you. You thrash and struggle with all your limbs trying to get free.

Some people feel helpless, enclosed, trapped, or beset with a myriad of seemingly unsolvable problems. This is often similar in effect to confusion or disorganization, but it is accompanied by a particular anguish. The individual usually perceives one person or entity as the agent of their situation, and they desperately fight to get free from either their influence or their oppression. This sense of desperation could be elicited by being physically stopped from leaving when a person wants to go, being socially or otherwise intimidated so that they believe that they cannot leave, or becoming enmeshed in an argument that gets worse and worse and continues to escalate. In the latter case, people feel unable to speak sensibly and make others understand their point of view. Arguments between intimates frequently evoke this type of anger or even rage, where whatever one person says is "checkmated" by a response by the other.

The fear of attack elicited by perceived invasion of personal space is often a precursor to assault (Chapter 4). Every human being has a sense of space, a "bubble" in which an outsider is only permitted if invited. Particularly in stressful or volatile situations, you will be perceived as an attacker if you encroach upon another's personal space, no matter your intentions or relationship.

A demand for what they perceive as justice. It is rare that an angry person does not believe himself to be justified. Demands for justice are usually a complex sense of victimization or grievance and can include the following:

- **The person feels they are losing personal autonomy and power**. The person feels dominated and oppressed, viewing themselves as fighting for their freedom. This sense of loss of power is personal: it doesn't have to be "true" in an objective sense.
- **The person feels that their rights are either denied or being taken away**. People who have a mental illness frequently have their freedom of action limited to keep them safe or to keep them from disturbing or interfering with other people. Many people experience a sense of violation when they are being limited or forced to conform to rules.
- **A "self-appointed" revolutionary who is revolting against an unfair world, system, or group of people**. The best sense of power that many people can achieve is in opposition to others. They welcome an opportunity to designate others as enemies. Such individuals, particularly those with paranoid ideas, believe that they and others are being oppressed by systems or powers beyond them. They are not fighting against interpersonal oppression, but against something they believe to be far larger, and "designate" you as a representative or exemplar of those larger forces.
- **Entitlement**. For many people, entitlement is intertwined with desire. Their formula of life is that "if I want something, I deserve it, and if I am not getting it, I have a right to be more forceful in my demands so that it is given to me." Such a sense of entitlement justifies itself.
- **Hallucinations, particularly "command hallucinations."** A person may feel compelled to act as their voices demand, or become violent while trying to make their hallucinations stop. On other occasions, the voices, visions, smells, or sensations are simply distracting and irritating. Imagine your increasing annoyance with a mosquito whining in your ear, and when you try to hit it, all you do is hit yourself over and over again.
- **Material threats**. People will fight to defend what they have or what they believe they deserve. If a person believes that someone is intent on depriving him of his home, job, or possessions, violence can seem to be a logical choice. Any time involuntary hospitalization is considered, you must remember that you are, thereby, threatening your family member's living situation and employment.
- **Organic stressors including loss of sleep, insufficient or un-nutritious food, and fatigue.** Brain chemistry changes when the human organism is stressed. This causes changes in perception, mood, and cognition, and among these changes can be an increase in irritability or hypersensitivity.
- **Recent stressors and losses**. Anything that elicits profound emotion can cause the person to become volatile, and hence, aggressive. This can include a recent death, a job loss, a divorce, an infidelity, or feelings of profound insecurity.

Intoxication. A self-induced delirium, intoxication leads to poor judgment. For other people, drugs and alcohol are not a "problem," they are a solution. They drink or take drugs to "liberate" their violent desires, something frequently observed among perpetrators of domestic violence.

Ideology. Religious and cultural factors -- whether the larger culture of a society, religion, or nationality or the smaller culture of a community or family -- can provide an ideology that legitimizes aggression, even violence. Many cultures offer their members an "operating system" that expects a violent response in certain situations. Furthermore, cultures often define certain people or classes as inferior, even less than human. All too many cultures sanction violence against women.

Family interactions. One of the biggest motivators of aggression is what occurs within families. Arguments about everything -- house rules, who "owns" the house, the irritation due to living too close together, past unresolved grievances -- can cause friction. An argument starts but it quickly degenerates into a demand that each concede that the other is right. Each feels emotionally flooded and becomes more and more irrational, furious by their inability to "get through" to the other. This becomes all the worse when a family member is mentally ill because what they are arguing for may be irrational or delusional. Families often function as emotional traps: there is no escape from the people who, although loved, cause one the most pain.

Romantic relationships. People in relationships often demand that the other person submit to their wishes. There are numerous grounds to fight, from money to sex to child care to infidelity. The rage is fueled by the same source: you will "love" me on my terms, even if the relationship is delusional, mere fantasy, or wishful thinking.

An individual who has already "given up." For some, aggression, like its mirror twin, suicide, is a "problem-solving" activity, a "what the hell" response when they cannot find any other solution. This is related to the person's belief that he has no effect on the world. Violence ensures that you will make an impact. Depressed people, particularly males, often manifest this type of aggression.

Shame and humiliation. One of the most powerful driving forces of aggression is a sense that one has been shamed. Shame is not a mild sense of social embarrassment; it is a sense of being exposed and victimized by others, with no hope of relief. Humiliation is a driving force for revenge-based aggression. This type of reaction often smolders for a considerable time, until the person explodes into rage or violence, like an underground coal fire suddenly exposed to the air.

The person is egged on by others.
- Some people are set up by others who are amused at getting them mad, a particular problem when some of your family members provoke others for fun.
- Other people are provoked by family members or friends, who use the person as an instrument of their vicarious desire to inflict harm. For example, one family member hears from his father, "I thought you were more of a man. I can't believe you let that case manager talk to you like that." Or a teenager in a youth program, who has been taunted over a period of time by other family members that she is a "suck-up" to the GED teacher, proves them wrong when she suddenly assaults her.

- Other people do this *to themselves* by "fronting," making a scene in front of others (friends or family, for example) to increase their status in their "pack." Then, out in front of everyone, they are afraid to back down. Others carry an "audience" inside their imagination. They require of themselves that they conform to a fantasy of themselves as a fearsome individual whom others will avoid or submit to.

Violence as recreation. It may be difficult for some readers to accept, but for some people, hurting others is perhaps the most pleasurable activity in their lives. There is a joy in making others submit, and for some, a delight in causing pain. Because they are your family member, it is sometimes very hard to accept that you are living with a predator. If you attempt to deny this ugly truth, you will convince yourself that you are safe or in control, and will remain for too long in the presence of such a dangerous person.

Surgical violence. This is a conscious tactic of intimidation. "I won't hurt you if you do X. But if you don't do what I say, I will hurt you very badly." This is criminal aggression, whatever diagnosis the person might have. This is the violence of criminals, and it is something done by some mentally ill people as well. As with recreational violence, you need to escape from people like this.

Protective rage. This is the rage expressed by one trying to protect another perceived as a victim. The closer one feels to the victim, the more one's identity is "merged" with theirs, and the more fiercely aggressive the person will become. For example, a family member yells at her doctor and is physically escorted out of a common room in the ward. Another family member begins threatening the doctor or other staff because he believes his relative is being treated poorly.

> **Create an aggression profile**
> Look back at the list of reasons for aggression listed above and consider which applies to your family member. This information will help clarify what preventive steps you can take and what strategies would work best for managing future aggressive behavior.

CHAPTER 35

What Does Escalation Look Like?

As a person escalates in their aggressive behavior, they are priming their bodies to posture, to intimidate, to fight, or to flee. They can display a variety of behaviors.

Changes of Affect (Their Mood as Reflected in Behavior)

Atypical physical and emotional withdrawal. This is typified by avoiding eye contact, no longer speaking to others, or responding only with short phrases and monosyllabic answers. Of course, some people are more naturally withdrawn and reserved: this does not mean that they are readying themselves for an aggressive outburst. I am discussing, here, a heretofore friendly or otherwise engaged family member who lapses into sullen hostility or refuses to engage in conversation.

If you notice a family member behaving in this manner, you should approach them and engage them in order to elicit a response. For example, you may ask, "Hey Tim, you say hello and ask how my day went every evening when I come home from work, but today, you turned your back and just looked at the floor. Something's bothering you today." Note that you do not ask, "What's going on?" Direct questions will merely give the family member an opportunity to ignore you or reply with simple answers such as "nothing" or "I don't know." By treating their behavior as meaningful, something about which you are concerned, you are more likely to get a truthful response, such as, "I just had a really bad argument with my mom, and I don't want to talk about it" or "You know what's going on! You know what you did!" Such a response is the quickest way of ascertaining if the family member is a threat to you or anyone else.

Nervousness, anxiety, and fear . Such people usually lash out in defense. They are not looking for a fight; they are trying to protect themselves.

Overwhelmed or disorganized. Family members who speak in repetitive loops, mutter incoherently, or pace are displaying symptoms of a chaotic mental state, whatever the cause. Family members in this state can be unpredictable, and they may react to your attempts to communicate with sudden, unexpected aggression.

Hostility. The open expression of dislike, hatred, or threat should immediately put you on guard. A plainly hostile demeanor can escalate into violence quite easily.

Seduction. Seduction is not reserved for just sexual expressions or desires. This is when an individual tries to get you to collude with them. (e.g., "C'mon. It was just a slap. You aren't going to tell dad just because I slapped my kid.") These individuals mask their aggression. Things will be "fine" between you if you agree to collude with them; if not, they frequently explode.

Mood swings. This means rapid shifts in mood from, for example, boisterous to morose, then depressed and quiet, and then belligerent (Chapter 15). Such individuals present a particular risk due to their unpredictability and their inability to control their emotions.

Hypersensitivity to correction or disagreement. Hypersensitive people are very reactive to other people around them. Paranoid people, in particular, may complain of being stared at, watched, or controlled, and feel under constant attack (Chapter 18). When there is no apparent enemy, they will find or even create one. The hypersensitive family member can react aggressively to even the most inoffensive and harmless attempts at communication, particularly if they believe there is a chance that they will be censured or a limit will be set on their behavior. Paradoxically, they do not feel right with themselves unless they discover who is attacking them. In their world, someone always is.

Authority issues. Such a family member becomes very frustrated or outraged, refusing to comply with rules. Limitations on their behavior are, in their view, oppressive or humiliating. Their motto of life can be summed up in the phrase, "No one can tell me what to do."

Electric tension. This is the feeling before a thunderstorm hits. <u>You must *always* trust this feeling, this intuitive sense that you are approaching a dangerous situation</u> (Chapter 4).

Cognitive Changes

Cognitive distortions. Cognitive distortions are thinking patterns where the individual makes global, negative assumptions. For example, a family member assumes that if he misses a single meeting at his substance abuse treatment facility, he will be dropped from the program and get in trouble at home. Therefore, when he sees his dad, he is already flamed up at the injustice he believes will be perpetrated upon him.

Interpersonal cognitive distortions. This occurs when the person hears the worst possible interpretation of what *another* person is saying. For example, if her mother says, "Tia, you have to start following rules here, or your father and I may have to ask to you to move out," she might respond, "You are throwing me out!"

Becoming less and less amenable to conciliation or negotiation. The individual focuses increasingly on dominating the conversation or situation, winning the argument, or taking out their frustrations on the object of their anger rather than trying to find a peaceful resolution. They focus on being "right," and not on the facts. By refusing to consider other perspectives, they value only their own ideas and desires.

Deterioration of concentration and memory. It becomes harder for them to communicate, solve problems, or recall past problem-solving skills. As their information-processing skills deteriorate, their judgment consequently becomes worse and worse: They cannot evaluate what is really in their own self-interest.

Changes in Patterns of Verbal Interaction

Silence. Potentially aggressive family members may lapse into a morose, sullen silence, often accompanied by hunched shoulders, knitted brows, and glaring at the floor or at other people.

Sarcasm. Sarcasm can be considered hostility shaded with humor or passive-aggressive phrases. The sarcastic person jeers at you, or sneers scornfully, demeaning your strong attributes and highlighting what they perceive as your weak points. Their goal is to make you unsure of yourself, or to hold you up to contempt in the eyes of others.

Cold rejection. Your peacemaking gestures are pushed away. The person makes it clear that there is nothing you can do to change their attitude toward you.

Deliberate provocation. The person says and does things to upset or irritate you. Provocation is a challenge, either to place you in the victim's role (if you do not respond), or to set you up as the "aggressor," through provoking a response on your part that will justify them becoming increasingly hostile, if not violent.

Word games. Such individuals will deliberately twist or misinterpret what you say, trying to confuse you or make you question your memories of previous encounters. They may act as if it is your fault and that you are provoking them. Everything you say is used as an excuse to further attack you. In making you feel increasingly unsettled, they are grooming you for aggression, for which you, preoccupied with their word games, will not be prepared to respond.

Becoming increasingly illogical. Rather than purposeful, this is a manifestation of increasing agitation. The angry person misunderstands or misinterprets what you are doing or saying. They often go off on a tangent whenever you try to offer calming words or a way to restore peace. Others only focus on one aspect of what you are saying. They become unable to explain what they are doing or trying to say.

Vocal tone. Many angry individuals become increasingly loud and demanding, either with a belligerent tone, as if trying to pick a fight, or simply louder, as if you cannot hear them. The latter is caused by their belief that they are not "getting through to you." Others, more calculating, assume a quiet, menacing tone.

Abusive or obscene language. (**NOTE**: Spitting, though an action, has the same effect on us and has the same intentions as obscenity.)

- Of greatest concern are verbalizations that are vile and degrading. The aggressor's goal is to make you "less than human," thereby giving them license to be violent. They might not do violence to a human being, but if you are a _____ (fill in the blank), then violence is no more wrong than it would be to exterminate vermin or a wild beast.

- Others use words as weapons, to shock or stun, so that you focus on what they say and not on what they are doing (such as moving ever closer, or surreptitiously reaching for a weapon). Imagine someone saying what is, for you, an unforgivable, absolutely out-of-bounds word. While you are preoccupied with their disgusting language, you don't notice that he is three feet closer to you, picking up a glass paperweight.

- Remember that some people use obscenities as adjectives and punctuation. A family member may swear to illustrate their own emotions and ideas, with no intention to use their words as a form of attack. If things are calm and you find that kind of language unacceptable, you should ask the family member to refrain from such talk. However, you must be able to distinguish between true aggression and simple speech patterns, as you may end up escalating what was a very benign situation.

Repeated demands or complaints. Of such a person, we often say, "They have an attitude." They may demand that you do things for them, or that you provide an excuse to, for example, their parole officer or doctor for why they missed an appointment. This family member is both trying to leverage others to do things for them and looking for a pretext to legitimize what is a pervasive sense of grievance, so that it can coalesce around an issue worth fighting about.

Refusal to comply with rules or directives. In their mind, it is "all or nothing." If they comply, they lose. Only resistance is victory.

Total denial. Such individuals deny either the facts or the implications of what they are doing. They are so angry that reality is irrelevant to them. All that matters is that they are right and you are wrong.

Clipped or pressured speech. Some aggressors attempt to hide their aggression by appearing to be polite -- overly so. They often use very formal or stilted language, presenting themselves as being in control when they are actually seething with aggression or a sense of injustice. It is eerie to have such a sense of menace when they are so polite! They are trying to present as someone in control even as they have the pent-up energy of a volcano. This is often the hallmark speech of someone with paranoid traits (Chapter 18).

Implicit threats. As with threatening sarcastic remarks, any implied threats made by a family member must never go unanswered or ignored. This includes people who boast of past acts of violence, or who warn you that they might not be able to stop themselves from reacting the same way in the future.

Physical Organization and Disorganization

Facial expressions. These can vary greatly, depending on the person's mode of aggression. Facial expressions will be discussed, as part of a total complex of behaviors, in Section IX. These are among the most significant facial expressions:

- Clenched teeth, usually an attempt to contain or control intense emotions.
- Bared teeth, usually a threat display.
- Frowning can have a variety of causes, but is often associated with anger or dissatisfaction with the person the frowner is facing.
- Staring eyes can be an attempt to intimidate, manipulate, or simply target the other as prey.
- Wide-open eyes, looking beyond or through you, can be a manifestation of extreme fear. Psychotic people may be gazing beyond you at visual distortions or hallucinations.
- Biting the lips, usually associated with barely controlled emotions.
- Quivering lips, usually associated with fear or unhappiness.
- Tightening the lips, associated with an attempt to control or contain intense emotion.
- Pulsating veins in the neck, often associated with building anger and rage.
- Dilated pupils, often associated with drug intoxication.
- Avoiding all eye contact, when coupled with other expressions of aggression, is associated with planning an attack, hiding intentions of an attack, or, paradoxically, attempting to disengage so that they will not attack.

Pain in the skeletal muscles and joints. Some people experience headaches and pain in the chest and joints, as there is increased blood flow to their tense skeletal muscles. This is sometimes accompanied by a rise in body temperature, resulting in sweating.

Voiding. Some people, when angered, have an urge to void themselves, clearing their bodies for the fight. Nausea and vomiting can occur with reduced blood flow to the gut. Other people feel a need to urinate or an onset of diarrhea. These behaviors notably occur when an individual is in a state of intense fear or otherwise full of adrenalin.

Changes in breathing. Those shifting into hostile, offensive anger often breathe deep in the chest and abdomen. This can be slow or fast, depending on how fast their anger is building. Those going into fearful, defensive aggression usually breathe in a shallow, rapid, and irregular pattern, almost like panting or gasping. Some hyperventilate, breathing so fast and so deeply that they go into a panic state. Such individuals often become violent out of the terror induced by the panic. This panic state is accompanied by a feeling of heart palpitations.

Actions

Tensing or relaxing. Most aggressive individuals become tense and/or agitated. Sometimes people try to discharge the tension by pacing, typified by rapid jerky movements or even exercising that clearly is not for fun. However, predatory individuals tend to relax when they are preparing for an attack. They are at home with violence, like a tiger or a snake. These individuals sometimes smile while making eye contact with you.

Posturing. Becoming angry, most aggressive people begin to posture: inflating their chest, pointing a finger, leaning into the other, and/or thrusting their chin forward. This is an intimidation pose rather than a fighting pose. Posturing transitions into ritualized behavior, particularly among men, many of whom go into a stereotypical "war dance," puffing up their chests and spreading their arms to make their torso look bigger, invading their "victim's" personal space, pacing, smacking their fist in their hand, breathing faster, and so on. They may move in quick jerky starts and stops, making movements toward their victim and then backing off, as if working themselves up to attack.

Positioning. Those looking for a fight or confrontation square off directly in front of their target, while those looking for a victim tend to move to the corner of the person, trying to get an angle on them so that they can attack more easily. This division of behavior conforms to the well-known formula of affective violence (driven by the intention to dominate) and predatory violence (driven by the intention of taking prey).

Fighting pose. A combative stance, unlike posturing, is often a crouch with the chin tucked in. In other cases, the person brandishes a fist or a weapon. Be aware, however, that those who are most skilled at violence can often attack from a position of complete relaxation.

Trespassing and power testing. An aggressive individual will intrude on your personal space, "accidentally" bumping into you. They may also test your ability to set limits by picking up, mishandling, or even breaking your possessions.

Visually raping. Men, in particular, will use their eyes to trespass on women, running their gaze over their bodies in what can only be considered a "visual rape."

Displacing. Angry individuals may hit, kick, or throw objects in an effort to discharge tension, display a threat, or "warm up" to an attack. Another displacement activity is scapegoating, expressed on living beings rather than on objects. For example, furious that the doctor will not provide him with narcotics, a family member verbally or physically abuses his wife and children.

Making a dramatic scene. The individual "acts crazy," either to get close to you or to get you so preoccupied with calming them down that you lose sight of larger tactical concerns (like their girlfriend, who is busy stealing drugs from your medicine cabinet, or victimizing someone else).

The Edge of Attack
As people continue to escalate, the risk of violence, of course, increases. They shift from anger to rage, becoming harder and harder to reach.

Skin tone. Angry people have a flushed face – the pale skinned turn red, and the dark skinned turn even darker. Blood at the surface of the skin is threat display, as if to say, "See how angry I am!" If people blanch – light skinned people turn bone-white, and dark skinned people get a grayish tone – this indicates *rage*; the threat is not potential, it is *now*.

Pacing. Increased pacing, while muttering to oneself, is arousing, bringing oneself closer and closer to the edge or attack.

Calm before the storm. Some people engage in more and more displacement activity, hitting, kicking, spitting, and throwing things. Others internalize all signs of incipient assault. In either case, right before the attack, many people stop breathing for a moment. This is usually accompanied by a "quiet" – the "calm before the storm." The person will "recede" into quiescence, or have a "thousand-yard stare," where they seem to look beyond or through you. It is as if you aren't there. They are very often depersonalizing you, and will attack very soon.

> When people go into a thousand-yard stare, you should, whenever possible, escape. If you are not able to do so, or circumstances demand that you remain, you should strive to bring them "back" to relationship. For example, you can say, "Sammy, listen to me. Put the chair down. You know me. Put the chair down. You don't need that here. You know me, Sam! You *know* me. We can work this out together. Sam, think about what you are doing."

Eerie smile. Some people – particularly, but not exclusively, a person experiencing a psychotic episode – get an eerie smile on their face, one that holds no mirth. This can be driven by a lot of things, but it is sometimes emblematic of the person cutting off human relationship with you and attending only to the voices or impulses within them that urge violence.

Losing it. As the attack is incipient, the person can "lose it," shaking, yelling, and acting berserk.

Explosion and Afterward

The crisis will be some form of assault, possibly explosively violent. Other examples would be stalking or verbal intimidation; however, most often, it will be some kind of dramatic aggression: physical or verbal. As described above, this requires you do whatever you must do to establish safety for yourself and those around you.

After the explosive episode, be it physically violent or not, the aggressor moves to the *resolution* phase, in which they gradually, sometimes *very* gradually, return to baseline. Their body relaxes, cognitions improve, and actions are less stereotypical.

After resolution, there is often a *post-crisis depression* that is partly psychological and partly due to the physical depletion one experiences after the adrenaline rush that accompanies any threatening situation. The individual may be remorseful, apologetic, resentful, or merely withdrawn.

As a result of their actions, a number of things might happen next:
- The person might go in the custody of the police or to a hospital or detox unit.
- You may have run out of your home, and the person is still inside, enraged: essentially a barricade situation. The police may have to enter or may have to negotiate with them to surrender.
- The person may have calmed down, and the crisis is not so severe that he needs to be arrested or restrained. See Chapter 59, concerning the aftermath of aggression.

SECTION VII

De-escalation of Angry Individuals

CHAPTER 36

Core Principles of Intervention with Angry People

Example: How things can go very wrong
Joseph suffers from schizophrenia. He has taken a variety of medications, and although some have taken the edge off his delusions, none has really given him ease. In addition, he has experienced a variety of side effects that are so unpleasant he frequently tries to cut down on his meds or quit them altogether. Joseph starts a relationship with a young woman at the clinic where he goes for treatment. She, too, is schizophrenic. The relationship does not go well. Joseph worries constantly that she is attracted to other men, to the point where she breaks up with him.

Joseph paces and talks to himself. When his mother says she is sorry to hear what happened, Joseph mutters, "You never wanted to see me happy anyway. You want me to live here, miserable, forever." Stung, she says, "Joseph, if you are not happy here, you are free to leave." He whirls around and yells, "You're throwing me out? You want her to move in! I know you want a daughter. You've tried to castrate me for years to turn me into a woman!"

His mother sighs and says, "You're being ridiculous, Joseph."

Joseph grabs a chair and throws it across the room, narrowly missing his mother. He yells, "Women don't throw chairs. Don't call me a ridiculous woman!"

Designing a Safety Plan

You must be prepared for the worst. No matter how skilled you may become at verbal de-escalation, you are dealing with another human being who may be unable or unwilling to stop from acting violently, not matter what you might say or do. Therefore, you should know what to do if things do go terribly wrong.

Such preparation has another benefit. When you already know what to do, you can focus on calming your loved one, because your mind is not divided, trying to figure out escape routes or whom to call *if* things get out of control. Preparing for the worst makes it less likely to happen. A safety plan should include the following components:

- **Have emergency numbers on the speed dial of your phone**. This should include police, fire, and medical emergency numbers. In addition, you may have second-level emergency numbers speed dialed, such as your family member's case manager, psychiatrist, or treatment facility.
- **Have a landline rather than just a cell phone**. In many countries, the moment you are connected to the emergency number with a landline, your address flashes on a screen for the dispatcher. Therefore, even if you are unable to speak, or the phone is taken from you, the police know the emergency location.
- **Have a backup phone contact**. There may be a situation where your family member will not allow you to call the police or any other emergency contact. However, you may be allowed to call a family friend. Arrange a code phrase with one or two of these people (i.e. "The weather is simply beautiful today.") that warns them to an emergency and alerts them to call the police to help you.
- **Maintain a cordial relationship with your family member's doctors and counselors**. Try to get your family member to agree to sign a release of information that allows unrestricted communication between other parties, such as physicians, therapists, drug/alcohol counselors, and you. Remember that if your family member is not willing to sign a release of information, the care providers will not be allowed to share information with you, but they can take information *from you*. If you have secured a release of information, not only will you be able to alert the care providers when things are beginning to deteriorate, but you will also be able to receive further education on what to do.
- **Go through your house and figure out the best escape route from each room**. If a confrontation develops, you need to be standing or sitting near that exit.
- **Consider aspects of your living space that might aggravate your mentally ill family member**, or might make it harder to escape if he or she is assaultive.
- **Review your house rules**. Some things are simply not worth arguing about. Others are quite important. Figure out which is which.
- **Go through your house again and look for weapons and objects that could be used as weapons**. If your family member has a past history of violence or is otherwise clearly dangerous, lock the weapons away!
- **Which other family members and friends can help calm your loved one when they are tired, stressed, angry, ashamed, or otherwise upset?** What family members tend to create more stress? Discuss this with your other family members and friends, and make sure that the latter folks are not around your loved one when they are having a difficult time.
- **Once you have developed a safety plan, you need to rehearse it in your mind every few days**. Make sure all family members know the plan.
- **Become very familiar with words, situations, and environmental factors that aggravate your mentally ill family members**. As much as you can, protect them (and thereby yourself) from these factors. If, for example, loud noises and the sound of arguments agitate them, do not watch such shows on television.
- **If your mentally ill family member is a child**, you may need to be trained in physical restraint methods to protect that child from self-harm or from hurting you. Not only must you be trained,

but you also must practice the techniques. The skills should not be mere information – they have to become trained reflexes. Consult with your child's treatment team, foster parent association, or therapist on how to acquire training in ethical and safe physical restraint methods.
- **<u>Spoken de-escalation skills are the same. Without practice, you will not be able to use them when you need them</u>**.

De-escalation of anger

All of the de-escalation techniques outlined in Section VII are for angry individuals who lie between 20 and 95 on the aggression scale. These tactics are not recommended for use with an enraged family member, whom I rate between 95 and 99 on the scale. In fact, using strategies designed for angry people with enraged or violent ones will likely result in a further escalation of the crisis, increasing the risk of injury or assault. Conversely, using strategies and control tactics that are suitable for enraged family members with those who are merely angry can also escalate them *into* rage. In any case, you must first center yourself before stepping into the conflict and establishing control of the situation and the family member. (If you have properly trained in the procedures in Section I, centering is an almost instantaneous act.) Once the family member is under control and their anger has cooled, you can attempt to resolve the situation that led to the aggression.

Deal with the current behavior, not the problem causing the behavior. You may be very aware of the anguish that your family member is suffering. You may find their desire to wreak havoc to be absolutely understandable. Nonetheless, if you do not establish safety for yourself and others, you can be of no assistance to them. This does not mean that you should cease talking, reassuring, or negotiating with them. However, you cannot solve a problem with an angry person. Therefore, your focus should be on what the family member is doing, rather than solving their problem. Remember, the angry family member sees the conflict as a win-lose proposition. He or she will view any negotiation or agreement as a loss of power. For this reason, first eliminate the anger, and then engage in problem solving.

Knowledge is power. Note any significant changes in your relative's behavior and life circumstances. Inform the other people who may be involved in the family member's care of what changes you have observed. Check out your perceptions and intuitions with others in the family, and also those at a little distance from the situation. Find out what might be disturbing your relative *before* a critical incident, not after.

Presence. Your presence, especially if you are calm and strong, can be enough to calm many people. What sometimes drives the angry person is a sense of being existentially alone. That you are nearby is sometimes all that is necessary. Proximity is not enough, however. Presence means that you have established through your stance and demeanor an authority that, as quiet as you may be, cannot be ignored.

Watchful waiting. A crisis always requires that you be mindful and aware, so that moment by moment you can decide upon the best course of action. It does not necessarily require that you intervene. Sometimes, all that is necessary is that you remain centered and ready, as the family member calms himself or herself without assistance. This does *not* mean that you ignore them, but in this case the best control tactic is letting the family member control himself or herself.

Trust your hunches. As has been noted throughout this book, you should listen to your intuition and "gut feelings." If you have a vague sense that something is wrong with your relative, or a feeling that he or she might be angry, you are probably right. Once you have such a hunch, you must pay close attention to their behaviors, both verbal and nonverbal. What do you see? How is the family member interacting with other people? Have they been having any recent problems? What is different now from the way they act normally? Remember the characteristic signs and behaviors that this person shows when he or she becomes angry: Are any of those signs showing now?

One point of contact. Only one person should be communicating with the angry family member. This becomes more relevant the angrier they become. Trying to talk to two or more people at once, particularly if *they* are not in complete agreement, will cause the family member to become more and more confused and make him feel surrounded and overwhelmed.

Be what you want them to be. When speaking to an angry family member, you should embody the behavior you desire of them. Speak to them calmly, control your breathing, and maintain an upright and nonthreatening posture, all the while remaining ready to respond to any attack. Your hope is that the family member will mirror your behavior and demeanor. This is not an unattainable goal. In crisis situations, people tend to mirror the behavior of the most powerful individual with whom they are interacting. If anyone else in your family is in crisis, your mentally ill relative will feel even more out of control. If you are calm, however, you can take over the situation with that calm.

You Are the Expert

The techniques in the following chapters are quite varied. Some are widely applicable; others may only be useful in very specific situations. Think of them like the scales and octaves of music that must be mastered so that you can improvise freely.

Above all else, remember that you are the expert. No one knows your family member like you do. What might work with another individual may not work with your loved one. You will have to decide what to do in an emergency. This guidebook, aside from offering some new techniques, is for the purpose of helping you highlight things that you "didn't know you knew." There are skills you have used instinctively. Now it is time to bring them to mindful awareness, so you can consciously use them when you need to.

These techniques live through your human presence. Without this presence, an amalgam of courage and respect, all the techniques in the world will be of no use.

CHAPTER 37

Physical Organization in the Face of Aggression

How you stand, how you breathe, how you use eye contact, and how you gesture are all essential factors in calming aggressive people. You can say all the right things, but if you look like you are afraid, irritated, or unsettled, your verbal interventions will have no effect whatsoever and the situation will likely get worse. You cannot successfully and safely de-escalate an angry person if you are overwhelmed by your own fear or anger. Such off-center emotions only give the aggressive person power.

Your goal is not a constant state of readiness, going through your day tense and hyper-alert to the slightest threat. Presence, as discussed in the last chapter, is manifest in how you organize your body.

Breathe smoothly. When you breathe rapidly, you tend to hyperventilate, while forceful, deep breathing activates the more primal areas of the brain for combat.

Circular breathing (Chapter 6) is strongly recommended. However, for those who are not able to use circular breathing effectively, use the four-four-four breathing, also mentioned in the same chapter. When you are centered, people tend to feel calmer in your presence.

Standing or sitting? Remaining seated when someone is menacing you is very unwise. Remain aware of potential avenues of escape, and do whatever you can to keep your exit route open.

Stand or sit at an angle to the upset person. This is sometimes called a "blade stance," because you stand with one foot in front of the other, the back foot at a 45-degree angle with some space between your legs. (Don't put two feet in one line as if you are standing on a tightrope!). In this angled stance, your appearance is neither overtly threatening nor fearful. People can actually tolerate your proximity better than if you were standing squarely in front of them, a more confrontational posture. Of course, this stance also allows you to react more easily to an attack, because when you square up to someone, they can knock you over with a simple push to the shoulder.

You can and should also sit with a blade stance. Sit on the edge of your chair, with your lead foot flat on the floor, your foot on the ball of the foot. You look interested and attentive, but in fact, you can easily get up without using your hands or needing to lean forward to get back on your feet.

Are you too close to the family member? (Chapter 4) Quite naturally, families exist in close proximity to one another. You must never forget that family members still have a sense of personal space, and some with a mental illness have an extreme view of this. Some will see any intrusion into their zone as an attack, and they may respond with violence. For everyone's safety, always be tactful when attending to required tasks that involve close proximity or physical contact.

This is all the more important if you are actually trying to calm an angry individual, where your proximity is for the purpose of controlling their behavior. As escalation and danger increase, establish the ideal space to create an authoritative presence, neither too close nor too far away. For adults, this is generally two to three arm lengths apart. With small children, try to assume a low posture so that your head heights are equal.

Beyond these basic metrics, don't get so wrapped up in communicating with your relative that you are not aware of their discomfort at your proximity. You will sometimes need far more than two arm lengths. When sensing violation of their space, mentally ill people may become more agitated, uncomfortable, or uneasy the closer you get, perhaps shifting back and forth, looking down or away, swaying backward, trembling, or their eyes going flat. Move back so that your loved one does not feel pressured or intimidated.

Is the person too close to you? Just as you must be aware if you have moved too close to someone, you also have to warn the angry person when he or she approaches you too closely. Calmly tell your family member that you are happy to talk about their problem, but they should step back; they are standing too close. You can also say, "I prefer to talk with us farther apart, so I can see you clearly. You are standing too close for me to do that." However, you are showing your relative that you are 1) aware of danger, and 2) taking care of yourself. You are also teaching those who, due to their own lack of boundaries, are unconscious of their trespasses.

Move slowly and smoothly. Agitated people startle easily. Anything that causes you to move rapidly or in an uncoordinated, jerky fashion will cause them to become more fearful and/or aggressive, increasing the likelihood of a physical altercation. By breathing and moving smoothly, you hope to induce the person to mirror your actions and attitude.

Use quiet hands. When communicating with an aggressive individual, minimize hand gestures and other movements that could be misinterpreted as an attack. Clasp your *wrist* with the other hand in front of your body. You can stand this way relaxed for a long time. Don't clasp one hand in the other because you may unconsciously begin wringing them if you get nervous. You will then look scared, and this will frighten people with paranoia, or tempt the predatory to victimize you, in either case evoking the aggression you are trying to avoid. By clasping your wrist, you slightly broaden yourself. You will feel solid rather than nervous. Furthermore, you can easily bring your hands upward to ward off an attack, <u>without looking like you are ready to do so</u>. In other words, there is no apparent fight in your stance: just strength. Another benefit is that many of us, when verbally or physically intimidated, don't know what to do with our hands. They tremble involuntarily, or we make unconscious gestures, some of which the other person may interpret either as a threat or as a sign of weakness or fear. Clasping them as described, rather than letting them hang at your sides, keeps your hands occupied.

Use your hands as a calming fence.[15] Fences lend a feeling of security. Even while leaning on the fence to talk to a neighbor, we also have a sense of privacy and protection. Similarly, when you extend both hands, palms out, in front of you, you establish a boundary between you and your family member. The arms should angle from the body at about 30 degrees, and the hands should be relaxed and slightly curved. If an angry person comes close enough that their body or hands touch yours, they are intruding within your personal space. Upon making physical contact, most people will back off. People sometimes do not even realize that they are too close until they bump into your "fenced" hands. They step back only when they feel the contact. If they do not step back, this means that they are either no longer aware of personal boundaries, or worse, about to attack.

In an emergency, you can also use these upraised hands to push the person back, "bouncing" yourself backward at the same time, to get some distance from them. <u>It is important to keep your hands and arms relaxed – like a flexible willow branch rather than like iron bars.</u> The hands should express, in their relaxed calm, that although you are closed off to physical contact, you are open to listening.

You can use your hands as a fence in a more natural way by "talking" with them. The hands are held in the same position, but with the backs of the hands forward. You move them in tune with what you are saying – sometimes turning one or both hands forward, or little-finger edge toward the other person. However, <u>remember to keep your movements slow and small</u>. You are, more or less, rotating your elbows, not swinging your arms from the shoulders. Agitated people will become more so if the person they are talking with is waving their arms in what appears to be threatening or chaotic gestures.

> Paradoxically, holding up *one* hand, although weaker from a combative perspective, is more likely to provoke the family member. Rather than a fence, a single hand becomes the leading point of a triangle, your shoulders being the other two points. For many people, it looks like you are saying "shut up" with your hand.

Establish eye contact. In most cases, it is best to establish some type of eye contact with the angry individual. As with the other aspects of body language, you must be both nonthreatening and non-threatened. Glaring at the family member with hostility or darting your gaze around nervously will just make them more ill at ease, and may actually elicit a preemptive attack, because they perceive you are about to attack them. To calm someone else, you must show that calm and strength in your own eyes.

There are several exceptions to the eye-contact rule:
- In domestic violence situations, the perpetrator may be assaultive if the victim makes eye contact. The perpetrator hates any manifestation of integrity on their victim's part and tries to destroy them for having it. <u>Given that this is a totalitarian dictatorship within a home, the only way to improve things is to escape as soon possible.</u> This is different from the situation of a family caregiver who is responsible for maintaining the safety of their ill family member, who may, on occasion, be aggressive.
- Some psychotic people find eye contact to be very invasive. Particularly when they are calm, or only slightly agitated, angle your body in such a way that they do not feel confronted or forced to make eye contact with you. Even in these situations, however, you will have to make eye contact to establish control if they escalate into real aggression.
- A disinterested "no eye contact" can be used with *aggressive-manipulative* people (Chapter 55).
- Some people are so frightening that you feel apprehensive about making eye contact with them. Others are so chaotic, manipulative, or disorganized that you find yourself unable to focus on what to do or say when you make eye contact. If this describes the person you are dealing with, <u>look between his or her eyes, at the center of their forehead</u>. When you look in people's eyes, you are revealing who you truly are and also seeing them in truth. This may be overwhelming for you with some aggressive people. When you look at their forehead, you are *literally* gazing at layers of dead skin. You will have, thereby, disengaged yourself from human contact with them. This may be necessary in the case of really intimidating or manipulative aggressors. You will find yourself far calmer, and the other, *if aggressive*, won't be able to tell that you are not making eye contact. You will just appear very strong.

Regardless of the exact nature of the situation, or the other's mental state, do not look away from them altogether. If you turn your attention away from the aggressor for even an instant, you have given them an opportunity to attack you. Remember, an attack takes but a split second, especially in close quarters. The aggressor must be aware that *you* are also aware.

CHAPTER 38

The Tone and Quality of Your Voice

Use a firm, low pitch. In most situations, try to pitch your voice a little lower than is usual for you. You do not need to drop your voice to a baritone or bass, simply a little lower in pitch. It should also be firm and strong. Do not betray any negative or angry emotions; an aggressive person will focus on your tone rather than the content of your words. For example, a bored tone with either impatience or condescension is guaranteed to evoke more anger, not less. If you sound angry, the aggressive person will ramp up their aggression even further, intending to overwhelm you.

You will feel a small vibration in your chest when you pitch your voice lower. When we are upset or frightened, we usually feel out of control of everything, including our own body. Our voices, under stress or intimidation, tend to go up in pitch. When you feel this vibrato in your chest, you get immediate feedback that you have taken back control of your own body. This gives you a sense of power. In addition, a quiet but strong, low-pitched voice communicates that you are in control of yourself and the situation.

Slow down. You should usually speak a little slower than the person you are de-escalating. You are trying to get them to resonate with your slower energy, and also to keep yourself from being swept up in their aggression. Do not, however, speak with an exaggerated slow motion quality, or in such a way that they think you are trying to hypnotize them.

Do not be overly "sweet" or condescending. Except when you are dealing with small children in distress, do not hover over them, trying to "nurture" them with a gentle, supportive voice, attempting to convince them that they want to do what *you* want them to do, or what you desire them to feel. That overly sweet vocal tone says, "I don't have high expectations of you. You are too weak, and I have to care for you like a child." This can provoke the person to regress to a more childlike state, which can easily deteriorate into hysteria or a tantrum, and a tantrum in an adult is usually manifested as chaotic rage. Others, insulted at what they perceive as condescension, become angrier.

Again, your tone of voice should be strong and pitched low in the chest, conveying this message: "I know this is really hard for you. I can't fix it. But I am willing to see if I can help you fix it yourself."

The use of a dramatic voice, an exception to the rule. In this case, you *do* make your voice a little louder, and you use drama and charisma to grab their attention. Here is an example: You are staying at a hotel, and your mentally ill family member is upset because she believes people in the lobby were laughing at her. She storms across the room where you are standing in a group of people. You say, "Claire, I *see* you are upset! I'd be upset too if I thought those people were laughing at me! Now *come on* over here!" Start moving as if you are absolutely certain she will follow (do not, however, turn your back so that you can no longer see her). "Yes, ma'am! C'mon. I want you to tell me *exactly* what happened! *Every* word. Let's go over here where no one can bother us!" You show her that not only are you giving her your complete attention, but also the drama means that she is important, the center of the action. By moving her somewhere else to talk, you remove her to an area where there are fewer people whom she might victimize or who might agitate her further.

Reserve the lion's roar for dangerous situations. There are almost no situations where you should yell. There is one exception, however. When an aggressor is moving toward you to attack, or is otherwise presenting immediate danger to another, roar like a lion to startle and freeze their motion momentarily with commands (such as "*stay back*" or "*step away*") so you can evade, counter, or escape.

- Open your eyes *wide*!
- "Slam" your stomach *backward* to try and connect your navel and your spinal column.
- Tighten your throat. (This will be a little painful to some people, leaving a raw throat for the next day, but it's worth it if it saves you or someone else from harm.)
- ***Roar*** a command. Remember that when an aggressor, already close to you, is moving toward you with hostile intent, do not command them to "stop" or "freeze." They may comply and still be too close. Instead, command that they "step back" or "move back." The command "stop" should be used to arrest an action that will result in harm -- for example, if an individual is about to punch someone, throw something, or run out into traffic.

CHAPTER 39

Preemptive De-escalation

In many instances, you can use preemptive intervention to calm a family member who seems to be brooding or obsessing over something. This can be anything ranging from a legitimate grievance to a delusion. You avert the crisis before it happens. This technique may be more useful with someone with whom you are familiar, as you will recognize subtle changes in their demeanor that have, in the past, indicated increasing anger. Several different tactics may prove helpful in these circumstances.

Greet them and work your way toward the subject. If the person seems to be brooding or preoccupied, a grievance or perhaps a delusion or an obsession, do not necessarily attempt to address their irritation immediately. Try to draw your family member into a conversation about a benign subject such as the weather, something aesthetically beautiful like the hummingbird that has been visiting the garden, the local sports team, or another area of interest to them. Such seemingly harmless topics are also an assessment tool. If they resist you, this informs you right away that the situation is becoming serious, and your primary goal now shifts to attempting to prevent further escalation of their anger and frustration.

Use a "door opener." Begin by stating dispassionately that you believe something is upsetting them, and that they do not appear to be themselves today. Do not pose your concern as a question, such as "What's wrong with you today?" or "Why do you seem so upset? Is there some sort of a problem?" By asking a question, you give the person an opportunity to simply "close the door" and deny that there is a problem. Instead, use phrases like, "You are really down today," or "Something is going on," or "You looked really sad when your grandfather dropped you off today." These phrases give the person an opening to present their problem to you without seeming to be interrogated. By making an open-ended statement as if it is self-evident, you are implicitly saying, "We are already past the argument whether my perception is real or not. At this point, we are discussing what this perception means to you and to me." Follow this question with *silence*, accompanied by an open inquiring expression on your face, leaving the person space to respond.

Express faith in their ability to solve the problem. If they open up to you and begin discussing the issue, use open-ended questions that require them to respond: "I see why you are so upset, but how do you think you can take care of it?" or "What do you think can be done to fix things with your sister?" Open-ended questions are intended to bring your relative into the conversation by making them consider their options and offer their own solutions. This also gives you openings to suggest other potential solutions to their problem, or to discuss the possible ramifications of their suggestions.

> **Important: Questions should only be addressed to a person who is mildly upset or agitated, not to one who is truly angry or enraged.**
> - Questions are used to "slow down" the person to make them think, but a very angry or enraged aggressor is beyond hearing and processing your questions, let alone being ready to think about alternative solutions.
> - Likewise, if you notice that your questions are making the person angrier, stop asking them, because questions demand answers, and an angry or enraged person will view your continued questioning as a failure to understand their problem, or as an abusive interrogation.

Assure them that you want to help. As basic as this might sound, the following illustrates the power of this intervention. Your two nieces, both very upset, are arguing. You approach and say, "Things are kind of stressful here. I don't know what you two are going through right now, but a lot of us have been having a rough time these days. How can I help you two?" People in the middle of an argument feel like they are in a zone of invisibility: when someone approaches, they realize that they are making a public display. Furthermore, by offering assistance without criticism or directly focusing on the subject of the argument, you ensure that you are not seen as a "part" of the fight.

CHAPTER 40

Across the Spectrum of Anger: 20 to 95 Percent

De-escalation of anger is about resolving everyone's problems. Your problem is the agitated family member, their problem is attempting to obtain a goal. After all, *people become angry and violent because they want something*. Successful negotiations will work to solve everyone's problems, although the angry person is not likely to achieve exactly what they want.

Mentally ill family members can present a somewhat different de-escalation problem, because their fears, concerns, and outbursts may be due to their mental illness, and not necessarily due to their desire for *something*. In other words, their problems are internal, although this may be difficult to distinguish at the moment of crisis.

This chapter will offer strategies for de-escalating angry individuals. Some are general principles for all de-escalation attempts; others are strategies for specific circumstances. You may only need to use one tactic, but it is more likely that you will use a combination of many. Those skillful at crisis intervention have an ability to shift from one tactic to another, all the while maintaining basic core principles.

General Principles

Honesty is golden. You must be honest and forthright, never making promises (or offering consequences) that you cannot keep, and always keeping the ones you do make. Do not try to fool the family member or agree to their demands in the heat of the moment. If you suggest a solution to the problem, be clear about the limitations. If they do not clearly understand their options, they will later experience a sense of betrayal when they are refused something they want.

If you think of de-escalation as negotiation, then you have the opportunity to achieve a compromise solution to the problem. Since the angry individual is often unlikely to realize their original goal, you can offer them a secondary goal or solution. However, since many people take negotiation as concession, believing they will end up getting everything they demand, you must be absolutely clear with them: "You want X, but X simply cannot happen, so how about Y?" Keep in mind that with de-escalation at this stage of aggression, you are not trying to force the angry person into compliance or capitulation; you are having them *choose* a second or third option because they eventually realize they are not going to accomplish their original intentions through aggression.

Don't try to win, try to establish peace. Just as you should be honest and forthright when de-escalating an angry person, you should also be respectful after the successful resolution of the event. Regardless of their motivations, strive to help the individual save face. Try to resolve the situation so that they can separate with their pride intact, increasing the likelihood that, even if they have not achieved their original goal, they will at least have a certain amount of respect for the way that you handled the situation. If they feel cheated or betrayed, they will likely be noncompliant in the future.

> The phrase "don't try to win, try to establish peace" is in reference to the de-escalation of anger, *not* to the terrible situation of a life-and-death struggle. In the latter, your intention must be "I will win. I will survive."

Make haste slowly. As described in Section I, *your* attitude is an essential component to de-escalation. The individual in crisis believes there is no time left. If you also believe there is no time, you are now enmeshed within the same crisis, and you will not be able to act as a stable person to help them back to a peaceful state. Consider the deliberate actions of an emergency room doctor or paramedic. They are calm and act with no wasted motion. <u>Above all else, try to move into the situation with the attitude that you have all the time you need</u>.

Stay concise and clear. Use easily understandable words, and keep it simple, using only one thought in a sentence, rather than long run-on, multi-leveled paragraphs.

Create an exit plan for both of you. Part of any problem-solving strategy is how you will disengage, and what each of you will do once you've done so. The angry person should have a clear idea of what he or she needs to do, how the problem is expected to end, what will result from the solution, and what they should now expect from you.

Try to get the person to sit rather than stand. Pacing and stomping around is stimulating. You are also more ready to fight when you are standing. In addition, we associate sitting and talking, and even more so, sitting and listening, with peaceful communication. When we sit together, we find ourselves more ready to solve problems and figure things out, not act things out.

Strategies for Specific Circumstances

Remind them of what they know. Sometimes the best thing to do is to remind your loved ones of what they already know, but have forgotten when they got angry. Remember, this is not scolding! You are not criticizing them for forgetting something: you are supporting them by reminding them what they do when their best aspects are active and aware.

- *Remind them that all problems can be worked out by talking.* There is no need to throw things or hit. Remind them that you've done it together in the past and are happy to do it again.
- *Remind them of the coping strategies they have learned from their case manager or therapist.* These can include walking away from what upsets them, deep calming breathing, changing activities to get their minds on other things, to give only a few examples.

Set Limits. Sometimes it is a good thing to reiterate house rules.
- Only set reasonable limits that the other person can do.
- If you can't give a good, understandable reason for the limit, then it's not a good limit.
- Once you have set a limit, give her time and space, if at all possible, to make a choice. The best way to do this is to give your relative a face-saving way to disengage. In other words, if they do agree to the limit, they should feel that they are getting something for doing so. This is not a bribe, however. An example would be when they say, "OK. I'll sit down. I will stop yelling. But now we'll talk about buying a dog, right?"
- Don't be impatient. Offer a choice and "withdraw." If you can, go to another room, so she has time to think.
- One limit that can be very important to reiterate is the "social contract," such as, "We can work this out. But you know and I know one important thing: nobody fights in this house. Nobody hurts anybody here. We will talk things through and figure it out."

A caution regarding limit setting

Many people get angry over power struggles, and they flare up when they are reminded that they are breaking the rules. A rigid insistence on adherence to rules is often linked to assaults on the rule giver. This should only be a gentle reminder. Do not scold or blame.

You can say, for example, "We can continue this discussion, but only if . . ." Understand, however, that, even as gentle as this statement is, you have just "drawn a line in the sand." Once you have made such a statement, it will possibly become the main focus of your interchange. The person will either accept the conditions or they will escalate into rage; then you will have to shift the conversation to control tactics.

Don't touch the irritated person hoping to calm them down. There are many circumstances where touching an angry person will make the situation worse. Do not put your hands on your angry relative unless you know that it will comfort or mollify them. Even then, be very careful, because things might be different today.

Demonstrate empathy. Empathy is not the same as sympathy, that feeling of sorrow for another person's plight. Empathy simply means that you grasp, approximately, what the other person is experiencing, based on their physical organization and what they say and how they say it. You can easily accomplish this through the use of phrases like, "I understand you are . . ." or "What you are saying really makes sense," or "I imagine I'd feel the same way."

> **Over-empathy will result in the family member becoming more rather than less angry**
> Do not overuse empathic phrases or you will sound like a parody of the worst kind of counselor. The angry person will either become extremely irritated with you, or, among the more antisocial or predatory, will perceive you as weak.

Help them get it off their chest. Sometimes people simply have to say their piece. There is no need to problem solve: just listen with a powerful, quiet attention. Given an opportunity to speak, they will. The only real requirement here is that you do not begin to intervene or offer suggestions until the person has been able to say his or her piece.

It is often necessary to encourage the person to speak in more detail, particularly if they are so upset that you can't understand what they are talking about. Some people rush through their explanation, expecting to be cut off. (That expectation, of course, fuels even more anger.) Some are so caught up in the situation that they assume you understand, and therefore, only give sketchy details. Other people are so agitated that they don't make much sense. Say to them, "Tell me more about that," or "Take your time. I really want to know what is going on. There's no hurry."

> You must differentiate between a person "getting something off their chest" and **venting** (Chapter 44). Venting can be viewed as a form of verbal aggression, albeit toward another individual or entity who is likely not present. The danger with allowing an angry person to vent for any length of time is that venting, in and of itself, becomes arousing to the person. As they begin talking about the issue at hand, they can become more agitated, and hence, aggressive. As will be discussed in later chapters, venting must be de-escalated and controlled in the same manner as any other type of anger or rage.

Filter out the static and leap ahead to the objective. Some family members present a particular problem – over-inclusiveness. These individuals do not merely tell you what is wrong. They will, in addition, tell you their life story, perhaps, or voice obsessions and delusions that either do not pertain to the current problem or obscure just what the problem is. It is often necessary to focus specifically on the problem right now.

Example: Filtering out the static and controlling a cascade of words

"Douglas, you are telling me too many things at the same time. I know you need help, but I don't know what kind of help. What is bothering you *right now*?" You will have to be calmly assertive, because the individual's delusions or obsessions are so fascinating or so dominant to them that they easily lapse back into them. "Douglas, stop. You may not tell me more about the Punic Wars. Not one more word about that. I know you are also upset with Francine. You and I need to speak about that now."

You may have to define your "scope of work." "Jesse, I do not know anything about alternative energy or about geology. I am your mom. We have to talk about your medications. Remember, your prescription was changed. I know alternative energy is a very important subject, but you will have to discuss that with other people who know more about that than I do. We have to talk about your medicine now."

Interrupt to clarify misunderstandings. If the person voices a misunderstanding and they are not so agitated that they can accept an interruption, you can sometimes interject and solve the dispute, saying something like, "Just a moment, Madeline. Before we go on, let me tell you something important. You are not being terminated from the day-treatment program. Doctor Masters thinks you are doing wonderfully. We are so happy that you are in that program."

> Clarifying a misunderstanding is *not* the same as interjecting to argue that they don't understand your position or attempting to save face by trying to explain *why* you did what you did. This strategy is used specifically to correct your family member's misunderstanding about the primary cause of their anger.

Team up with them, creating an alliance. When you team up with the angry person, you make the situation a common problem. This is most effective when they see you as an ally. It does not work well in a situation where the angry person views you as an adversary. Teaming up requires more than words. Your offer should include a request that the person does something with you; if they refuse, it is unlikely that you will be successful with this tactic.

> **Examples: Creating an alliance**
> "Let's you and I sit over here. Yes, we do have a problem. Let's see what we can do to figure this out."
>
> Ask the person to come with you down the hallway to continue the discussion because others might misinterpret the loud voices and get frightened, or overhear private information. One way to do this is to make a request: "Let's go outside the house on the porch where we can talk without anyone bothering us."

One aspect of teaming up is finding something – anything – that the two of you can agree upon.

> **Examples: Finding something to agree upon**
> - "Look, I know things have been hard, but your kids are here. Let's move over here so they don't have to hear this."
> - "Yep, I have no doubt whatsoever that you are angry. Furious. Let's get a drink – coffee? Tea? Soda? And you tell me about it."
> - "I am aware you don't agree with me, and I don't think we are going to get anywhere further now. How about if we speak tomorrow, and you tell me, after thinking about it, if you still disagree." (Note here that the agreement is to separate and return, not to agree with your position.)
>
> **Simpler examples:**
> - "Will you, at least, think about it?"
> - "Does that make sense to you?"
> - "I understand you disagree here, but do you see how I might come to that sort of idea?"

Separate. Suggest that the two of you take a break, and promise to return to the subject later. Phrase it in a way that puts the responsibility on you, such as, "I'm having trouble concentrating. Let's take a break and we'll talk about this later. If we continue, I'm not going to make much sense, and nothing will be resolved. Let's set a time. It's two o'clock now. Let's talk again at four."

Do not tell the person to take a "time-out," because angry people may believe you are patronizing them and talking to them as if they were children. Disengaging is particularly useful when you both are at an impasse and continued discussion will increase the level of frustration between you. It is also the right thing to do when you feel flooded -- helpless to get through to them, overwhelmed by emotion (any emotion), or confused.

> **Caution!**
> Many people who choose separation feel a sense of relief that the confrontation is over and, because they feel better, assume that the problem is solved. Understand that the person you separated from may be fuming, planning his or her responses when you reinitiate the discussion. The longer they wait, the more their anxiety and anger increases. When you do not reengage, either at a promised time, or worse, if you left the timing of your follow-up discussion open, the other person interprets this as a sadistic control tactic on your part, making them wait, even "making me come to you to ask for a little attention!" To make matters even worse, the people whose default is "out of sight, out of mind" often act surprised when the other reinitiates the conversation or confrontation. If you initiate the separation, give the other person a clear idea of when you will reinitiate it, and keep your promise. If you don't have all the answers for them at that time, you still must give them a status report.

Give praise for their good ideas. Don't be over-effusive, but highlight any positive moves the person makes. If they find this rewarding, this will encourage them to offer more productive solutions. It is important not to merely praise them, as if a few compliments will solve everything. "Ride" the praise into a problem-solving solution.

> **Example: Giving praise for a good idea**
> "I like that idea. I think we can make it work. What we have to find out first, however, is if we can get permission for you to use that room. You are absolutely right. You are in a much better mood when you can play your guitar. You need to understand, however, that I do not make decisions on who gets what room. The whole family has to decide. So let's you and I also think of an alternative, if that room is not available."

Take responsibility. Sometimes the best thing to do is to take over: sum up the situation, tell your family member to wait in the living room or go back to their book or the TV. You promise that you will take care of the situation. This requires a statement that includes the following:
- A realistic idea of what to expect.
- A specific time when you will return with results.
- A promise that if you are not able to accomplish what you have committed to within that time, either you, or your delegate, will return to the person with a progress report.

If you do not follow these steps, the individual will, very likely, become anxious and then angry when things seem to be taking too long, or if a solution, too long awaited, doesn't conform to their fantasies, which have time to percolate in the interim.

If they try to disengage, let them. Assaults commonly occur when one person tries to disengage, often doing so with yelling an obscenity, and the other person insists on working things out *right now*. This is almost always a mistake. That person is leaving to calm down. The only time you might insist you stay engaged is when you have a legitimate concern that they might harm someone or get hurt themselves if they leave.

Use self-revelation carefully. It is occasionally helpful to describe a situation you went through when you experienced something similar: fear, embarrassment, anger, and so on. You must be careful and use this strategy very sparingly, as there are a number of ways it can backfire:

- The angry person should not feel that you expect to be comforted. You are demonstrating your understanding, not expressing a demand that they take care of you the same way you take care of them. If they perceive any pressure to take care of you or feel sorry for you, you will probably be vehemently and angrily rejected.
- Self-disclosure can trigger anger in some individuals because they feel that you, in telling your story, you are pushing them off their "stage." The family member essentially says, in outrage, "This is for me! You are taking the only thing that is just for me."
- You can implicitly trivialize the other's distress. When you say you went through something similar, you can, if not careful, also imply, "And here you are, all messed up while I, with the same problem, am doing fine."
- Finally, if you make a spurious comparison, the person will either blow up or blow you off. To use a silly example, if someone tells you about the death of their child, you should not try to establish common ground by revealing your pain at the death of your cat.

Ask what they think would make things better. Ask for their ideas on what would make things better, then repeat it aloud "just so I've got it clear." This can help someone feel like you are taking them seriously.

- Surprisingly often, the angry person has a wonderful idea about how to fix things. You may have gotten so involved in solving the problem for them that you neglect to ask.
- People sometimes get stuck on irrational ideas that they won't let go of until they propose it to another person. The utter absurdity of an idea can only be grasped when they hear it coming out of the their own mouth, or the person sees the look of astonishment on your face after they say it. At the same time, make sure that you convey that you are truly listening and trying to understand, not mocking them.

Try to acknowledge some or all of the other's point of view. You do not lose any power when you concede someone is right. However, an angry person, particularly one who uses manipulation as a strategy, can interpret this as submission and escalate further, so your concession should be made assertively and strongly.

> **Example: Set parameters, only acknowledge what is true or right**
> "Roger, you are right here. No, listen to me carefully. I agree with your complaint about the noise, but I do not agree with what you are planning to do about it. Yes, you *are* right, and therefore, I want to help you. But I will not help you go across the street and get arrested, which is what is going to happen if you stomp over there and break their stereo."

Distract. Particularly with young or cognitively impaired people, it is often best to simply distract them. This is sometimes useful even with people who are experiencing a delirium state, where you distract them long enough so that they can be safely restrained. The anger of disorganized people is often driven by inchoate feelings and sensations, rather than what they are thinking. If you can change the focus of their attention, their anger can dissipate. This can include food or drink, or sometimes simply pointing something out that is fascinating. "Look at that bluebird! I haven't seen one all year. What a beautiful red and blue color!"

Giving something has a number of ramifications beyond distraction. Let us consider offering food, juice, or a toy. When you give someone a gift that is meaningful to them, this transaction has symbolic importance far beyond the distraction, the monetary value, or what momentary pleasure the item may offer. For most of humanity, a gift accepted is an emblem of a relationship that should not be violated.

Use humor carefully. The ability to see a situation from another perspective can sometimes work like magic with an angry person. <u>However, you must be very careful: it is helpful only when the person is at low levels of escalation</u>. If they are too upset or agitated, their response to a joke or humorous comment is likely to be, "You are making fun of me," or "This is serious. You think this is a joke?"

Apologize. When you hurt the other person's feelings, have to break a promise, or otherwise do something wrong, *apologize*! It will not compromise your authority. It shows that you are a gracious and strong enough person to take responsibility for your own mistakes:
- If the person has a good reason to be upset, or has a legitimate complaint, accept the criticism and apologize.
- If the person is partially right, concede that point, but continue to differentiate where you are responsible and where you are not.
- If someone will not accept the apology or concession, or is making unreasonable demands, do not continue with more and more apologies. If the first apology is rejected, reiterate in a stronger voice: "I meant what I said. I am sorry for what I did." But if the person continues to berate you, then say, "I have already apologized, and I meant it, so I can't do it again. <pause> James, we have fifteen minutes left before I have to go to work. We can use that time to figure the problem out, or we can end it now. But as I have already apologized, there is no point in doing so again. It will not help to just repeat myself."

- If you cannot disengage, then you will have to use other tactics – depending on their level and mode of aggression.

Give two choices, both of which are, in fact, positive as far as you are concerned. For example, "Do you want to give the book to me or put it down over there?" or "Do you wish to continue to talk about this now, in a low voice, or would you like to discuss it peacefully tomorrow?" This gives the individual a sense of control, although, in fact, either one of the alternatives is acceptable to you.

Withdraw strategically. There are some situations when you absolutely *cannot* engage with the person. For example, let us imagine that your family member wants to initiate an argument.
- **State firmly**, "I'm not going to discuss this right now." Do *not* say, "I don't want to discuss this."
- **Immediately give the reason**. "I *will* talk about this, but not right now. This isn't the time or the place. Something as important as this shouldn't be news to all the people at the community center. I love you too much to have other people listening to your private business."
- **Set conditions when you can discuss the problem**. "We can go out on the porch in half an hour. We can sit down and talk about it until we figure things out."
- **Disengage, do not talk about it further**. Do not make eye contact that would indicate that you want to discuss it further. However, keep aware with your peripheral vision and your ears wide open in case the person becomes aggressive or even violent.

Beyond the above form of disengagement, there are times, such as when confronted by an individual who is much more powerful, who may be armed, or is on display in front of his confederates, where a "tactical" retreat is the very best means of control. You take the target of his rage, *you*, out of the picture. You can gather your thoughts to return later, feeling in control. You can also use the separation to call for help.

CHAPTER 41

Diamonds in the Rough: Essential Strategies for De-escalating Anger

Codes for Living

People live by codes. Some of those codes are based on the culture into which they are born, and others are based on the culture or lifestyle they adopt. Some of these codes are passed down within a family. Other people may develop their own codes, unique to themselves. Mentally ill individuals may develop an eccentric set of rules congruent only with their mental illness or character disorder.

The heart of their code can be a phrase of one or two words, a core metaphor that sums up their deepest values. The phrase is often interwoven throughout their speech. This is especially true with an angry person whose reason(s) for outrage is their belief that their code is being threatened or compromised:
- They perceive that others are demanding they violate their code.
- They believe they are facing a choice that forces *them* to violate their code.
- They take offense when others do not conform to their code.
- Another's actions require them to respond, lest they violate their code.

Angry people will often proclaim their values and code for living in their explanation or tirade. You should be able to identify their core metaphor in one or two words or phrases.

Examples: Various codes of living revealed in peoples' speech
- "I'm a man. He can't talk about me that way."
- "Think of how I feel. If someone did that to you, wouldn't you be upset?"
- "Are you saying I'm not going to get paid? Whether you like it or not isn't the issue; you made a promise to pay me when it was done!"
- "I was standing there. Everyone was looking at me, talking about me. I was just 'out there,' and I couldn't make them stop."

Take some time to think about the core metaphor of these individuals. Try to describe it in one or two words. What is most important to each person in the above examples? Notice that in the last two examples, a code has "coalesced" into a specific issue – in the third example, into debt and promises, and the fourth, into humiliation.

Using the code to reach the person. The code is an access route to the person. When you incorporate it in your response, you are recognizing their values (however misguided or antisocial). When you do so, the other person feels understood. That is what most angry people mean by "respect." Another way to think of this is filtering out the static and noise to get to the real music. Consider these examples:

- If you realize that personal integrity is a core issue of concern to a man, frame your responses with the same theme. "I wouldn't want people talking about you as a man who can't control himself."
- To a young man who believes someone treated him with "disrespect," you could say, "I can see how angry you are. I'd be angry too if someone said that to me, but if you try to hurt him, you'll end up losing. You'd lose your room and you'd be out on the street. Yeah, I know you think he disrespected you, but if you attack him, you would be letting him *own* you. He says three words, and your response means you lose your room here? This is the nicest place you've ever lived. No, I'm not saying to let it go. Let's see what we can do, so you win in a real way, so you keep your room and your self-respect."
- Sometimes a core metaphor is situational, something as apparently benign as the weather. "Look, Frank, it's a hot day, I'm tired, and I guess you are too. I don't even care who's right about who was late. I just want to finish this paperwork so you can get that appointment with your psychiatrist. The computers are down, so we have to figure out some other way to get you an appointment. Gosh, these hot days are awful. Here we are, all stressed out just cause we're both hot and tired."
- A mentally ill person, in particular, can get so focused on an issue that they get "tunnel vision," and it is all they can think about. In effect, the problem becomes their code at the moment. "You are absolutely right, those meds are disgusting. They must taste terrible, but if they didn't work so well, I'd never tell you to take such foul-tasting things. But they do work, don't they?" (Of course, knowing this may help you design effective treatment plan interventions, such as offering applesauce or a beverage to counteract the bad taste of the medications. But your family member will probably not be interested in such a solution unless they clearly believe that you understand how awful the meds taste.)
- Here, the person's outrage is based on his code that he is a helpful person: "Of course you are upset! You were trying to help Esther, and you made a simple suggestion. She told you to shut up. She didn't see that you were simply trying to help. She didn't understand that you weren't bossing her around. You were just trying to be helpful!"

Break the Pattern

We often find ourselves in the same arguments over and over again, and often with different people! In order to detect any patterns or behaviors that may have negatively affected your communication with family members or other people, you can easily perform a review of your own actions and responses in past disputes, noting, in particular, your hot buttons (Chapter 5). Honest self reflection will reveal any patterns of behavior, personal style, even *your* personal codes, that may have had a detrimental effect on your relationship with a particular individual, or group of similar people. You can get "caught in a rut" that only deepens with prolonged interaction with aggressive people, especially those who are mentally ill.

There are many occasions when an aggressive person attempts to enmesh you in an inescapable system. Consider the following:
- Aggressive man: "What are you looking at?" "Nothing," replies the intimidated person. "What! You called me nothing?'
- Aggressive man: "What are you looking at?" "I just looked in your direction," replies the intimidated person. "What! There's something on my face you don't like? Or are you just calling me ugly?"

Any time you can alter the dynamics of the communication system between you and another person, you change everything. For example, if you flinch whenever the person swears, resolve to keep a peaceful body. If you become defensive when the person calls you a name, do not argue or object: change the subject instead. If you typically start lecturing when verbally attacked, keep an open frame of mind this time.

At times, however, you may be forced to more dramatically break the pattern of interaction between you and an aggressor by doing or saying something that makes it impossible to continue the dispute. In many cases, you will use a dramatic voice or display somewhat uncharacteristic or unexpected behaviors. Jumping out of the system can be effective because many aggressors expect their victims to react in a somewhat predictable manner to their displays of anger and/or violence. By reacting in an unanticipated manner, you can throw the aggressive person off balance. Here are a few examples of breaking the pattern:

Example #1: Breaking the pattern
A case manager was visiting the home of a woman and her very dangerous son, who was suffering from schizophrenia. However, he was never violent in the presence of his mother, so she believed she was safe. The three of them were baking cookies, when his mom suddenly said, "We need more milk," and bustled out of the house to go to the corner store before the case manager could tell her to stop. The young man began glaring at her, saying, "I know who you are. You are a serial killer. You deserve to die, because of all the people you killed." He grew increasingly agitated. The case manager, keeping the table between them as he stalked toward her, replied, "You are right! I am a cereal killer! This morning, I drowned my Cheerios in milk, and yesterday I crunched my Grapenuts between my teeth. I kill cereal every morning for breakfast." He tried to return to his menacing theme, but she maintained a cheerful rant about the breakfast cereals she ate. Finally, he said, "You don't make any sense at all! You aren't doing this right!" His mother soon returned, the son pretended nothing happened, and the case manager left soon afterward. (In future meetings, she got a guarantee that the mother would not leave the house while she was there.)

> **Example #2: Breaking the pattern**
> A police officer was arresting a drunk when he called her a word that, more than any other, makes many women incensed. With a look of puzzlement on her face, she said, "Jimmy, do you spell that with a K or a C?"
>
> "K," he replied.
>
> "Jimmy, if you are going to use big-boy language, you should at least know how to spell it. It starts with a C."
>
> "It does? Damn, they didn't teach me that one in school."

Determining the time and necessity for breaking the pattern may seem like magic, but instead, this is a skill that will develop with time and experience. Because future behavior is unpredictable, you cannot prepare an array of specialized catchphrases to disarm an aggressive family member. This technique is pure improvisation, like jazz or rap, grounded in a powerful calm. If you consciously try to be creative, or if you are excited about a cool or funny thing you are about to say, you may indeed say something witty, but it will be at the wrong time, to the wrong person. When you are centered and in control of yourself, such improvisation will simply emerge when it is needed.

Silence

Sometimes the most powerful thing you can do is to keep silent. Be sure that you are not being passive-aggressive, fuming in silent anger, or appearing to ignore or dismiss your angry family member. Instead, you should powerfully, quietly *wait*. Such silence can evoke curiosity, anxiety, or a desire for a response. Keep your facial expressions calm and your posture centered, and listen carefully. Nod your head calmly as you listen, slowly and intermittently. In many cultures, including the United States, nodding your head too rapidly indicates that you want the other person to hurry up and finish, or worse, just shut up.

Silence, however, is not that easy, particularly for the person who is suffering the brunt of another's anger. There are three ways to listen silently, and two of them will escalate people even further.[16]

Contemptuous silence. You are tired of the dispute or may be tired of the person. You fidget, you sigh, and most significantly, you roll your eyes upward to one side. You twist one corner of your mouth. In almost every culture, this facial expression and behavior express an attitude of contempt, and is guaranteed to provoke anger, even rage, in others.

Stonewall silence. When you stonewall, you ignore the other person or otherwise make it clear that you wish they would be quiet. Your demeanor shows that you have no interest in what they have to say or why they are saying it. Such dismissive behavior, whether intended or not, evokes incredible anxiety, even anguish, in the other person who wants to communicate with you, only to find that there's a "wall" in the way. They will do anything to get through to you, including trying to tear down that wall.

The right way to listen silently: interested silence. When you have been listening well, angry people often interrupt themselves to ask, "Aren't you going to say something?" or "Don't you have any ideas?" If they continue to talk and talk, however, *you* may have to interrupt them.

Do this by advancing a hand slightly at your waist level or a little higher, fingers curved, palm down (you don't want the person to interpret your hand movement as a "shut up" gesture). You should also lean toward the family member slightly, indicating that it's your turn to speak.

<u>After interrupting the angry person, the first thing you should do is to sum up your understanding of what he or she just said</u>: this proves that you were indeed listening to them, and you are interested in solving their problem.

CHAPTER 42

Paraphrasing: The Gold Standard in De-escalating Anger

Paraphrasing may be the most important technique for calming angry people.

Paraphrasing simply establishes that you are truly listening and have understood what your loved one has said. You sum up in a phrase or sentence your understanding of what the family member has just said, as disorganized or confused as that might be. If you paraphrase accurately, you've established that you've "got it" so far, and they do not have to repeat themselves or try to express themselves in other words.

There is another component, however. Use a slightly activist approach, selectively summing up *the healthiest aspects* of your angry relative's complex, multifaceted communication and statements. If you sum up the healthy aspects of your family member's communication, you will direct them toward resolution and draw out the part of them that *does* wish to resolve the conflict. On the other hand, if they are bent on causing mayhem, they will correct you by escalating what they are saying, believing that you are not getting the message. After all, if they are angry and talking to you, they are trying to communicate with you. Similarly, if you sum up a person's worst impulses, they will perceive that you are in agreement with what is most primitive and aggressive within them, and this may lead them to further escalate.

> **An over-the-top example of choosing what to sum up**
> Angry person: "I am so mad at my daughter that I could just wring her neck!"
>   1. Incorrect paraphrase: "You want to murder your daughter."
>   2. Correct paraphrase: "You are *really* furious with her!"

If you have, in the second example, accurately summed up the meaning of your relative's statement, they will go on to the next layer.

Angry person: "You will not believe what she did. I came home and found her on the couch lip-locking that punk from down the street. You know, the kid who epoxies his hair in corkscrew spikes?"

If, however, you are *inaccurate* in your summation of the second example, the other person will correct you with more vehemence.

Angry person: "No, not 'really upset.' I honestly want to loop a belt around her neck and strangle her. Seriously! She better not be home when I get back."

NOTE: Lest there be any misunderstanding, in the second example you have, through paraphrasing, revealed that the father actually does intend to commit homicide. Of course, your next step would be either dissuading him from this action with very active verbal intervention or calling the police. Or both.

Why Paraphrase Instead of Asking Questions?

More often than not, asking questions is not a good idea with really angry people. They are already using anger in an attempt to make you "get" what they are saying, and a question shows that you don't. This makes them try harder, usually with even more anger as well as less organization and coherence than before. They experience your questions as a failure to successfully communicate, and this combines their anger with a sense of powerlessness and frustration. In this state of mind, the angry family member feels like they are in a fight, one that they are losing. In essence, they experience a question – a demand for an answer – as putting you in a dominant position.

> To illustrate how even the simplest, most innocent question can lead to feelings of annoyance, irritation, or even an explosion of anger, consider the following.
>
> Imagine coming home after a bad day; you are hot, tired, and frustrated. You walk into your house, drop your bags on the floor, sigh loudly, and walk toward the shower. Your spouse says, "Did you have a bad day?" Isn't this irritating? Isn't it *obvious* you've had a bad day? After all these years together, he or she doesn't know when a bad day just walked into the house!
>
> On the other hand, imagine that your spouse observes you and says, "Bad day, huh?" You don't have to explain anything. You continue walking toward the shower and say, "I don't want to talk now. I just want to take a shower. I'll talk to you later." You are not forced to explain yourself or to provide an answer.

Layers of Anger

One useful image to associate with anger is an onion: layer upon layer. All that shows, however, is the top layer. You may think you know what is inside: "I know what you are really upset about. It is not about her standing you up on the date. It is your essential insecurity based on mom leaving when you were six." However, your angry relative did not ask for your invasive "wisdom": such a statement is an outrageous taking of liberties *even if you are right*. Furthermore, the underlying layers of the person's anger, and more centrally, character are unpredictable. Not only will you be wrong even when you are "right," but you will also, very often, be wrong altogether.

However, when you properly use paraphrasing, you sum up in a phrase or sentence what the person has just said in a paragraph. If you paraphrase accurately, you've established that you've "gotten" it that far, so that the person does not have to repeat what they've said, or try to say it in other words. It is like peeling off a single layer of that onion, so that you can see the next one.

On the other hand, if you *don't* show that you get it, the person will feel compelled to repeat and/or elaborate that layer of the problem with more and more vehemence. The wonderful thing about paraphrasing is that you don't have to be "smart" and interpret anything. You simply have to listen carefully, layer by layer, until you reach the core level that is driving their anger. Frequently, this is their code of living (Chapter 41).

Example: Paraphrasing
Shoshona: "I can't believe it. He is so stupid!"

You: "You are really upset!"

Shoshona: "Not upset. I'm furious!"

NOTE: *When you sum up imprecisely, the other person usually corrects you, as if she were tuning up the signal rather than arguing with you.*

You: "I haven't seen you this mad in a long time."

NOTE: *You can include extra information ("in a long time," for example). This is for the purpose of gently steering your relative in a positive direction. It also helps to assess how responsive she is to you. In other words, if you add a little something, is she even able to hear it? In validating that she hasn't been angry in a long time, you are indicating that you are aware that she has shown that she is able to maintain control of herself.*

Shoshona: "I know. But nobody's ever done anything like this to me!"

You: "This is something new, huh?"

Shoshona: "Yeah, I asked him out last week, and he said yes, and then, in front of everybody, he said he was just joking."

You: "You must have been so embarrassed!"

Shoshona: "I was ashamed. It was just like when my mom left. I felt like I wasn't good enough for anybody."

NOTE: *Notice how Shoshona reveals the very thing we discussed above in the previous "outrageous" example several paragraphs above.]But she did it herself, because she, voluntarily, peeled off the intervening layers. And at each step, all you did was sum up what she just said. Rather than feeling invaded, she willingly offers you that deeply personal information, as an act of trust.*

How to Use Paraphrasing Successfully

- Your voice must be strong and firm, yet also calm. You speak to the person as someone who has the power to resolve the problem safely for all concerned, not as someone who is fragile or volatile (even if they are).
- Contact the strong, positive aspects of the person, that which is striving for strength. If you focus attention on your loved one's weaknesses and insecurities, you may foster behavior regression, which is often impulsive or violent. One of the easiest ways to encourage such regression is a soft, tender voice.
- Sometimes, you can use a *dramatic paraphrase*: "You are really ticked off!" Here, you sum up the individual's mood with your voice and posture, in addition to what they are saying.

Author's Example: How I learned what not to do

I was interviewing an acutely suicidal fourteen-year-old girl in a detention facility who had witnessed her mother murder her baby brother. Furthermore, her mother was manipulating her from prison, writing, "I didn't kill him, the alcohol did it. I've forgiven myself, and you have to forgive me too." The young girl told me that she had one wish: to commit a serious enough felony that she would be put in the same prison so that she could care for her manipulative mother. My heart broke for her as she cried; I said softly and tenderly, "It's been really rough for you, huh?" She picked up her head, tears on her cheeks, and snarled, "Tell me something, do all you therapists learn to talk like that in school, or were you born that way?" In essence, she was saying, "I have just told you that I am bereft of a mother. I have no one to care for me. And you? How dare you come into my cell, a man I will never see again, and talk to me like you are going to be my new mother?" I put down my head a long moment then looked in her eyes and said, "I'm sorry. Can we start over?" Beginning again was not easy. It took a long time before I could regain her trust, although eventually, we did establish enough rapport that I could help her through her suicidal crisis.

What should I have said had I done things right? *The problem wasn't my words – it was my tone of voice.* Instead of speaking in a soft, gentle voice, I should have said, "It's been really rough for you," in a strong tone that expressed the following message: "Kid, this is a terrible situation. It's not fair, and it's not your fault, but let's not have any illusions, you and I. I can't save you. All I can offer you is a few tools to help you save yourself. It's up to you to pick them up."

By speaking with a strong voice, and not asking insipid questions, you are far less likely to further agitate your relative or cause them to stare at you in disbelief at the folly of your attempts to communicate. Remember, angry and agitated people are not looking for your sympathy. I earlier mentioned the oft-used word "respect." When we treat someone with respect, we are not trying to make them into something we'd like better, or reframe the situation in a way that would make us more comfortable. A true paraphrase pays respect to the person as he or she is.

Using Paraphrasing to Communicate with Severely Mentally Ill Individuals

Paraphrasing can be remarkably effective for communication with severely mentally ill people. Given the internal chaos that people experience when psychotic, manic, or disorganized, it is essential that we do not add to their sense of confusion by barraging them with questions, or attempting to solve their problems by "taking over" and telling them what they should feel or do. Using paraphrasing, you can usually guide the mentally ill family member toward a state of mutual understanding and an agreement that the immediate crisis needs to be resolved safely.

Example #1. Paraphrasing with a psychotic family member

Emily, soon to give birth, is in a midst of a psychotic episode. When her mother visits her to check if she'd signed a release of information, she finds Emily in a decompensated state, saying, "There were pink rose petals, rose petals flying all around my head, clouds and clouds of roses." Rather than ask her a lot of questions, her mother sums up the only thing she can grasp. (**NOTE**: This is not the *only* possible response. Her mother could have paraphrased in many other ways.)

- Mother: "Pretty confusing, huh?"
- Emily: "You are darned right it's confusing. How'd you like to be in my head?" (This is the second layer of communication.)
- Mother: "I wouldn't want to be in a confused head. It must be hard to think."
- Emily: "Hard to think and scary. The roses spin and fly away, and I fly apart."
- Mother: "You can't keep things together."
- Emily (nodding): "I might fly to pieces, me and the baby."
- Mother (sums up what she believes to be her mood): "Pretty scary, huh?"
- Emily: "Yes, if the baby dies, I'll be apart forever."
- Mother: "You are worried about the birth, huh?"

NOTE: *"Huh?" is not really a question; it is an invitation to correct a summation.*
- Emily: "Not worried. Terribly, terribly, terribly terrified."

Example #2 – Paraphrasing with a treatment-resistant family member

Perry: "I never get enough sleep."

Father: "You look really tired."

Perry: "I don't know how I look, but I feel exhausted!"

When you are inaccurate in your summation, the other person usually corrects you. He is not arguing with you, just tuning up the signal.

Father: "You've been up late the last couple days, waking early, and now you are really tired, aren't you?"

You can include extra information that sums up the experience the other is having. This is for the purpose of slightly steering the person toward problem solving without giving advice. It also allows you simply to assess how responsive the person is to you. In other words, if you add a little something, is he even able to hear it?

Perry: "I am not tired at night."

Father: "You can't fall asleep when you go to bed, huh?"

Notice the taglines "huh?" or "aren't you?" These are not really questions. They follow statements and give the other person an invitation to correct you or give you more information.

Perry: "I don't even bother going to bed. I just lie there looking at the ceiling if I do."

Father: "It seems like a waste of time, and then you wake up early anyway. It'd be fine if you weren't tired."

The father's response is an attempt to paraphrase what he believes are Perry's feelings about his sleep cycle. It is also another assessment: he offers Perry something to agree with or to correct.

Perry: "Yeah. I'd be fine if I wasn't tired. I'd just sleep less and do more. But I'm too tired for that. I wonder if I need to talk to Dr. Montour about my medications. I think I need something to help me sleep."

Imagine that Perry is a young man who is very resistant to talking about his medications. If his father had immediately responded to his initial statement by suggesting he go to the doctor ("problem solving"), Perry might have angrily stopped talking or argued with him. By listening and showing step-by-step that he understood him, his father allowed Perry to find the "deeper layer" of his concern by himself.

Reaching the Core of the Problem: Spinning Your Wheels
We know we have reached the core level of the person's problem when we stop making progress. The person "spins his wheels," using different words but essentially saying the same thing over and over again. On other occasions, they express relief at finally being understood, or exhibit an intensification of emotion, because you have reached that which is most distressing to them. When you reach core, and it is clear that you are on the same wavelength, *then* you can begin problem solving. Reaching the core problem can be achieved by the following:

- **Further validation.** You continue to show greater and greater understanding about their problem(s).
- **A summation of the core problem, followed by a puzzled "why?"** (**NOTE:** "Summing up why" is the only time that a "why" question is tactically sound.) For example: "You trusted him, and told him about the situation with your wife. He told the entire agency after you asked him to keep it secret. I can understand why you'd be so furious at him. What I am confused about is if you do break his arm, he wins. He gets hurt, sure, but you will go to jail. Given that this is the situation, why would you want to go after him instead of figuring out a way that you would really win, without getting in trouble?"
- **Establishing trust.** With some individuals, validation establishes you as a person of trust. In such cases, you can now be quite directive, because the family member is often willing to accept advice or instruction from someone they trust.
- **Collaboration.** After reaching the core of the problem, you can engage in a collaborative process of problem solving: trying to figure out a way to resolve the situation that is in everyone's best interest.

"Socratic" Summation: Guiding Them to a Logical Conclusion
Here you guide the person to a logical conclusion. Imagine that each statement in the following sequence was preceded by a statement, perhaps one line, perhaps several paragraphs.

Through Socratic summation, you paint the person into a corner: actually, using their own logic, the person paints themselves in a corner, and they "have to" accept your help, based on their own logic that you summed up.

Example: Socratic summation followed by a problem-solving suggestion
So let me make sure I got this straight. You think Dr. Glazer doesn't like you.

You aren't sure, though, because he smiled at you.

But you think maybe he doesn't like you because the meds upset your stomach, and you wonder if maybe he prescribed them to do that.

You like the trip to his office because it's so pretty by the river, and you wouldn't want to change to another doctor unless you had to.

You haven't been able to figure this out on your own, and it's making you really nervous and angry.

And you are talking to me about this because you want to figure it out together, right?.

"So here's my idea. How about you and I visit your doctor together, and we can tell him about the upset stomach. And if you think it's a good idea, you can ask him if he likes you or not. You can tell him why you are concerned, and I will be beside you so you won't have to worry that you will get in trouble for asking."

Don't Waste It

While paraphrasing is a useful and necessary tool for de-escalation and communication with an angry person, this technique is too important to waste on everyday interactions. If your family members become accustomed to your paraphrasing as your primary method of discourse, they will soon become jaded, seeing it as a rather spiritless and irresolute response. It is "cold fare" compared to a rich dialogue, a combustible exchange of views, or a lush conversation. If your family member is calm and is attempting to find out what you think and who you are, be human in return! Simply talk with them.

If there is a crisis, however, and your loved one does *not* believe they are understood, paraphrasing becomes an important tool. It can have an almost electrifying effect on an angry person. Imagine the feeling of relief you get when trying to remove a splinter from under your fingernail, and after ten long minutes of aggravating struggle, you finally get a hold of it and pull it out of your nail bed. That is the sense of relief that an angry family member, desperate to be heard, feels when they realize that the other person "gets it."

> **How to master paraphrasing**
>
> As you as you view paraphrasing as a 'specialized,' technique, you probably won't want to do it—and you won't be good at it anyway. When you are hit by adrenaline, dealing with an angry loved one, perhaps in the throes of mental illness or intoxication, you will stumble over your words if you try to remember to say things like:
> - "So what you are sharing with me is . . ."
> - "What I hear you saying is . . ."
>
> **Don't do this!** Many people will find you irritating, and you will be in your head at a time where you must be aware of what's going on in front of you.
>
> You are, in fact, a master of paraphrasing. You do it all the time simply keeping a conversation going, saying things like:

PARAPHRASING: THE GOLD STANDARD IN DE-ESCALATING ANGER

- "Your kid flunked out, huh?"
- "You're not getting a raise."
- "You hate that guy."
- "She's the one."

In short, the natural statements you intersperse in any conversation are perfect paraphrasing. However, because you do this unconsciously, it's hard to tap into as an *emergency technique*. It's easy to perfect, however. Consider this—how many conversations do you have a day? Twenty? Thirty? Forty? <u>In each and every conversation, at an arbitrary moment of your choosing, decide to paraphrase the next thing they say.</u> Just once. Your conversational partner won't even notice. But because you made a conscious decision to do this, your brain notices. That means you have practiced that skill twenty to forty times a day. Consider how good your skill at any physical activity would be if you do twenty, thirty, forty perfect repetitions every day—it would become automatic! Similarly, if you do this every day, you will be able to step into crisis oriented paraphrasing without hesitation. It will be so natural to you that you do not even have to think about it.

CHAPTER 43

Guidelines for Limit Setting

Sometimes you have to draw a line. Once you have done this, however, it will become the main focus of your interchange. Therefore, set limits that are reasonable and simple to understand. Whenever possible, give your relative time and space to make a choice. This also includes time for them (and you) to formulate a graceful way of disengaging.

Limit setting is often a kindness rather than oppression. Beleaguered by mental illness, struggling with substance abuse, beaten down by poverty or unemployment, your mentally ill relative may experience his or her life fragmenting into pieces. When the rules shift, they can become profoundly anxious.

Other people, more calculating, unilaterally change the rules by applying tactics such as pure intimidation or passive-aggressive manipulation. This hurts the entire family; even the manipulative person loses. If the rules are fair and enforced with clarity and strength, our loved ones also have a chance to become clearer and stronger. Consider limits similar to the stakes we tie to a sapling, so that it grows straight and robust. It is when you know *where* you stand that you can actually gather your resources to stand on your own.

You must tell your family members what the rules are and do your best to ensure that they accept and then comply with them. Simply state what is required, or on other occasions, offer two choices, either one of which is acceptable to you. Then withdraw yourself from the exchange, so that they have time to think.

There are times when you should physically withdraw. Don't be impatient. Offer a choice and "withdraw." Go to another room, if you can, so they have time to think.

Other times, you simply withdraw from the debate itself, without leaving your family member's presence. Let us say that you set a limit, but they continue to argue with you. Your reply should be something like this: "I do understand you are upset, but there is nothing more to debate about the subject of shouting. The only thing you have to decide is this. You can lower your voice so that we *can* continue to discuss the problem, or we can end this for now and talk about it again another time."

Try to give your loved one a face-saving way to disengage. In other words, if they do agree to the limit, they should feel that they are getting something for doing so. This is not a bribe, however. An example would be when the person says, "OK, I'll sit down. I will stop yelling. But now we'll talk about my boots, right?"

When setting a limit, your tone of voice should be matter-of-fact. You should not scold the other person, or criticize them. Simply remind them of the rule or set a proper limit (a new rule, so to speak – something that may have been implicit, but has not been clearly enunciated).

Rules should be fair. They should also be possible for your family member to do: otherwise, it is a set-up for failure. If you cannot clearly explain why the limit is necessary, then it's not a good limit. One limit that is often very important to reiterate is the "social contract," such as, "We can work this out. But you know and I know one important thing: nobody is allowed to hit anyone in this house. Nobody is allowed to hurt anybody here. We will talk things through and figure it out."

CHAPTER 44

What Doesn't Work
(or the Big Mistakes that Seemed
Like Such Good Ideas)

Interacting with an angry family member can be intense, even frightening, if you are not both mentally and physically prepared. De-escalation requires on-the-scene improvisation, often with a volatile and unpredictable person. In such a highly charged atmosphere, where clear communication is necessary to prevent any misunderstandings that may worsen the situation, you must be able to think quickly and calmly before speaking.

That's the ideal. We all are less than perfect, however. Many mistakes are very obvious, and the moment something leaves our mouths we think, "Uh-oh. I shouldn't have said that!" Fortunately, you can prevent mistakes by taking a moment to gather your thoughts before responding to your angry relative. Sometimes you can hold up your hands (Chapter 37) to give them pause, gather your own resources, and then reply.

Some mistakes are subtler. On certain days, you may be tired, not feeling well, or distracted by family matters, and de-escalating an angry family member is the last thing you wish to do. Not surprisingly, risk increases when you are at less than your optimum ability and awareness.

The following topics are areas you should note to avoid making a blunder that leads to an escalating encounter.

Ingratiation. Do not pretend that a potentially aggressive situation or encounter is not developing by continuing to engage with them as you would normally. Do not ignore the aggressive behavior or language while calmly going about your business in the hopes that they will eventually tire out. It can be very scary dealing with a threatening family member. At other times, we are just tired: we don't have the energy to continue the argument, or we are sick of the subject and we give in, letting the person have what they say they want, hoping that this will end the dispute.

Others fool themselves. They let their family members vent feelings, making everyone uncomfortable, but they try to tell themselves and others that they are just helping their loved one "express their emotions." In short, such people cover their eyes and hope for the best. One of the paradoxes of ingratiation is that people who allow their aggressive family member to control interactions in the home often present themselves as having a "special rapport" with the person who, in fact, intimidates them. These same intimidated people often suppress a lot of anger at being controlled by the person who frightens them.

They displace this on those who call them on what they are doing. Thus, one of the first signs that the person is ingratiating him- or herself is an attitude of self-righteousness, a defense mechanism that enables one to avoid questioning the violations of one's own integrity. The following factors are also signs of ingratiation:

- You worry about "how things are going" between yourself and your aggressive relative, and act or react accordingly. In particular, you worry if you are saying or doing the right things to make the person happy, calm, approving, and so on.
- You are sometimes ashamed of your actions, or believe that you act cowardly in your interactions with your family member.
- You believe you are caring and nice, so you react with shocked outrage when a family member is unkind, cruel, or aggressive toward you, as if the two of you had made some sort of agreement that they have now betrayed.
- You allow the other to speak to you with rude or demeaning language. Don't not let this pass unchecked: "Michael, I'm your mother. Don't call me that ugly name. I don't like that. I would like you to speak to me with the same respect that I speak to you."

Do not let the abnormal become normal. Sometimes, your home becomes so pathological that the abnormal becomes normal. You no longer react in a natural way, tolerating or not noticing covert or even overt aggression.

For others, even thinking about being in danger is so aversive that they blind themselves to boundary trespass, manipulation, or even blatant threats.

> **Example: When the abnormal becomes normal**
> During a party, a mentally ill person began approaching her relatives with a smile, giving them a bone-crushing hug, effusing how much she loved them. People, both unsettled and physically hurt, would firmly tell her to stop. However, because there was no general consultation that would have revealed these behaviors as "practice runs" for an assault, others were similarly grabbed. They had no plan to deal with her: everyone was on their own. Some fended her off, some tried to stop her verbally when she came close, and others tolerated the forceful embraces. Then, suddenly, the "hug" turned into a tackle and several kids were seriously hurt in the melee.

The mistake of mind reading. Some people will try to connect with their potentially aggressive relative by telling them how they must feel, claiming to have gone through a similar situation. As noted elsewhere, personal comparisons normally make the family member even more indignant at your assumed familiarity. Statements like, "I know how you feel," "I know you love your son," or "When I...," are statements that the angry family member may not agree with at all.

When you make such a generalized statement, people may feel compelled to prove you wrong by doing or saying exactly the opposite. If you do want to say something positive, praise a specific action and say it like this: "I know you are really mad, so I really appreciate how hard you are trying to not yell." And of course, only praise them for something that is true.

Do not talk down to the person. People can feel trapped by words, and all too frequently, people talk to their family member using vocabulary or explaining concepts that confirm the mentally ill person's low sense of self-worth: "Gosh, my uncle is so nice, and explains things in such detail, but I cannot figure out what he is saying. I'm so stupid!" In other cases, the family member or family experiences your elaborate sentences and arcane vocabulary as condescending. Do not, therefore, be "smarter" than your family member. Your brilliant insights will be experienced as off the mark, confusing, or invasive.

Another dreadfully insulting thing to do is to talk to other family members or to professionals as if your relative is an object, or too mentally incompetent to understand what you are saying.

The dangers of venting. Venting is different from the situation described in Chapter 40 where you let someone "get something off their chest." In that case, the person has something that they have to say aloud: a complaint, a shameful secret, or a lot of frustration.

Venting is somewhat different, a kind of verbal aggression. Many people have a false idea about aggression, imagining it is some kind of psychological fluid that builds up pressure inside of us. When we vent (hence the word), these people believe that we get rid of the anger and then become peaceful, similar to a valve releasing pressure from a water line. Aggression, however, is not a fluid; it is state of arousal. Just like any other state of arousal – sexuality, happiness, excited interest – <u>additional stimuli elicits more arousal</u>. When one shouts, yells, complains, kicks, or the like, one is stimulating oneself to greater and greater aggression. Therefore, if you allow a family member to vent angrily, the more aroused, and, hence, dangerous they become.

When you let an angry person vent about other people, they perceive that you are giving implicit approval to their verbal complaints and abuse; they believe you are on their side. If you listen to their venting silently, without de-escalating or controlling their verbal escalation, they see it as a form of alliance or approval. However, when they get so angry that they start to become dangerous, and *then* you object, they will turn on you, feeling betrayed. Thus, if an angry person begins to vent, de-escalate and control them.

Head nodding. In western culture, we generally nod our head once or twice followed by an interval of immobility while we listen to the other person. If we nod our head more than twice, particularly in rapid succession, this means we are not interested and wish the person would be silent. In some cultures, Japan being a prominent example, rapid and almost continuous head nodding and brief interjections like, "really, really, imagine that, yes, yes . . ." denotes interest. In other cultures, nodding while someone is talking is considered rude, and people will, instead, hold their head still and look directly at you as a sign of respect. It is examples like this that illustrate the necessity of "cultural information training." Nonetheless, if you wish to be perceived as truly listening with interest to someone in mainstream American culture, nod once or twice.

Reframing. Reframing is a therapeutic technique in which we attempt to assist the other person in perceiving their situation from another perspective, -- a less negative perspective. For example, Johnny Cash's famous song "A Boy Named Sue" is the story of a man who is forced to grow up tough because his father names him Sue, shortly before abandoning the family. The "reframe" is that his father did it for his own good, because in such a hard world, naming him as a girl served to make him strong enough to handle anything. You must be very cautious with reframing, because it can serve to trivialize the other's experience. One example of the latter is to *impose* the appellation of "survivor" on a victim of rape or abuse. The *victim* deserves and needs the presence of someone who can face horror head on, standing beside them, not someone who tries to make it more palatable. It is often only when a person can accept the full implications of their victimization that they can begin to figure out how to survive. <u>Reframing, done incorrectly, can outrage a traumatized family member as they feel betrayed by a relative undermining their perception of what happened to them</u>.

Other Really Obvious Mistakes that We Shouldn't Do, But We Do Anyway

Although some of the information included in the following list has been discussed elsewhere in this book, it is repeated here as a reminder of the de-escalation **strategies to avoid**. *Do not*:

- **Make promises you can't keep**. This will be experienced as betrayal. If your angry loved one is already aware that you cannot enforce a consequence or keep a promise, you will have damaged your credibility, perhaps irrevocably.
- **Bombard them with choices**, questions, and solutions, as this will only overwhelm them.
- **Ask the upset person "why?"** Asking a "why" question demands an answer or an explanation, something they may be quite unwilling or unable to do. "Why" questions should only be used when you have used paraphrasing to successfully reach the core problem (see Chapter 42).
- **Talk down to people as if they are stupid**. Do not roll your eyes or sigh heavily while your family member is trying to communicate with you. Do not interrupt as they speak, particularly to correct what they are saying.
- **Speak to them as if they are fragile**.
- **Use global phrases such as "calm down."** Do not use "social services scolding" such as "That's not appropriate." Phrases like this color you as someone uncomfortable with confronting aggression head on.
- **Analyze why they do something**. Analyzing is "cutting apart to examine." People, particularly upset or angered people, experience someone analyzing them not as a mark of the analyst's brilliance, but as a violation.
- **Expose their private information** in front of others.
- **Take things personally when your angry relative attacks your character**. A measure of the strength of your character is *not* taking things personally.

WHAT DOESN'T WORK (OR THE BIG MISTAKES THAT SEEMED LIKE SUCH GOOD IDEAS)

- **Allow the angry person to trespass on your personal boundaries**. When we allow others to trespass upon us, we are implicitly giving them permission. Any territory we relinquish is free to whoever chooses to occupy it.
- **Touch, push, or try to move** them from one place to another with your hands, or point at them.
- **Adopt an authoritarian or demeaning attitude**, particularly in front of their peers.

SECTION VIII

Communication with Mentally Ill and Emotionally Disturbed Youth

CHAPTER 45

Communication with Potentially Aggressive Youthful Family Members

De-escalation of Youth: Are There Any Differences from That of Adults?[17]

> Generally speaking, you will use the same de-escalation strategies with youth that are outlined in the rest of this book. The differences are often more on nuance than on major details. I have, however, "subdivided" youth in some general categories based on behavior that will help both in understanding young people and using the best strategies to help stabilize and calm them when they have become aggressive or are otherwise in crisis. As in other sections of the book, these categories are largely independent of diagnosis.

It's hard being young – it always has been. Young people begin to look to their peers to define what is an acceptable way to exist, and if those peers are not of the best character, our own children will begin to slide as well. Parental influence recedes, and parental authority is challenged. Hormones sweep through every cell of the body, making biological demands on both young men and women to mate and to reproduce. Testosterone, along with growing muscle and bone, encourages both risk taking and aggression in boys, and with the flood of both estrogen and androgens, girls often begin to see other girls as rivals rather than friends. And these are in the best of circumstances! Things can be far worse for our children.

Ostracism, for example, was once the equivalent of a death sentence: in earlier times, cut off from one's family and tribe, one had nothing left to do but die. Yet children are ostracized all the time. Some children have no way to escape this. With their social life centered on the Internet, harassment and ostracism can explode like virulent fungi, poisoning every relationship the child has and leaving him or her no escape but total isolation.

Bullying makes one tough, some people say. Yes, it is true that to grow up strong, you must, on occasion, stand up for yourself. Yet how can a child stand up to systematic bullying, where a much stronger person or even a group makes a single child the object of incessant torment? The child is also trapped within an "ethic" that utterly condemns anyone who tells on his or her tormentors.

A couple of generations ago, parents mulled over how to introduce the topic of sexuality, and the timid might leave a book on their child's pillow that explained in some detail what happens between a man and a woman. They would also leave a note, saying, "If you have any questions, just ask." Kids used to look up "intercourse" and "sex" in the dictionary, and checked, just to be sure, that "f---k" was not there as well. Today, he or she Googles "sex" and gets tens of millions of hits, with films of transgressive sex, some of which, truly, had never been conceived of before a combination of drugs, money, desperation, and degenerate imagination enabled filmmakers to coerce people into doing just about anything. With the Internet the normative touchstone of youth culture, many children and teens end up attracted to sexual behavior that is uncaring of one's partner, and/or skewed far from the standards of ordinary human sexuality. I am well aware that the panoply of sexual fantasy and activities is not confined to a single norm, but do your own browser search! Something has gone terribly wrong when our children's sexual education enlightens them that sex, as often as not, often involves acts that border close to torture, and pushes well over the line in terms of contempt and degradation of everyone involved, particularly women.

Drugs are everywhere, and not only do they affect children directly, but far too many have been affected *in utero* by their parents' drug use. This is not only the fault of their mothers: there are questions about genetic changes in the sperm of male drug and alcohol users as well. Furthermore, parents who regularly drink and do drugs offer limited attention and caring toward their children in the "best" of such circumstances. In fact, abuse of all kinds increases exponentially in drug- and alcohol-abusing homes.

Street gangs metastasize within a community just like cancer. There is a putrescent vitality to gang life that is both charismatic and compelling. Despite the terrible things one may do, the gang offers solidarity and a life committed to something bigger than oneself, however damaging that might be. Once initiated, one crosses a line that is hard to cross back over.

> Gang charisma, by the way, is not only attractive to children from broken or abusive homes – the vitality of a warrior culture, no matter how violent and destructive to both it victims and its own members, seduces children from loving families as well. It is only when "the good" has a power and charisma greater than that of gang culture that youth find it easy to turn away.

We live in a culture that bombards us, not only with images of sex, but also of impossible romantic love. Kids get the message that without a relationship, life is empty. Furthermore, everyone is lovable if only we smell right, look right, walk right, dress right, think right, perform right, talk right, are shaped right, and make sure to drink the right beer. The major preoccupation of many teens – no, much earlier, preteens, even children -- is whether one is in a relationship, is doing what he or she has to do to stay in a relationship, or what to do now that one has lost the relationship. School, rather than a place of learning, is, for many, an enclosed environment, where a preoccupation with who likes who achieves cosmic importance. Many kids are labeled as useless for relationships by their peers and themselves. Others squander much of their waking hours obsessing on their looks, their weight, and all the rest of the artifices that, applied correctly, might make one worth spending time with.

Enough, yes? One could write an Ecclesiastes, a dirge for the innocence of our children lost. Suicide? Violence? Why not? Both are problem-solving activities, when one cannot think of another viable solution to the problem that traps them. Do many of our children find themselves so trapped? Yes, beyond counting.

One significant additional factor that plays into our relationships with young people is the particular dynamic that exists between teenagers and adults in Western culture. Modern Western culture is unique in its "creation" of teenagers as a special class. In most societies, one was a child until, through some initiation usually connected to one's ability to procreate or fight, one became an adult. Such "young adults" might still have had a lot to learn, and they have been quite low in a social hierarchy regarding their elders or family, but they were expected to fulfill an adult's responsibilities.

These days, due to the requirements necessary to educate someone for a mature role in our far more complex society, the assumption of adult responsibilities is quite delayed, compared to other cultures – including America and Europe of a century ago. With financial support from their families, youth have become commercial targets. There is a multi-billion-dollar industry that focuses all its attention on how to please young people. In traditional cultures, youth idolized adults because with adulthood came both responsibility and privilege. The creation of a commoditized youth culture has reversed this: far too many adults envy youth, trying to dress and be like them. All of this causes many young people to affect an arrogant stance: they assume that they are eye-to-eye equal with their elders. They speak to adults as if they are peers or even inferiors, and sad to say, far too many adults agree.

Nonetheless, there is a deep desire within every human being to become a person of dignity and integrity. Young people have a passionate desire to find individuals worth respecting. Think, for example, of the worldwide admiration for such people as Nelson Mandela.

However, when children emerge into modern teenage society, they are not *primarily* concerned with either maturity or integrity as an adult, or security and happiness at home as a child. They desire to stretch their wings and feel powerful. They measure power by their effect on others, particularly their peers. If youths view adults as their peers, they will be preoccupied with who is more powerful and will vest considerable energy in not being powerless in relationship to them.

To make matters more difficult, power, too, has been commoditized. It has been made synonymous with violence and the ability to intimidate. Many teens see intimidation (everything from violence at the extreme end to such subtle gambits as the "silent treatment," where a teenager makes an adult anxious and overeager to reach them) as a means of achieving a powerful role in this world.

What so many teens tragically lack are "true adults," individuals who do not believe that power is merely a dynamic between predators and sheep, who understand that there is a power of humanity that does not resolve itself around violence or terror, but is manifested by integrity and dignity. Because we have, among all our drives and desires, this innate passion to mature, such true adults will have charisma, even among very volatile and troubled youth. They draw kids to them without any effort. Their attitude is not, "How can I please or reach you?" Instead, it is a simple invitation: "Here I am. You are welcome here. But I don't need you here either. It's up to you."

Many parents, faced by a young person who is living a life of terrible pain, are moved to comfort and nurture them. This can make the youth "soften" and feel childlike. Even though a part of them may desire this, as it is often a missing experience growing up, they very likely will also feel disarmed, no longer able to protect themselves. Imagine trying to make friends with a wolf. You do not roll it over and try to rub its belly. Instead, you sit quietly, with the back of your hand out, and wait for the wolf to carefully come close to smell and get to know you. Rather than hoping he will roll over, it is far better for him to be able to quietly sit, his wolfish identity not threatened, and yet feel safe enough to let down his guard and appreciate who you are and what you can offer.

Because so many aggressive youth use negative attention as the means to engage adults, you must have a spacious enough attitude to powerfully respond to dangerous behaviors without *overreacting*. Furthermore, it is imperative that you "seize" and validate positive interactions. The danger is in going overboard. These kids do not need gold stars and a lot of praise. They do *not* have a problem with self-esteem, per se. Their biggest problem is that no one notices when they are acting decently or simply not provocatively, events that, due to their lack of drama, often pass right under the radar. Some recognition, even praise, is needed, but *less is more*.

Teenagers, especially, experience fear and rage as being out of control, yet they'd like to believe that through aggression they will *take* control. Every time you can deal firmly and effectively with an angry teenager without losing your temper, you demonstrate a kind of power that is at variance to loss of control, something very attractive to teens who may have never seen it before. This is contained power, power expressed with dignity and grace.

Youth and young adults show mental illness in much the same manner as adults. If a young person is displaying psychosis, mania, latency or any of the other behaviors described in Sections II to IV, the strategies described there apply. In this section, you will learn the character traits that are often related to different modes of aggression in youth

View each chapter in this section as a quick step-by-step process. If the approach in the first chapter (Chapter 46) does not work, move on to the next. It is quite likely that you will intuitively grasp that a youth is in one mode or another and start with the tactics appropriate to that behavior. This section will take things, however, as a step-by-step process. To reiterate, this section offers information on what approach to take with youth to de-escalate them. Beyond that, specific de-escalation methods for any person – youth or adult – are discussed in Sections VII and IX.[18]

> **Caution**: Don't become a chameleon and try to be "one of them," ineptly mimicking the child's body language, slang, or dress. You will only look ridiculous. Your task is to give them the gift of a genuine relationship with an adult who can offer support and even guidance. Imitation means that you are conceding guidance and authority to them.

CHAPTER 46

No Brake Pads: A Consideration of the Impulsive Child

Children in the United States have been allegedly plagued by an epidemic of attention deficit disorder (ADD)/attention deficit hyperactivity disorder (ADHD). Per orthodox theory, attention disorders come in two major forms. In the first type, the main manifestation is a short attention span. In the second type, hyperactivity is also present. Although beyond the scope of this book, the diagnosis of ADD/ADHD, now so common, deserves more debate than it currently receives in both media and clinical sources.[19]

In any event, let us here consider the impulsive youth, one who tends to act before he or she thinks.
- He is in a store and sees a video game he wants, and without considering the consequences, shoplifts right in front of the security camera.
- She gets in an argument with her sixteen-year-old painfully shy sister, and blurts out something embarrassing about her body to her new boyfriend.
- Another boy bumps him in the hall and he stabs him in the hand with his pencil: he is as surprised as the victim; both of them look at the bloody pencil tip with their mouths open in shock.

Due to their difficulty in deriving satisfaction by methodical step-by-step work as opposed to the thrill of immediate gratification, many impulsive youth engage in disruptive or thrill-seeking behaviors. Beyond any interventions, from educational and vocational planning to cognitive therapy or medication, the impulsive youth needs an activity that consumes their interest. They are able to focus with remarkable intensity when something fascinates them, about which they can say, "This is me." This activity gives purpose and meaning to their lives, a touchstone they can use to help them manage those more difficult situations where they do not feel at home.

The impulsive young person gets angry or aggressive for the same reasons that any other person would, but they get particularly upset and frustrated when someone interferes with the gratification of an impulse. Swept away by this anger, they find it difficult to stop. Impulsive youths hear very little of what you say, particularly when they are angry, upset, or confused. Paraphrasing (see Chapter 42) is particularly valuable, as you prove that you understand their desire and frustration, rather than argue with them.

However, impulsive youth track very little of what you say – particularly when they are very angry. If they are too escalated for paraphrasing, keep a calm demeanor and use simple, short commands: it is not the time for explanations, attempts to elicit empathy, or moral preachments.

> **Review: Dealing with the impulsive youth**
>
> When dealing with an upset or aggressive youth, assume that he or she is in "impulsive" mode until proven otherwise. How do you know that they are *not* merely impulsive or upset? If the strategies suitable for de-escalating an impulsive youth don't work, go on to the next strategy. Remember, we are talking about an approach that takes only a few moments.
> - Paraphrase.
> - Give them firm, brief commands; help them regain control by directly telling them what to do. This only works, however, when you keep firm control of your own behavior by centering yourself.

CHAPTER 47

Conduct Disorder: Fierce Youth

> Conduct disorder is a term/diagnosis that delineates behaviors in children and youth that, in someone over the age of eighteen, would merit the diagnosis of antisocial personality disorder or even psychopathy. However, because the child/adolescent brain is still so changeable, we properly do not give them a diagnosis that indicates that change is unlikely, if not impossible. <u>The majority of children who fully merit the diagnosis of conduct disorder do *not* grow up to be psychopaths</u>. Nonetheless, to understand a youth who is conduct disordered you must also understand manipulation (Chapter 20) because their behaviors, even if not fixed throughout the span of their lives, are the same as adults who manipulate. This section focuses specifically on youth who display ferocious, manipulative, or predatory behaviors.

This is a disorder of childhood and teen years and is often, though not definitively, a precursor of criminality, even psychopathy. Such youth often seem to be without conscience or caring for most other children or adults.

The conduct-disordered youth typically displays rages in three major categories: fury, aggressive manipulation, and predatory behavior (Section IX). Conduct-disordered character traits can develop from a myriad of reasons, some of them heart-rending. This is relevant in future treatment, but not for the de-escalation and control of their anger or violence: someone will be seriously hurt if you contextualize or excuse their behavior.

Fierce youth strive to defend themselves against any need for other people, as well as building up a callous attitude in which they extinguish any concern for other's pain. Some actually take a sadistic delight in the harm they cause. Attempting to establish a sympathetic or nurturing connection with an aggressive young person is often a mistake, especially during a rage state (and this is *particularly* true with such fierce youth). They experience these gestures as an attempt to soften their defenses and/or a sign of your weakness.

In the most basic sense, such youth are profoundly isolated, without human ties. They are left with an inflated and easily bruised sense of pride and respect, their most important "possessions," something for which they will live and die. This pride, however, can be an access route for communication and de-escalation. <u>The formula for communication with such fierce youth is "respect outweighs sympathy."</u>

In other words, enforce the rules with calm gravity and strength, and never try to ingratiate yourself, as this will invite contempt. Similarly, trying to "prove" that you care will have a negative effect. If you manifest yourself as a strong and dignified adult who does not make it "personal" when you give advice or set limits, you will sometimes draw their attention and curiosity. The youth might begin to question: "How come she has nothing to prove? Why is she not weak? Why isn't she, like so many others, 'sucking up' to me, trying to please me?" If there is hope for such youth, it lies in their fascination with power. You present to them a world unimaginable, one where power and human decency can exist within the same body. If you do not behave in this manner yourself, such a fierce young person will be unreachable.

> **Review: Dealing with conduct-disordered (fierce) youth**
> You first approached the youth as if their aggression was impulsive, and you tried to exert authority over them. That didn't work -- instead, the youth becomes more focused and directed in his or her aggression toward you.
> - Let them know where they stand, that anything you are requiring isn't "personal," you are doing what needs to be done.
> - Dispassionately express your authority.
> - Respect before sympathy! Don't try to *prove* you care.
> - They may become threatening or violent: be prepared at any moment to call the police.

CHAPTER 48

Dynamite under a Rock: Explosive Youth

These young people can carry a variety of mental health diagnoses. Not all, or even most, have the typical attention problems that we note with the impulsive youth. The term "explosive kids" also includes youth with head injuries, fetal alcohol spectrum disorders, and other neurological problems. The hallmark quality of these young family members is that once their fiery temper is unleashed, it is very hard for them to stop. They rage and rage. When something sets them off – usually a personal affront – they shift into hot rage (Chapter 55). They *know* what they are infuriated about, but they cannot let it go. Unlike the impulsive kid, simple commands do not calm them down. Imagine a fire so hot that anything – even the blanket you throw over the blaze – is new fuel that allows the fire to burn hotter.

Despite their explosive personality, many of these younger family members do not necessarily have general attention or impulse problems, and they can pay attention when they choose to. Others, such as those with fetal alcohol spectrum disorders or a history of head injuries, cannot pay attention very well in the best of circumstances, in addition to their explosive tempers. Regardless, they are the kids of whom one says, "Billy lost it again today," and everyone nods, imagining the slung chairs, classroom supplies, and the young person raging for over an hour *after* they were restrained on a gurney or in a quiet room.

Orders or even firm commands do not work well with these young people. In fact, they may view such commands as further provocation, heightening their anger instead of calming them. The watchword, instead, is containment. You *do* give commands, but your voice must be firm and calm, even quiet. The command is to get their attention to focus everything on one being – you. In favorable circumstances, try to guide this young person to a quiet area where they can calm down on their own. Your task is to stay nearby so that they do not injure themselves or damage property. You cannot, however, problem solve or otherwise work things out while they are still on fire. If you are unable to accomplish this, you should avail yourself of the strategies in Section IX on rage and violence.

Examples: Children with neurological deficits who are explosive

Some youth, particularly those with neurological damage, can suddenly shift into an "organic rage," apparently unmediated by cognitive processes. However, these kids often show small microchanges of behavior right before assaults. Learn these signs so you can help them shift gears into another activity or process, thereby heading off the explosion. Discuss organic rages with the youth's treatment professionals as well.

A young girl had enacted a number of apparently sudden severe attacks against family members. We found that when she focused on an intellectual task too long, she would begin scratching at her forearm. The "sudden" explosion of aggression followed a few minutes after this "tell."
- Another youth would knit his brows and glower in a stubborn manner when he didn't understand a conversation. He interpreted this as people "making me feel stupid," an attack in his view. This facial expression was a clear sign to slow down, lighten up, or change the subject.

Review: Dealing with explosive youth

You attempt to exert authority on someone you think is an impulsive, aggressive youth, and when that doesn't work, you use the respect, command presence, and distance that are best with the fierce youth. When the youth continues to ramp upward into further aggression, assume you are dealing with an explosive youth. They get more and more aggressive, without a "circuit breaker" that helps them turn off. They become very reactive to just about anything you say or do.
- Rage is usually explosive. They often have no fear of harm when in an explosive rage state.
- Don't get flamed up yourself, no matter what they say (which will frequently be pretty bad!).
- If you speak at all, use paraphrasing (see Chapter 42). The explosive youth, however, will often react with more rage even to paraphrasing. In their rage, they view paraphrasing as mocking them.
- Silently, implacably, take them somewhere safe, where they will be contained and unable to harm anything. Wait them out, so to speak.
- In some such situations, you will need to call police to provide the containment they need.

CHAPTER 49

"Even if You Force Me, I'll Still Make You Miserable": Opposition-Defiant Kids

Oppositional defiant disorder (ODD) is considered a behavioral disorder of childhood. ODD often develops with upbringing typified by poor boundaries (too invasive, too lax, or both). Aggression is typically against family members and those familiar to the child. Dictatorial parents, in an effort to "break" the child to their will, often "create" ODD youth among those who are too strong-willed to crumble. The ODD kid's motto seems to be, "You will not break me. And even if you make me do it, I still say 'no.'" Other parents, who are not consistent or who do not enforce reasonable discipline (either overly permissive or chaotic), also elicit such behaviors. In this case, the child is implicitly saying, "I will act out until you are forced to give me some limits." It is very possible that you recognize yourself in one of the previous descriptions and are now reading this book, trying to make things right. You know that the way you chose to raise your child was significantly off the mark, and now you are trying to make things right.

However, even youth from solid homes can display this type of behavior. Our culture, supported by a toxic media, has taught many of our young people horrible behavior and attitudes. They may have perniciously bonded with other young people, as well, and both their friends and the media encourage defiant behavior. Furthermore, exacerbated by drug or alcohol abuse, many previously loving young people turn nasty indeed.

Negative reinforcement – giving most of your attention to their negative behavior – will elicit more. Punishment, the most forceful type of negative reinforcement, particularly that which is either out of proportion or inconsistent, teaches the child that discipline is an attack and that the parent is unpredictable, but that acting out at least gets the parent's attention. Sadly, the child experiences a kind of "social power" when punished. They see the punisher as having the right to define good and bad, but at the same time, they see themselves as having impact (if they are not utterly broken in spirit or in body by the punishment): "If I 'make' you mad, I am in control of your moods."

Oppositional-defiant youth are surpassingly argumentative, fighting over fine points while claiming to be misunderstood. They apparently thrive on conflict, and they look for any pretext to continue the argument. Such behavior is not a search for truth or understanding: it is a power tactic. Unfortunately, once adults have given the child power in this manner, the youth gets a grandiose sense of his or her importance, and frustrating and defying adults becomes its own reward. They hold in contempt people whom they are able to easily upset or anger.

This need to argue, at its extreme end, seems related to obsessive-compulsive disorder; their brain, apparently, will not let go of their place in the argument. Right and wrong do not matter; only their definition of "right at the moment" matters.

The watchword in dealing with these kids is to pick your battles. Do not waste energy arguing about anything that is not important. When it is important, become implacable. They put energy in their argument, you respond with a calm, yet unwavering resolve. As an adult, you should never argue with such a youth as an "equal"; instead, tell them what will be, with no negotiation whatsoever. If you are correct in what you require, it should be experienced as a force like gravity – not a debate.

These youth are used to a lot of attention when they argue or resist. Because this drains so much energy from those responsible for them, they are often ignored when they are not making trouble, much less acting positively. Therefore, be sure to notice when they are acting with integrity, agreeableness, or respect, so that they experience positive attention for these actions. All people involved with such youth must maintain consistent boundaries with *no* deviations. The oppositional youth will test these boundaries over and over again to see if the limits have changed.

Review: Dealing with oppositional-defiant kids

These young people argue for argument's sake. Their reward is the negative attention they require from adults, and the sense that they have you – at least your moods – under their control. They believe they've won if they anger you or make you upset.

- Pick your battles. Disengage from those not worth arguing.
- If it is an issue worth confronting, require them to follow your instructions. Be like a force as unyielding as gravity – there is no argument with that.
- Whenever possible, give extra energy (positive attention) to the young person who is doing something worthwhile or worth respecting.

CHAPTER 50

PTSD in Young People

For both children and youth, post-traumatic stress disorder, experiencing or witnessing severe violence, is often physically enacted rather than verbalized. In particular, young men who would adamantly deny ever experiencing trauma seem to live by Nietzsche's adage, "that which does not kill me makes me stronger." Yet they show trauma in their behavior.

There is no unique de-escalation method for use with traumatized youth, because they can display aggression and violence in a variety of modes, from terrified and chaotic rage to purposeful predation. However, traumatized children, in particular, often display terrified rage (Chapter 54).

The more predatory or furious rages that some children and teenagers exhibit are a kind of reaction formation; they have found a way to cease experiencing the pervasive dread of the victim. Tragically however, this often results in their only feeling safe in the role of the victimizer.

Circular breathing (Chapter 6) contains a method that you can, on occasion, teach to traumatized youth that can help them turn trauma (lived experience) into memory (past experience). Circular breathing is particularly useful with those who are guarded against both therapy and help from others, because it is a do-it-yourself procedure, which allows them to feel in control. You can, quite honestly, introduce it as a martial arts technique to control the mind rather than as a therapy method – the latter being something the youth may resist. [20]

Finally, hold them to the highest standard of behavior. If you allow this a traumatized youth "off the hook" because of what may be, admittedly, a horrible history of abuse, they will begin to use their "abuse excuse" to license violence and predation on others.

> **Review: Helping traumatized youth**
> - Teach them how to calm themselves and manage their emotions – or get them access to a counselor who can do that.
> - De-escalate rage based on the mode of aggression they are displaying (Section IX), not their history.
> - Hold them to the highest standard of behavior. In other words, "Yes, this happened to you. But that's not all you are."

CHAPTER 51

Pseudo-Nihilism

By definition, nihilism is a general rejection of customary beliefs and the belief that there is no meaning or purpose in existence. Such a youth, who may affect a posture that includes self-destructive behaviors or affected disinterest, is in fact striving for power "through the back door." Juveniles who adopt this outlook feel a sense of control when they horrify, disgust, or offend others. Nihilistic youths may also display an aloof callousness, with a distinct lack of sympathy for the feelings and emotions of others. By making themselves outcasts, they are inviolate vis-à-vis the larger society and its goals.

When interacting with these young people, you should not be emotionally bland, distant, or apathetic. Instead, pay attention to what the youth presents and offer a human reaction. If you try to make yourself impervious, pretending that their provocative behaviors do not affect you, they may escalate until they do evoke a reaction. If you do succeed in "stonewalling" them, all you have succeeded in doing is establishing that you, like they, don't care.

One is most concerned about such nihilistic youth by what they hide inside. These kids, in particular, need an adult to be a "fair witness" (Chapter 8) to their world -- someone to provide feedback in a way that he or she does not feel compelled to resist. They need to talk with someone with more life experience, someone who is not going to abuse them, abandon them, or treat them unfairly. At the same time, do not imagine this as a heart-to-heart discussion, facing each other, with the youth "opening up" to your unconditional positive regard. You are far more likely trusted when you do not try so hard, when you sit side by side in a car, for example, with only occasional eye contact. You must be neither detached nor eager. By being at ease, you manifest a state of being that these young people crave above all else.

Beyond a "human reaction," you must demonstrate that you are inviolate, but not in the sense of becoming disinterested or uncaring. You demonstrate that you don't *need* them to change, and that you are, in your own way, free. One of the most striking things about rebellious youth is how they clump with others, assuming the same fashion. Your ability to be unique embodies what they claim they desire.

They are most dangerous when left alone to stew in their own juices. Be the adult that they almost surely do not have in their life, so that they have a moral touchstone.

> **Review: Dealing with pseudo-nihilism**
>
> Not only may they be aggressive, but they may also be focused on *not* making a link with you, treating you with withdrawn or sullen indifference. Other youth may be very much at odds with you; they may even rage or curse at you —or try to cut themselves off from you.
> - Don't try to make them change or "feel better" by telling them, for example, that they are young and these things pass, they have a lot to live for, and so on. They will regard "put ups" (and you) with contempt.
> - They may try to repel you with what they say, or say they have done. Give them a human reaction, but not an overreaction.
> - Be the adult that they almost surely do not have in their life.

SECTION IX

Control of Rage and a Response to Violence

CHAPTER 52

Preface to Rage

Rage and anger are not merely different in degree; they are different modes of being, just as water, once past the boiling point, becomes steam. Angry people posture to establish dominance or to force agreement or compliance from others. If nothing else, their goal is to communicate their feelings, although, due to their lack of interpersonal skills, their mental illness, or the effects of drugs and/or alcohol, they often resort to anger in an attempt to make themselves heard.

The reader will recall that anger is denoted as falling between 20 and 95 on the aggressiveness scale (Chapter 33). This represents a very broad range of arousal, ranging from mildly irritated to truly irate. Rage, however, occupies a much smaller fraction of the scale, from 95 to 99. An enraged person desires to commit mayhem. Enraged family members are in a "threshold" state: their anger and rage escalate until they have overcome any moral or personal constraints that may prohibit them from committing the ultimate expression of rage – violence.

Taking into account that the numbers in the aggression scale are images rather than scientific measurements, you still may use some of the de-escalation for anger when, for example, the person is at 93. For example, the tactic of "breaking the pattern" (Chapter 41) can be effective at just these moments; you can say something so unexpected that the fight just "drops out" of the person. Past a certain point, however, the enraged individual is truly intent on committing mayhem. Their only focus is overcoming what is holding them back: fear of consequences, damage to their self-image, and innate morality. Their internal restraints are "fighting" a battle inside them with their primitive desire to maim and destroy. At this point, all the strategies for dealing with the angry person are more or less useless.

Rage is an internal war. When we are facing an enraged person from whom we cannot escape, or our moral responsibilities require us to stay, <u>our task is to control the situation *and* the other person so that their inhibitions are strengthened</u>. In this sense, what we refer to as "control" is actually supporting the best aspects of the enraged person until they are able, once again, to live in peace without that imposition of control.[21]

Example: The power of internal restraints

As one man who had been in a manic psychosis told me half a year later, "You came into my room and I decided to kill you. I was just about to make my move, and a voice in my head said, 'You are not allowed to kill him. He's your friend.' I couldn't remember exactly what a friend was, but the voice said, 'I don't care if you remember. It's against the rules to kill your friends.'" Only aware of his hair-trigger tension, I left his room, perhaps saving my life in the process.

There are various types of rage. It is very important to recognize what type of rage the person is expressing, because we have different strategies to deal with each type. At the same time, do not worry that you will have a lot to remember. Enraged people's behavior is quite obvious – after reading this section, you will be able to identify what type of rage they are in and know the best strategies to control them.

IMPORTANT CAUTION

Here, and in several other areas of this book, I have used animal symbols to aid in the understanding of rage or other behavior. For example, we use the image of a leopard or a shark in describing predatory rage. These are thought devices and are not intended to be used to refer to people. In our hypersensitive times, such a reference to a person may be misconstrued as stigmatizing them as "being an animal." Nothing could be further than the truth – the images are to assist in understanding modes of behavior, not character. Nonetheless, such images should remain aids of understanding, not terms of reference.

CHAPTER 53

Chaotic Rage: A Consideration of Rage Emerging from Various Disorganized States

Signs of Chaotic Rage

Disorganized individuals (Chapter 21) enter into chaotic rage states for many of the same reasons that prompt agitation and anger in anyone: frustration, fear, confusion caused by too much stimulation, and feelings of invasion (for example, when you must carry out a necessary medical or hygiene task that they do not understand or that is physically disconcerting). Chaotic rage is typified by profound disorganization of cognitive and perceptual processes, and can be engendered by severe psychosis that has "crossed over" into a delirium state, mania, intoxication, drug withdrawal, severe intellectual/developmental disabilities, senile dementia, overwhelming emotions, or a result of brain injury or trauma. The individual is profoundly disoriented, often experiencing severe hallucinations, illusions, and delusional thinking.

> Lest there be any confusion, I am not asserting that syndromes such as severe intellectual/developmental disabilities, senile dementia, intoxication, and so on, are the same. I am, however, asserting that the manifestation of rage in a variety of people – chaotic rage, whatever the cause – requires a similar response.

<u>Unlike a classic psychosis, the most salient characteristic is the near impossibility of establishing *any* lines of communication with them.</u> Individuals in this state often cannot logically string words together, communicating in ways that are comprehensible only to them. They may utter nonsensical cascades of words or grunts, moans, or mumblings. Others make sentences based on rhymes, puns, or cross meanings, their brains capriciously linking words together based on sounds, not meanings. The delirious individual may laugh or babble without any clear object of mirth, or completely at variance to the seriousness of the situation. They may speak in repetitive loops, fixating on one subject, which could be real, delusional, or a manifestation of their disorganization.

People in chaotic rage states can easily become quite frightened or irritable, especially if they are overwhelmed with stimuli, such as a large group of onlookers. They may begin yelling, screaming, lashing out physically, engaging in such self-injurious acts as scratching and gouging their own flesh, striking themselves repeatedly, or banging their head against the wall or ground.

Their rage sometimes explodes, seemingly, out of nowhere. People in a chaotic rage state often strike out in all directions: they are not coordinated, but they are disinhibited. What this means is that nothing, no fear of injury or consequences, holds them back from their attack. They may grab, scratch, bite, kick, and strike in flailing blows. They are often indifferent or unaware of pain or injury to themselves. Some disorganized people target people to harm: combat with them is like fighting a tornado of arms and legs. Others are so lost that they are not fighting, per se. They are "swimming through people": it is as if they are drowning, trying to struggle through a river, choked with wreckage -- the people and objects around them are the debris they are forcing their way through. A helpful image is Taz, the whirlwind character in the old Warner Brother's cartoons.

Such behaviors should be considered a medical emergency, and proper medical attention must be summoned as soon as possible: ideally, they should stage nearby while staff and/or law enforcement are establishing the safe de-escalation and resolution of the crisis. The chaotic state can be a sign of a life-threatening emergency.

It is possible that chaotic rage may be part of the behavioral profile of a severely disabled family member, one who is not necessarily in a delirium state. If such an individual is in long-term care, you must have expert consultation to ensure that staff can differentiate between an emotional storm and a medical crisis.

De-Escalation of Chaotic Rage
- **Disorganized or delirious individuals are among the most difficult to verbally de-escalate**, because comprehension and coherent cognitive processes are among the first faculties they lose. Because of their impulsiveness and unpredictability, you must be on guard against a sudden attack. Therefore, knowledge of anything that might have set them off in the past is useful. Every one involved with them must be aware of what sets them off and what calms them down.
- **Use calm movements and a firm but reassuring voice**. People in chaotic states, most notably delirium, often experience poor motor control, vertigo, disorientation, and so on. Slow movements and a soothing tone of voice help them orient physically and emotionally.
- **Use simple, concrete commands** with no more than a single subject in each sentence; complex sentences or detailed instructions will be confusing, overwhelming, or irritating. Repetition is almost always helpful. For example, slowly say, "Sit down, William. Sit down. Sit down. William, sit down."
- **One of the last things the disorganized person will retain is recognition of their name**. Use their name repeatedly, interspersing it in your commands in order to get their attention before attempting to redirect them to another activity.

- **They are susceptible to being deflected to another topic.** You can sometimes simply distract the family member, although this is unlikely when they have entered fully into chaotic rage.
- **Use paraphrasing to validate and acknowledge their confusion and/or fear.** For example, "Really scary, huh?" or "You are really worried, aren't you?"
- **Be very cautious about touching those in chaotic rage**, as this may be experienced as invasive or even as an attack.

> **Physical contact: Guidance and restraint (relevant only for families where physical guidance and restraint is part of their safety plan and training)**
>
> You need specific training to understand if and when to touch someone who has lost control and needs to be moved or restrained. This is *never* a one-person operation. You must not only know the plan, but you must also regularly practice physical guidance and restraint procedures to keep everyone safe.
>
> If you need to touch a family member in a chaotic rage state, for example, to guide them to another room, be sure to touch them firmly. However, do not curve your fingers inward, because digging your fingertips into their flesh will be interpreted as an attack. Do not stroke, pat, or caress them: although you may intend to comfort them, you do not know what emotions such touch can elicit. The proper firm touch tells the person, "Here is your body. Here's where it stops. This body contains you. It is that which holds you. My hand is only to inform you of your bodily existence and to show you a safe way to go."

- **Do whatever you can to minimize environmental stressors.** Disorganized individuals often become agitated due to light, noise, and a chaotic environment. Try to clear the area of onlookers.
- **Minimize your extraneous body movements and other distracting behaviors.** Your movements should be calming and helpful to the person so they understand what is going on.
- **Make "invasive" procedures** that must be carried out as gentle and safe as possible.
- **Because of their difficulty in attending to what you say, nonverbal communication is a paramount concern.** A calm, reassuring presence, manifesting both strength and assurance, is truly your best hope of helping to stabilize an individual in chaotic rage.

Catatonia: Special Considerations

People may be immobile for many reasons, among them being a variety of medical concerns. Catatonia, however, is a very rare, very bizarre condition in which a person stays in a fixed posture, not congruent with injury or seizure. Catatonia is caused either by mental illness (schizophrenia) or an organic condition (drug toxicity, for example). The catatonic person's posture may be quite awkward or twisted, seeming to require great flexibility. A classic symptom of true catatonia is "waxy immobility" -- if someone else moves the body or limbs, the person maintains the posture into which they were moved. Such individuals are often totally unresponsive to speech, touch, or even pain, and there seems to be no way to establish communication with them.

Considerable caution is needed in dealing with immobile individuals for several reasons. First of all, they may be injured or having a seizure and are in need of medical attention. A second consideration is safety. One way to regard catatonia is to view the person as exerting 100 percent of their will to *not* interact with the outside world. Trying to help, you may be tempted to make physical contact or speak forcefully to them in an effort to get them to respond when they are unsecured. This can be a disastrous mistake. Imagine the incredible exertion of will required to maintain immobility for hours, even days, without movement, without response, without even blinking in some cases. Now imagine disturbing this equilibrium. The result is what is clinically called "catatonic rage." The individual shifts from 100 percent quietude to 100 percent explosive motion.

> I am aware of one incident in which a law enforcement officer's career was ended by such an individual who, all of 110 pounds, grabbed hold of his arm and yanked as if he was cracking a whip, ripping through all the ligaments of his shoulder and shoulder blade.

Although you may think the person is unaware, they *can* hear you. Therefore, speak calmly and respectfully. People can have very long memories of being shamed, and if you speak about or treat the catatonic as an object rather than a person, you may evoke a terrible sense of humiliation. They may not be able to respond in their "frozen" state, but months or years later, encountering another person like the one who verbally demeaned them (another family member or even a stranger), they may target this individual as a stand-in for their postponed rage. Beyond that, everyone, even a person in a coma, deserves to be treated with respect. Even if it seems that the person cannot hear a word you are saying, act as if they are listening to everything you say.

When police and emergency medical services arrive, do everything in your power to ensure that they are aware that they are dealing with someone who is very likely catatonic, and that they should not disturb them any more than is necessary. They need sufficient numbers to move them onto a gurney, for example, and should not try to arouse them or otherwise assess their responsiveness before they are secured in restraints.

CHAPTER 54

Terrified Rage

> Be aware that the line between terrified and chaotic rage can be very fine. The terrified person, overwhelmed, can shift into chaotic rage. When facing an individual in a state of either pure terror or terrified rage, be prepared, therefore, to shift to protocols suitable to assisting individuals in chaotic states (Chapter 53).

What Does Terrified Rage Look Like?

Terrified individuals believe that they will be violated or abused. They appear apprehensive and furtive, looking halfway ready to run, halfway ready to strike. Their voice can be pleading, whiny or fearful, and their eyes are often wide-open or darting from place to place. Wide-open eyes do not always indicate fear, however. When fearful, the muscles under the eyes are slack, giving their face a pleading look. Even though the terrified person is looking in your direction, they do not, usually, look *into* your eyes, nor do they want you to look into theirs. The enraged, aggressive individual with wide-open eyes, on the other hand, displays tension around the eyes. Furthermore, they often look penetratingly into your eyes, or *through* you.

The mouth of some terrified people gapes slightly as they breathe in panicky short gasps, high in the chest, while others press their lips together in a quivering pucker. Their skin tone is often ashen or pale. Some make threatening gestures with a flailing overhand blow, while others primarily use a fending off gesture, as if trying to ward off attack. Their body posture can be described as concave, as they pull away from you, or hold themselves tightly in fear. Their body is usually tense, preparing to either defend themselves or flee. They also exhibit heightened levels of physical arousal, accompanied by panting, sweating, and trembling. They may back into a wall or corner. They may also yell, threatening and pleading at the same time, using such phrases as "Stay back! You get away from me! I will hit you! I will! You stay back!" There is a hollow quality to their voice, as if it has no "foundation." This is due to the tightening of their abdomen and diaphragm, so that not only their breathing, but also their speech is high in their chest.

What Causes Terrified Rage?

Severely frightened people often suffer from paranoid delusions, a fear of the unknown, or frightening hallucinations. At other times, they are afraid of a loss of control, of being laughed at or humiliated. Some people are afraid that they are in terrible trouble with some agency, be it police, mental health professionals, or even the family. Finally, for any number of reasons, they are simply terrified of you. <u>Imagine a snarling wolf cornered, backed up against a cliff face.</u>

De-Escalation of Terrified Rage

Try to reduce the terrified person's sense of danger. Maintain a safe distance and relax your posture. Make sure your movements are unhurried, and your voice is firm, confident, and reassuring.

Notice if their body relaxes or tenses in response to your eye contact or its lack. If direct eye contact is reassuring for the person, do so; if intimidating, do not. Of course, you should never take your eyes *off* the person: the point is that you should not look penetratingly into their eyes if such contact terrifies them.

Initiate a litany of reassuring phrases, speaking slowly, with frequent pauses: "I know you are scared – that's OK. - - - - Put down the chair. - - - - You don't need that. - - - - - - <u>I keep it safe here</u>. You can put it down now. - - - - - - I'm way over here. - - - - - - Go ahead. Sit down. - - - - - - - I keep it safe."

<u>Do not</u> say "I'll protect you" or "I won't hurt you." Many people who shift into terrified rage have been hurt by people who said those kinds of phrases. However, when you say, "I keep it safe here," you are implicitly telling them, "This is my territory and no one, including you, will be hurt on my territory. I am taking responsibility now, and because of me, you will be safe."

Furthermore, by saying something similar to what they expect to hear, yet somehow different, you cause a "glitch" in their thought process. "What did he say? He didn't say, 'I'll keep you safe.' What's different in what he said?" By getting the terrified person to question what you said, you cause them to re-engage the parts of the brain that actually think things through as opposed to just reacting.

Their body language will also indicate that they are calming down. Their breathing will get a little shuddery or be expressed in short, high-pitched gasps. They may slump into a chair or onto the floor, as if physically exhausted, or they may even begin to weep. Maintain your reassuring litany and slowly approach them. If they show signs of becoming frightened again, pause, move slightly back, and continue to speak reassuringly.

As you approach the person, move in "half steps." For example, move the right foot a full step, then bring the left foot *up* to the right foot. Pause. Move either right or left foot forward, and then bring the other foot forward *up* to the lead foot. Pause. The advantage of moving this way is that you stay balanced, in case the individual suddenly attacks. Furthermore, you can ease backward, creating more space between you if the person becomes startled or reactive.

Attempting to hold or hug the person to comfort their fears should *not* be your first choice. <u>Particularly with adults, this will be a very rare option.</u> There are some times, however, when that is the right thing to do.

With adults, touch usually occurs at the end, when they are calm, close to baseline, or even further into post-crisis depression. If touch is in order, it should be firm. Be very careful: many adults will still be frightened and confused, and can misunderstand your intentions. Therefore, <u>do not</u> try to touch them unless you have a strong sense that you will be experienced as comforting and welcome. Do not curve your hand so that the fingertips "dig" inward: your hands, particularly to the hypersensitive person, will feel like claws. You must not stroke or pat them: these are gestures that are meant to *evoke* feelings. <u>A firm touch will help the person dampen down their emotions</u>. If you feel any tension in their body in response to your touch, calmly remove your hand. To reiterate, in such situations, touch is the <u>rarest</u> of options, but this is how to do it in cases where it is warranted. In such cases, the best touch to an adult is a firm palm of the hand on the shoulder – in particular, the deltoid muscle. If you place your hand on their trapezius muscle, you are too close to their neck. This may very likely be experienced as threatening or intrusive.

With small children, it is often effective to wrap them firmly in your arms, containing their rage within your kind strength. At the same time, reassure the child that you are holding them to keep them safe.

> If you do wrap a child in your arms, it is often very effective to "shove" a beloved toy – a teddy bear or doll, for example -- into their arms, and wrap their arms around the toy. They will thus be holding the toy in the same way you are holding them. At this time, you can repeat such phrases as, "You hold onto that dolly. Hold onto her so she won't get hurt. Hold her tight." You are subliminally suggesting that you are holding the child in the same way.
>
> This can also be done with terrified developmentally disabled people.

When Should You Allow the Terrified Person to Leave?

Fearful people feel trapped: this is one of the primary reasons why they are frightened. Remember the image of a "cornered wolf." The last thing you should do with a wolf is to block it from escape. There are many situations where you tell your family member, "You can stay or go if you want. I am concerned for you and want to help you. But you do not have to stay if you don't want to." On the other hand, you may have a responsibility to protect both the terrified person and other people. If you are concerned that the person may run out and harm either themselves or other people, you have a moral responsibility to keep them safe by keeping them close.

CHAPTER 55

Hot Rage

When we think of people on the edge of violence, hot rage usually comes to mind. Imagine an individual with muscles writhing, yelling or screaming, fist brandished, threatening to harm you. They throw things, tip over desks, and spit in your face. They want to beat you bloody, stab you, or pound you into a pulp.

Such behaviors are often thought to be instinctual, a product of our primitive drives – almost a reflex. However, instinctual aggression is usually uncoordinated and flailing, and falls under the category of terrorized or chaotic rage.

Hot rage, however, is coordinated: learned through modeling, trained through repetition, and reinforced through success. It is most productive to think of hot rage as a "pseudo instinct," a behavior that is a combination of primitive drives and trained actions. Such pseudo-instinctual behaviors are actions that have either been repeated so often or are so ingrained through powerful early experiences that they function almost like reflexes.

Hot rage also leads to deterioration in judgment, and at higher states of arousal, even basic cognitive processes. For example, some people with a history of abuse lash out in rage whenever frightened, with no ability to evaluate whether or not they are currently in danger. At the same time, they target where best to hit, and frequently choose a time and a place where they believe they have the best chance of success. On a more functional level, a good street fighter does his best to knock his opponent senseless, but he automatically takes a stance with chin tucked in, shoulder rolled forward, and punches in such a way that the power of the blow is amplified by his body weight and the torque of his hips.

General Information about Hot Rage

Hot rage is typified by emotional arousal or excitement. Arousal breeds arousal: the more often people go into hot rage states, the more comfortable they are with their rage, and the easier it becomes to be violent. There are also organic contributors: low blood sugar levels, head injury, or the use of drugs and alcohol that act as disinhibiters.

Hot rage is often a behavior that has led to short-term success in the past, such as scaring and beating a selected victim for criminal gain or just for the joy of the violence. In a state of rage, such a person has no concern about longer-term consequences, much less guilt. Individuals who need a lot of intensity to feel alive will amp up aggression to feel this energy and power. For some people, there is a sense of liberation, even a paradoxical kind of joy when they peak into rage. All their fears and insecurities disappear, and they merge into the ecstasy of the pure act. Such individuals desire rage because that ecstatic state is, to them, the best thing they ever feel.

Displacement is a common factor of hot rage, meaning the family member's anger is displaced, at least temporarily, toward an inanimate object instead of you or another individual. This also includes picking things up and slamming them down; throwing things; and punching or kicking walls, furniture, or other nearby objects. More predatory individuals use displacement as a tactic to make the target of their aggression more fearful, while warming themselves up for an attack.

Hot rage is also associated with peer group influence and masculine display, a primitive attempt to gain status in an aggressive group or win a perceived competition over an object of desire. This becomes especially problematic if the family member begins acting out in front of a group of onlookers, friends, or family -- they must act aggressively toward anyone representing authority in order to save face.

Some therapeutic professionals claim that hot rage is a result of frustration, but this alone does not usually elicit rage in normal people. When frustrated desires are coupled with something personal, as when the family member believes they are being impeded by another *person,* they are more likely to become enraged.

Three subtypes of hot rage, each typified by almost unendurably intense feelings, will be discussed later in this chapter. They are fury, bluffing, and aggressive manipulation.

General De-Escalation of Hot Rage: The Ladder

The primary method of de-escalation for hot rage is called "the ladder." This is an ideal technique for someone who is beginning to get threatening. It is used *only* for rage, that gray zone between anger (even extreme anger) and violence. The person is presenting a danger to you, and is no longer trying to communicate with you. Instead, they are right on the edge of assault: in a sense, they are doing a war dance to overcome their inhibitions against committing violence.

The ladder technique itself is simple: identify the most dangerous behavior and repetitively demand that it cease. Use a short sentence with no more than four or five words. Your tone must be strong and matter-of-fact. Once they stop that particular dangerous behavior, identify the next problematic behavior and use the same technique. Continue until the person is de-escalated. <u>This technique is only effective right before, during, and after the peak of the crisis</u> because it is a control tactic rather than a "lining up" de-escalation tactic. Control tactics will provoke rage in a merely angry person, someone you might have overestimated, due to his loud tone or dramatic behaviors. <u>As described earlier, facing an enraged person causes us to experience fear in a way that anger does not</u>. With the enraged family member, the danger is not just a possibility, it is *now*.

> The ladder should *only* be used with an enraged individual. Using this technique with an angry individual, even an extremely angry person, will cause them to *flare up* in rage. To give a sense of proportion, despite a twenty-year career in which I have dealt with many very aggressive, profoundly dangerous people, I have only had to use the adder twice. In every other case, de-escalation tactics suitable to dealing with angry people were absolutely sufficient.

Establish a Hierarchy of Danger

The general hierarchy from most to least is as follows:
1. Brandishing an object or a weapon in a menacing way. (**NOTE**: If they are too close or are trying to use the weapon, this is *violence*, not rage. In this case, try to establish *safety* not control.)
2. Approaching or standing too close to you with menacing intent.
3. Kicking objects, punching walls, or throwing things (displacement activity).
4. Pacing, stomping, and inflating the body in an aggressive manner (posturing).
5. Shouting *or* talking in low, menacing tones.
6. Using language that is intended to violate, demean, or degrade.

The ladder is not merely a verbal intervention. Like any other control tactic with an aggressive family member, you must move as needed to maintain the optimum space to defend yourself and exert maximum influence upon the aggressor. If they are very close or threatening, put your hands up, palms out and fingertips curved, and prepare to ward off an attack -- this gesture is both calming and dominant. Give the aggressor a straightforward command to stop their most dangerous behavior. You should not scream or shout: that will not get through to the person. Instead, they will ramp up on your screaming tone, and this, alone will increase their aggressive energy. Rather, your voice should be strong, low, and commanding (Chapter 38).

After every couple of repetitions, always add, "We'll talk about it when you . . ." followed by the same command. Once that behavior is stopped, pick the next most problematic behavior (the next "rung" of the ladder) and command that it stop. If the person does calm down and stops *all* the aggressive behaviors, including assaultive language, then set a firm and direct limit.

This is not the time to try to think of something brilliant or life changing to say. By keeping it simple, you can continue to look for escape routes, identify potential weapons, and attempt to get help. Frequently intersperse their name in your sentences, using this to pace and break the rhythm of your commands and "call them back" to a more personal interaction. By holding to a demand, you display clarity and strength and help focus *their* mind on the most problematic behavior, then the next, and on down the rungs of the ladder.

> **Do not:**
> - Explain yourself.
> - Use a scolding or nagging tone.
> - *Request* that they comply.
> - Use "psychologese," such as "It's not appropriate for you to . . ."

Continue working your way down the rungs until the family member is no longer in a state of fury. If the family member re-escalates to a higher and more dangerous activity, simply return to that rung of the ladder and begin again. Remember to stand and use your voice as described in the previous sections. The last rung is probably swearing or other obscene language. Remember, many people swear as punctuation, without hostile intent. They may sound crude, but they are not trying to be verbally violent. If the person is swearing in this manner, it is not a problem. That is something you will deal with at another time, during moments of calm, saying, for example, "Jamey, I don't like to hear that kind of language. I'd appreciate if you don't swear around me."

However, if the swearing is an attempt to violate you, you must deal with it in proper order. However, do *not* focus on the language, no matter how vile, if the person is *doing* something dangerous. Remember that predatory individuals will use language to shock, distract, immobilize, or terrorize. What they are *doing* is far more dangerous than what they are saying.

> If a family member becomes violent, do not hold back from any action to keep yourself and others safe. If you do have to protect yourself and others, do so! Escape, evade, restrain, and even fight back if that is what you have to do. Verbal control tactics are, of course, ideal with people in a state of rage, but if they cross the line into violence, do what you have to do to stay safe.

Example: The ladder technique

Your voice is firm, low pitched, and commanding, as you "descend" the rungs. Each statement is, of course, a response to something the aggressor has done or said. Do not talk too fast. (Note the <pauses> in the first couple of phrases. Do this with every statement. The pauses should be of different lengths, breaking the rhythm, rather than counting cadence.)

"Step back. <pause> Step back. Robert. <pause> We'll talk about it when you step back. <pause> Robert. <pause> Step back. Step back, Robert. <pause> We will talk about it when you step back." <etc.>

"Stop kicking things. Robert. Stop kicking things. We'll talk about it when you stop kicking things."

"Robert, I cannot follow you when you pace around. Sit down and we'll talk. Sit down, Robert."

Notice the paradoxical message that you cannot "follow" them. Aside from this having a double meaning ("follow" also means to understand), of course you can follow them. You are also trying to catch their attention as they try to figure out what you said. This draws in the higher areas of the brain – the neo-cortex – that actually tries to think through a problem. Once re-activated, the person is less likely to be assaultive. (This is similar to the "I keep it safe" statement in Chapter 54.)

Imagine they have stepped forward again, thus ascending to a higher rung on the ladder.
"Step back! Robert! Step back and we'll talk. We will TALK about it when you step back, Robert. Step - - - - - back."

"Sit down, Robert. We will talk about it when you sit down. We cannot talk when you are walking around. We will talk about it when you sit down."

Lower your voice. I cannot hear you when you yell that loud. Lower you voice and we will talk."

Here is a second paradoxical communication: of course, you can hear a person who is shouting. Once again, you are trying to create a "glitch" where the aggressive person tries to figure out what you mean when you say you cannot hear him when he is yelling.

"Talk to me with the same respect that I talk to you. We will talk about it when you stop swearing. Stop swearing. Robert. Talk to me with respect, the same way I talk to you."

You continue to work your way down the rungs until the person is no longer in a state of fury. <u>If the person re-escalates to a higher and more dangerous activity, simply go up to that rung of the ladder and begin repeating that command again</u>. Remember to stand and use your voice as described in the previous sections. Usually, the last rung is shouting, or even further down – swearing and using demeaning, ugly language.

Limit Setting after De-Escalation
Once the person is stable and willing to talk, it is important to clearly set a limit. Remember, you have not merely de-escalated an angry individual – you have *controlled* someone on the edge of violence, someone who almost assaulted you or another person. You must not relinquish that control now. Depending on the circumstances, here is what will happen next:
- If there has been property destruction or near assault, the person may need to be escorted off the premises by police or even immediately arrested. In other circumstances, they may be taken to

a hospital for an evaluation. The aggressor can be given a trespass warning by police, forbidding them to return to your home. You may also discuss other charges with the police, such as assault or destruction of property.
- Sometimes you will require the person to leave even without police or security response.
- You will sometimes set up a meeting for later. When this will occur depends on safety issues. Before you talk with your aggressive family member, determine the meeting parameters: who will attend, where it will be held, and what you will talk about.
- With cognitively impaired individuals, you may merely request that they sit quietly and continue to calm themselves, that you will talk with them in five, ten, or twenty minutes. It is usually *not* a good idea to process or discuss the recent incident. It is very likely that they will feel that you are attacking them. Education on better ways to handle upset should take place at another time, when they are totally calm.

Example: limit setting

Each person and situation is different, so you will adapt as needed. In the example below, the family member has mostly postured, but they also brandished a fist. They did not become so aggressive that they needed to be physically restrained.

"Robert, you have physically threatened me and used obscene language toward me. I will not accept anyone trying to intimidate or abuse me. I would like us to take a break from each other. You can go to your room or take a walk – that's up to you. I am going back to my room to work on my taxes. At two o'clock I will call you on your cell phone or come to your room. Then we can discuss your travel plans. But not right now. "

If he objects ("You said we would talk about it!") be ready with your response.

"We are talking about *it*! What we are talking about is that you threatened violence. We cannot get anything accomplished if you are going to do that. *I know* you were very upset. *You know* that we never solve any problem when that happens. Let's talk about it again when both of us are feeling peaceful. As I said, we can talk at two o'clock. But I expect you to treat me with the same respect I treat you, without threats, and without cursing or yelling. We can and will talk about your concerns. But that will be later. Not now."

Hot Rage Subtype #1: Fury

What does fury look like? Furious people are very tense, looking as if they are about to explode. <u>If they are large in stature, imagine a grizzly bear; if they are smaller, imagine a wolverine</u>. In either case, the image suggests a being that will tear you to pieces if it perceives danger, is provoked, or is cornered. Many people, both with mental health diagnoses and without, display fury, and it is particularly common

among people who have suffered head injuries. Furious family members may show some of the following physical manifestations of their rage:
- Their skin tone is flushed as they become angered, turning red or purplish. As they become even more enraged, however, their skin blanches and they turn pale or gray (depending on their skin tone), as the blood pools in the internal organs.
- Their voice, whether loud or low and quiet, has a menacing and belligerent tone.
- They often pace, inflate their upper body, hit or kick objects, or strike their hands together ominously, punching one fist into the other hand.
- They tend to stare into your eyes directly, glowering from under their brow, with a furious and hostile look on their face.
- Their eyes may appear red or inflamed; usually their eyes are wide open, with tension around the eye sockets and facial muscles.
- Physical arousal, blood pressure, and muscular tension all increase. You may notice veins popping out of the skin, particularly around the neck.
- They may display a smile that shows no humor or joy. Others snarl or compress their lips with a twist, as if they have a foul taste in their mouth. Still others bare their teeth or clench their jaws so tightly that the muscles stand out in bunches.
- They are very impulsive and unconcerned with possible consequences.
- Their breathing is often loud and straining.
- They may claim to be disrespected, humiliated, or shamed. Others will allege that they are not getting their questions answered and their problem solved, or that no one is listening or cares. They may rant about "the system" and claim that they are out of alternatives or solutions. (These verbalizations are for a particular audience – themselves – functioning as a feedback loop to further escalate themselves.)
- At their most dangerous point, they may become calm, breaking off eye contact or adopting a thousand-yard stare.

Control of Fury

When confronting a furious individual, no matter how frightened you are, your posture and tone should be confident, commanding, even imposing. Maintain direct eye contact and frequently use their name.

Stand directly in front of the individual, but out of range of an immediate blow. If you stand too close, you will appear to be challenging your aggressive family member; if you stand too far away, you will be seen as fearful, a potential victim. You may have to move forward or backward to maintain this spacing. In either event, move smoothly, without flinching on the one hand or making any sudden or threatening gestures on the other. When you move with a relaxed body, you are more ready to protect yourself, yet you do not appear as if you are trying to initiate a physical altercation.

Do not square your feet so that you are confronting him in full frontal fashion; stand with your feet in a "blade" stance, with one foot advanced and the other behind at about a 45-degree angle. (If you drew the back foot forward, there would be one or two fist's space between the heels: do not line the feet up one behind the other as if you were on a tightrope.) This position prepares you to escape, to ward off blows, and, if necessary, to fight back. With the blade stance, you are already "chambered" to do this. As described above, either put your hands up in a fence or clasp the wrist of one arm in the hand of the other, in front of you at waist level (Chapter 37).

Keep your voice strong and forceful but do not shout. Instead, keep your voice low-pitched and calm, dropping it into your chest where it resonates; enraged people, in particular, react violently to threatening or angry vocal tones. The only time you would shout is a "battle cry," that lion's roar of outrage and strength that you use only when you are trying to stop an actual attack.

You will use the ladder in its most orthodox form, with your voice pitched low and powerful. You should feel it vibrate in your chest.

The individual will exhibit one of three actions:
- They keep on coming: you are now being assaulted and you must do what you have to do to ensure safety.
- They get close, and when you tell them to step back, they say, "Make me." This, too, is an assault of a different kind, and you will do what you have to do to ensure safety.
- They comply. When individuals in hot rage comply with the command to step back, they usually do so yelling and screaming, "You can't tell me what to do!"

Once you have them de-escalated, you must maintain control. As previously stated in the section on limit setting, only after setting very strong limits will you shift into problem solving, even with a mentally ill individual. Otherwise, they will assume that the best way to get a reward – your attention or help – is to abuse you.

Hot Rage Subtype #2: Enraged Bluffing
<u>In keeping with the "animal behavior" analogies, the aggressively bluffing person is like a gorilla beating his chest, a display of aggression designed to keep you at a distance.</u> There is a sense of bluster rather than the pent-up pressure of the enraged person. They are like a wind blowing against a stone wall rather than pent-up explosiveness of dynamite under a rock. However, their *manifest* behavior appears much the same as the

individual displaying fury, hence the terrifying image of the enraged gorilla. At 50 yards, could you tell the difference between a charging gorilla and a charging grizzly bear? Both are huge, hairy beasts that apparently mean you harm. In all likelihood, the gorilla would prefer to be left alone rather than engage in combat, but he postures as if he wants to tear you to pieces. If he perceives no other alternative, he will do so.

The enraged bluffer often displays aggression for the benefit of friends or family. On many occasions their friends or family members have provoked them to "prove" they are tough. In reality, they are actually <u>frightened that they will be found out as being frightened, intimidated, or as succumbing to authority</u>. Perhaps they are trying to impress others or convince them that they are to be taken seriously. Such people can become quite violent if they feel a strong sense of peer pressure to resist your commands and efforts to de-escalate them. Because they are performing in front of an audience, they will often attack to protect their image.

Sometimes bluffers are alone, but they still have an audience, one inside their own head. They have an image inside their mind and they believe they must conform to that image. You will often hear this in their self-talk as they amp themselves up: "You don't know who you are talking to. Do you believe this guy? Do you have any idea who I am?"

Many bullies who have a long record of violence actually function in bluff mode. They are in a perpetual quest to prove to others, and even more insidiously to themselves, that they are not frightened. As a result, they repetitively solicit situations where they must either intimidate or beat someone bloody. It is essential, therefore, to short-circuit this behavior before it escalates into violence. Whenever possible, separate the enraged bluffer from his or her audience. At the same time, you should not, thereby, isolate yourself with the enraged person without sufficient backup.

How can you tell the difference between a person in hot fury and one who is bluffing, if their behaviors are so much the same? When you are facing a furious person, fear is a natural and likely response. Your instinctual mind, that part of you that puts survival above all else, demands your immediate attention and it uses fear to accomplish this. An aggressive bluffer, in a state of hot rage, may also elicit fear, but this fear will be accompanied by another emotion: you will find yourself a bit irritated, thinking how stupid (yet potentially dangerous) this incident has become, and that if the bluffer was not with his friends, or in another case, if he was not trying to prove to his brother that he was just as strong, this dangerous situation would never have developed.

Do not try to "out tough" the bluffer by refusing to back down or leave the scene. This is merely bluffing behavior on your part, and the aggressor's audience will only amplify their calls for them to be even more resistant. Try your best to not personalize encounters with your aggressive family member, and if prudence dictates that you should retreat, then do so!

Control of Enraged Bluffing

These individuals are not really in confrontation with you. They are *pretending* that they are. But this is a pretense that can kill. This pretense is usually for an audience, but sometimes they are trying to stand up the image they wish to project to the world. They may believe they need to prove themselves by refusing to back down. Another aspect of bluffing is that when frightened, the bluffing aggressor will move forward, toward you, so that no one will see how frightened they truly are.

De-escalate and control using the ladder much as you would with an individual in fury, but with a much more matter-of-fact tone. Your eye contact, too, is matter-of-fact, as if you are having a conversation rather than a confrontation. Rather than having your hands in front of you (clasped or in a fence position), open your hands, slightly to the sides, palms up. You can still protect yourself, but your posture appears nonthreatening, more open and relaxed. Your body language says, "There is no need for a fight here." Remember, enraged bluffers will attack out of the fear of being "found out" by their peers. Your task becomes helping them save face, rather than issuing forceful commands and instructions. In doing so, you will greatly reduce the risk of violence.

In some situations, you can short circuit things by helping them save face in front of their audience. Include in your strategy some information and re-assurance. For example, you can say, "Look, Frank. I know you thought I was making fun of you, but that wasn't the case at all. I was just pointing out that you forgot your meds so you wouldn't have to come back for them later." However, if they have ramped themselves into true "bluff rage," they may view concession or agreement as backing down, and only by taking control will you be able to ensure your own and other's safety.

When exerting verbal control upon the enraged bluffer, remember the following:
- Do not point out their fears in front of others. They will feel the need to defend their honor.
- Do not try to be more forceful than they are or appear overly domineering or condescending, as their self-image may require them to strike out.
- In some situations, let them have the last word. By letting them feel a semblance of control (the half step of space that you give them), they can satisfy their need to appear unafraid. When given a face-saving way out, they don't feel the need to further bluff or aggress.

> **NOTE:** When you have handled aggression well, aggressive bluffers often strut with a smirk, sometimes glancing around and making eye contact with onlookers. This is for the benefit of the audience and for their own self-image. They are trying to show that they are unafraid and in control of the situation.

- If they are not responsive to your more low-key approach and continue to escalate, you may have a furious person who happens to be in front of other people or a bluffer who has *shifted* into fury. In this case, you "turn up the dial," adopting a more powerful tone and stance and shifting into the more forceful version of the ladder technique for the furious individual. In essence, you would say, "Move back, Stephen. We will talk about it - - - - *move back.*" You shift from calm ease to a powerful, adamant stance.

- Remember, it is the audience that makes them so dangerous. If possible, separate them from their audience so they can calm down on their own. Whenever possible, do not allow a confrontation to take place in front of a person's retinue of friends and any family members who are encouraging the aggression.

Setting Consequences with a Person Who Has Enacted Enraged Bluff

Just as with the furious person, you must set limits at the end of the confrontation. However, you should also include some "ego building." These individuals are most dangerous when they believe that they must create a fearsome or frightening impression on other people. Therefore, draw them aside and say something like this: "Bernard, I'm glad this worked out with no one getting hurt. Had you not chosen to sit down and talk, you very likely would have ended up being taken out of here. Mom was just about to call police. No. Listen to me for a minute. I'm not disrespecting you. That's *why* you and I are over here talking instead of in front of them. Police haven't been called, but I'm telling you, it was a very near thing. Again, I'm glad this has worked out that you and I are standing here talking.

"Next time, though, don't do this in front of them." (*Them* refers to his friends for whom he was on display. Actually put a little *contempt* in your voice when you say "them," as if to indicate that Bernard is better/cooler/stronger than those people he is, in fact, trying to impress.) "Come to me and talk to me one man to another. You shouldn't put your personal business in front of them." You will see him visibly puff up, feeling flattered. You continue, "OK. Are we clear for next time? Good. Now as for this time. . . ." Then set the same types of limits as you did with the person in a state of fury.

Remember, it is the audience that makes this person most dangerous. If he feels that he will get his "respect" by himself, if he believes his status will actually improve if he comes in alone rather than with his crew of friends or family, he will be far less dangerous next time.

Hot Rage Subtype #3: Controlling, Aggressive Manipulation

Aggressive manipulation is a *strategy*, not a symptom of illness. Such people are calculating, trying to monitor the effect of what they are doing. They are not constrained by feelings of honor, integrity, or pride; their goal is win any way they can. You can sometimes tell when you are being manipulated ("played") because you are confused about why the person is upset or the purpose of his argument. The aggressive manipulator frequently changes either his mood or the subject of the complaint, displaying some or all of the behaviors of manipulative individuals (Chapters 20).

The image of a large rat is very useful when discussing the aggressive manipulator, because rats are the ultimate survivors. They will do whatever it takes to win. This image is not intended to be demeaning. It merely underscores that aggressive manipulators, like our furry, long-tailed cousins, are infinitely adaptable: whatever the conditions, they will attempt to find a way to endure or win.

Aggressive-manipulative people may have a long history of losing control, particularly when their desires are frustrated, or when they don't get what they feel entitled to. These individuals may approach you with flattery, or a plea for something, with detailed laments about their suffering. Once their request is denied, however, they blame or criticize you for their troubles, inferring that your refusal will result in furthering their suffering or cause them irreparable harm. They might try to make you feel guilty or begin to demean you, then shift into threats of violence. They may talk in an arrogant manner, trying to make you look incompetent to others or stupid to yourself. They often claim to be a victim, based on either real or imagined issues. Furthermore, they make demands in a whiny, accusatory voice. They will footnote old grievances, bringing up trivia, accusations, and old history. They will tell you how you are just like someone else who did them wrong. They will ask frequent or repetitive questions. They will try to frighten you or make you feel unsure of yourself.

Manipulation does not mean false threat. Manipulative people will often harm others: some will even kill. The difference between an aggressive manipulator and those in a state of pure fury is that the furious person's inhibitions are swept aside by their rage. You will often hear terms like, "He just lost it" to explain such behavior. The aggressive manipulator, on the other hand, attempts to monitor your responses and the situation as a whole to assess if their actions and behaviors are successful. Although the family member's behavior may be calculating, that does not mean they are in control. As they becomes more and more agitated, their judgment deteriorates, and they may concoct a rationalization for violence that makes sense to them in the moment, even if it makes sense to no one else. The idea of "intimidation for next time" is the driver of some aggressive manipulator's behavior.

Examples: An aggressive manipulator's thinking process
- "They say I'm mentally ill. So, just like last time, they'll plead it down to a misdemeanor and I won't really get in that much trouble."
- "If I hit him, mom will be scared of me, and next time they'll do what I want."

Control Tactics for Aggressive Manipulators
If you recognize manipulative aggression early in your interaction with the person, you can often cut it off at the onset. For example, in a firm tone say, "Shauna, let's not even get started with this. No. I have nothing to do with the medications your doctor prescribes; therefore, not only will I not talk to the psy-

chiatrist about your meds, but you and I should not speak about it either. If you are concerned, speak with your case manager. I am the wrong person to talk about this, and I don't want to waste either your time or mine." If, however, the manipulative person begins to escalate his or her strategies, you may have to use the ladder as a means of control and de-escalation. In this case, however, your tone of voice should be matter-of fact and slightly detached.

Making eye contact enables another person to truly see you as you are, and in return, you see them as well. Aggressive-manipulative people do not care about you, and they use apparent feelings of contact and intimacy to "read" and control you. They are interested in gaining information that they can use to their benefit. Similarly, they will use their eyes to create a (false) sense of trust to confuse you, misdirect your attention, or dominate you.

Rather than making eye contact with such people, look past one ear. Do not look away, however. While looking past an ear, you can still see what they are doing. If you look away, you will be assaulted before you even know what is coming. Your disengaged look indicates that you will not collude with them or participate in their manipulative behaviors.

The Ladder for Aggressive Manipulators
If your attempts at control and de-escalation of their manipulative strategies are unsuccessful, they may ramp up into a rage state. What distinguishes this from pure fury is that, even now, they continue to try to read and monitor you for advantage: Are they intimidating you? Have they succeeded in distracting or throwing you off balance so that you are open to an attack? Have they got you trying to "bargain" your way to safety? At the same time, they begin to "lose it," as it becomes more apparent that their strategic application of intimidation is unsuccessful. Furthermore, they get increasingly frustrated because they believe their manipulation *should* be working, primarily because it has worked so well in the past.
- Stand relaxed and ready to evade a blow and counter the attack.
- Express flat disinterest in their demands, accusations, and complaints.
- Use the repetitive commands of the ladder technique. Your vocal tone should be flat. Do not negotiate. Do not discuss other matters as long as the manipulative behavior continues.

> **Important: Locking eyes -- the "loop"**
> If the manipulative family member is noncompliant or escalates into *fury*, shift from looking past their ear to looking right in their eyes, accompanied by a firm command to stop what they are doing. When you turn your head, roll it slightly up and then down, locking eyes with them. Speak powerfully and directly, just as you do with the family member who is in a state of fury. In essence, once you make eye contact with the aggressive-manipulative family member, treat them as you would the furious type.

With the aggressive-manipulative individual, several things can happen when you attempt to control their escalation:
- Your flat disinterest shows them they cannot "get to you." After trying several different avenues, they give up: leaving in frustration, shifting to another strategy, or sagging in defeat.
- In more heated situations, they will flare into a fury (or pseudo-fury).
- When you "loop into" eye contact, they may "bounce" off into another tactic: sudden tears, for example.
- If you "hit" them with your eyes and they do not stop immediately, they are likely to attack. You will shift into the de-escalation for fury or take action to ensure your safety in the event of violence.

CHAPTER 56

Predatory or Cool Rage

This type of person is, thankfully, rather rare. They are intimidators who threaten either with vague innuendoes or explicit threats. Their aggressive behavior is calculated, but unlike the manipulator, violence is often their first choice rather than one of many options. The predatory individual delivers threats in cool, dangerous tones, often *after* a clear and strongly stated demand. Then they offer you a chance to avoid injury if you comply. A variant tactic is pretending to be out of control. (This is in contrast to a genuine attack, an action that they are eminently capable of and willing to carry out.) <u>A symbol for them is either a leopard or a shark, depending on if they present as "warm-blooded" or "stone cold."</u>

While predatory individuals seethe with hostility and/or contempt for other people, they have developed these emotions as a deliberate weapon of terror, perhaps even enjoyment. Paradoxically, their physical arousal is often low. Their heart rate can actually go down as they become more aggressive, and they can be charming and engaging, even as they are preparing to commit an act of violence. This disconnect between appearances and intentions can cause you to lower your guard because you may have a hard time believing that they are so willing to psychologically terrorize or physically hurt others.

Predatory individuals actually have no inhibitions about their aggression other than tactical calculation or self-interest. They have no capacity for sympathy or guilt, and many experience low levels of anxiety in situations that would frighten ordinary people. Every time they intimidate someone successfully, their behavior is reinforced, and they view your non-action, either during the confrontation or afterward, as either weakness or tacit approval of their behavior, thereby increasing the likelihood of similar behavior in the future.

Your Response to the Predator

> If you are living with a predatory individual, you must escape! Do whatever it takes to move out safely or get them moved out. This often requires the use of police and the legal system.

If you are trapped by a predatory individual and unable to escape, demonstrate that you are not prey, that you are not a ready victim, and that their attempts at intimidation will not work. Most predatory individuals do not wish to fight with someone whom they *do not* intimidate or otherwise control through emotional abuse or physical posturing. Instead, they seek more conciliatory and subservient victims, where their chances of success are great. If you demonstrate that you are not prey, why don't they want to attack? It is enough that they simply see you as not "edible," like an animal with quills or one that would taste bad:

Stand or sit ready to move. Be poised, but do not appear fearful or too defensive.

Avoid gesturing or using expressive movements. Fear often causes your movements to be awkward, and a predatory individual will see this as confirmation of their control over you.

Be open and strategic in everything you do: the way you position your body, your voice, and your posture. The predatory individual is well versed in reading body language and assessing weakness. Protect yourself openly, and do not change your actions based on what they say (for example, they may try to put you at ease or make promises of compliance). They may also use anything you do against you, either deriding you or pretending that you are out of control, paranoid, or acting strangely. Ignore all that and openly act to keep yourself safe.

Do not overreact to vague threats or they will interpret your reaction as a victory. An explicit threat is a criminal act. Contact law enforcement for help as soon as you can.

Cryptic Consequences

Keep your voice matter-of-fact, and give clear and direct statements of *potential* consequences. If you can, slightly smile. <u>These consequences are of a special type, clear, but cryptic</u> (i.e., "You know what would happen if you did hit me."). In this case, do not tell him what would happen. Let their imagination take over. These vague consequences are a mirror of their own method of intimidation, and they may likely react to you as "not prey, not edible, not worth the trouble." Do not make explicit or unrealistic threats, such as, "If you come near my family, I will kill you!" To the predator, that tells him what you will *not* do. In his mind, if you really meant it, you would do it now. An explicit threat is an empty threat.

- If they say, "What are you talking about?" you should reply, "You know exactly what we are talking about." When the predator responds to your cryptic consequence with questions or with confusing statements that would make your statement illogical, simply say, "You know what is going on here. You know what is happening."
- You may have to intersperse your vague consequences with ladder commands if they escalate their behaviors.
- Try to minimize eye contact. However, you need to look directly at them, so look between their eyes, or look at them with a flat stare. (Imagine turning your eyes to buttons. They will begin to look like a cutout or silhouette.) Your eyes are flat, with no attempt to "penetrate" or make contact.

- You should make sustained eye contact only if in a fight for your life. Then, you must shift focus, trying to penetrate their eyes as if you were a laser beam.
- Do not overreact to their threats or they will interpret your reaction as a victory.

> *Only* use the strategy of cryptic consequences with the openly predatory, that most rare of people, *only* when they are escalating into predatory rage, <u>and *only* when you have no way of escaping and summoning help</u>. In other words, it is very unlikely that these circumstances will happen, but you need to know what to do if they do.

Your entire goal is to convince them that it is not worth it to hurt you. Once you have succeeded and are free, you need to get help, surely from the police. To reiterate, you do not have to prove that you are bigger, tougher, or more dangerous. You are merely establishing that you are on to their game and are not, by nature, someone to victimize. Like a leopard that chooses *not* to chase an antelope because it is moving too smoothly, obviously showing that it is healthy and strong, the predator will likely disengage if you do not act like vulnerable prey. Therefore, do not give them anything to discount (an attempt to directly intimidate him with a threat) and do not try to find middle ground. (Negotiation is something they have no interest in – all negotiation means to them is that "you have given me half of what I want, let's discuss how you will give me the other half.")

If at any time you can separate yourself from the predator, do so! Similarly, if you use these cryptic consequences and, as is very likely, they leave, dissuaded that you are not easy prey, get help! Do not keep the incident to yourself. You and other members of your family are being threatened, whether the tone is velvet or harsh. You will need advice on how to be on your guard and how best to keep safe. Such an incident is sometimes a one-time affair, but on other occasions, they can go on for a long time, with further threats, stalking, or other dangerous behaviors that require you to get professional assistance and protection.

It's awful to imagine being threatened by a family member who is a predator. The best way to avoid this is to escape or make it difficult or even impossible for the predatory individual to get access to you.

If you must respond with cryptic consequences, it will be a one-time interaction: you must never allow anyone who treats you in such a way that you need to use this strategy to ever again get close to you.

Do not hesitate to get help from police. I understand that this is a family member, very possibly someone you love. But he or she means you harm: you have a right to be safe.

CHAPTER 57

De-escalation of Developmentally Disabled Individuals: Special Considerations

Developmentally disabled people can present special challenges when they are aggressive. Many of the standard de-escalation tactics described in the previous chapters are useful, but you must be aware of their limitations. Keep your communication simple and direct. If you use language that is too sophisticated, either in terms of meaning or nuance, you may elicit more frustration and anger within the person by making them "feel stupid." In addition, many developmentally disabled people are subject to "magical thinking," (Chapter 21) and their beliefs about the world and their own powers and vulnerabilities often don't conform to reality. You can sometimes use these beliefs to help calm them, as you would calm a child. On other occasions, you must be aware of these beliefs to keep the situation from escalating out of control.

If you try to control an agitated developmentally disabled individual based on their physical age and appearance – for example, a 250-pound, 35-year-old male -- things usually go very wrong, very quickly.

However, once you make eye contact, you can usually estimate the emotional age of the developmentally disabled person: small child, young kid, preteen, or teen. <u>In ordinary conversation, speak to them as one does any child, drawing them "up" toward maturity: in a crisis, speak to them at their emotional age level.</u> Regardless of the person's emotional age, you cannot allow their apparent childishness to compromise your physical safety. As with children, developmentally delayed people can be quite impulsive and unpredictable. Unlike children, however, they have the physical strength of an adult and, even more dangerous, they often do not recognize their own strength. For this reason, always be ready to evade an attack and protect yourself if necessary.

You can still use paraphrasing (Chapter 42) with an enraged developmentally disabled person. However, do not just calmly sum things up. Use an almost dramatic voice, overemphasizing words. For example, you can say, "*You* are *realllly* mad! You are *so* upset about dinner." Your voice is a combination of drama and enthusiasm. In essence, you are trying to catch their attention with charisma, a kind of energy in which you change the dynamics of your relationship through your voice and demeanor. Your dramatic voice validates how important the situation is to the angry or enraged individual.

You can use this same communication style with a developmentally disabled person who is disappointed or unhappy. "Wow. You *realllly* loved that puppy! I *know* that. You really wanted to take care of him!"

Your dramatic voice validates how important the situation is to the other person – and it is the voice, here, more than the words, that provides the validation.

> **Example: De-escalation of an assault by a developmentally disabled woman**
> A developmentally disabled woman grabbed my finger, trying to break it. I neutralized her attempt by shifting the angle of my hand as she yanked. Because she was the emotional age of about an eight year old, rather than forcefully commanding her to "let go!" I said, "I know you want to hold my hand. You don't have to twist my finger. We can hold hands as much as you like. Sure, we can hold hands." She suddenly let go and dropped to the floor crying.

Talking with Your Developmentally Disabled Family Member after a Crisis

It is certainly reasonable to validate feelings, both for yourself and for your family member, after a crisis. For example, you might say, "Franny, that was really scary. I was scared too. I'm glad that's over. I'd like you to go to your room and have a rest. No, you are not in trouble."

A detailed critique or discussion, however, is a mistake. The cognitive limitations of developmentally disabled people affect their memory, particularly in regards to emotionally charged events. Their feelings, also, are not under their control, and they very likely will react to your debriefing as if it is a new attack, especially as you may be somewhat upset yourself by the recent incident. Your concern should be behavioral stability (no new attack) and reassurance (because they are likely afraid that you want to get back at them).

You may impose consequences in some situations, after things are calm. It's very important that you do not make it a punishment. Your attitude should not be, "I'll show you! You won't try that again!" Instead, consequences are a kind of reminder, something that they bump up against, in the same way that a closed door reminds one simply to not walk through it. Unless they have done something entirely new and unexpected, they should have been warned about the consequences of an unwanted or forbidden behavior. Consequences should be predictable, consistent, and not for the purpose of breaking their will or hurting their feelings.

CHAPTER 58

When Facing Violence

Establish Safety: What to Do If an Enraged Person Becomes Violent
Safety is defined by what you must protect. This includes protecting yourself, other vulnerable people, and the family member as best you can within the circumstances you are facing.

When confronted by an individual who is more powerful, who may be armed, or who is on display in front of his confederates who may also attack, a "tactical" retreat is the best thing to do. You take the target of that person's rage, *you*, out of the picture.

Tactical retreat strategy is important with people across the range of aggression, whenever it is clear that the situation is only going to get worse and there really is nothing you can do to make it better. Whenever you can, escape and get help.

The Right to Defend Yourself: A Message Worth Repeating
If you are responsible for the protection of others, such as small children, or if you are trapped, you may have to fight back. In the event of an actual assault when escape is impossible, it is an absolute human right to fight to protect yourself and other potential victims, even from a family member whom you may love. That the aggressor may also be a suffering individual does not abrogate this right. I, like you, hope that you will never face such a horrible situation. At the same time, it is necessary to be clear with yourself, on a mental and spiritual basis, that you are willing to act to defend yourself and others. You must do this now. Trying to discover this within yourself once the assault is occurring is far too late. Remember that protecting yourself is not only a personal matter. You are protecting everyone who cares for you from the harm that they will suffer if you are maimed or killed.

Self-defense tactics are well beyond the scope of this book. If you are interested, consult with recognized experts in the field to find a self-defense program suitable for your needs.

The essential principle of self-defense
Imagine a door with seven locks and no keys. You are locked behind the door, and all that is good in life – your family, your love, your dreams, your values, even your integrity and dignity – is secured on the other side of the door. How will you go through the door? The answer, of course, is any way you can – with tooth and nail, and any implement you can reach. A violent aggressor is that "door." You have a perfect right to be on the other side.

CHAPTER 59

The Aftermath: What to Do Now?

Rage, and even more so, violence, are exhausting experiences – both emotionally and physically. Many people get the "shakes" after such an incident. So much blood has "pooled" inside the core of their bodies to prepare for combat that they feel cold and start to tremble.

Most individuals have a significantly impaired ability to remember what happened in sequence. One way the sequence gets out of order is that they recall your act of defense as the initial attack. They may have a patchy memory of a few events. Much of the rest of the incident is a blur. Although they may be remorseful, they usually do not remember what happened, how it started, or who was responsible.

Even more drastically, they can lapse into a state of defensive confusion where they no longer recall what happened at all, or they completely distort the incident in their memory, thereafter taking no responsibility whatsoever.

Others may feel profound guilt. This might be positive, if it were to lead them to reflect on their own responsibility, but for most people, this guilt is so noxious that they project responsibility onto the person who "makes them" feel so bad. Thus, they shift to resentment and blame the other person.

Humiliation, the feeling of having one's faults or vulnerabilities involuntarily or forcibly exposed to others, is quite common, and here, too, many people quickly become defensive. People describe humiliation like being flayed and exposed. Some people respond to shame by becoming enraged all over again. Their thinking seems to be, "If I feel this bad, someone must be doing it to me."

What is almost universal is a post–crisis fatigue, a combination of the depletion of the body's energy stores and the cumulative effect of all the mood and cognitive changes described above.

Taking Care of Your Family Member
If the person is still in your home after the crisis, your tasks are to maintain control, establish limits and consequences, and possibly regain rapport and provide reassurance, as long as the latter is not a "reward." In other words, you reassure your relative that you are not going to seek revenge, but neither are you going to pretend that nothing serious happened nor are you going to reward them just because the aggression is over.

If the person is someone who can accept conversation and help after the crisis is resolved, your first responsibility is *clarification:* clearly delineating what you consider abusive, aggressive, or otherwise unacceptable behavior.

If the situation continues to be volatile, if they have clearly violated rules or other people's rights, or if safety or tactics demand it, you must go right into *limit setting*. You will inform your relative of the severity and the consequences of what they did. Consequences can include being required to leave (for a relatively brief period of time – staying at another relative's home, for example – or even permanently), or simply being required to sit alone to reflect on what led them to act aggressively. Limit setting and offering consequences must be differentiated from "holding a grudge." The aggressive family member needs to experience consequences for their actions, but we must strive to keep them from experiencing this as punishment or attack. Your tone can have disappointment or outrage, but you are trying to communicate that what they did was wrong, not that they are bad or evil.

If the person is really frightened or devastated by what happened, the first priority is *reassurance and orientation,* letting him or her know that they are not going to be harmed or punished. For people who are experiencing dementia, psychosis, or other fragile mental states, you may have to let them know what has happened, where they are, what is going to happen, who you are, and so on.

Although *educative follow-up* frequently must be deferred, individuals who are calm enough to understand should participate in the following:
- Discussing what other tactics they might have used to get what they desired
- Assisting them in becoming aware of patterns that led to the aggression or assault
- Negotiating agreements on how to avoid future incidents
- Helping them return to a sense of dignity and integrity

Some people are *not* suited to participate in such a debriefing. Developmentally delayed individuals or others with dementia or cognitive impairments cannot really remember what happened, and they may re-escalate, thinking they are under attack. With people who do not have the mental capacity to understand the details or implications of the incident, it is better to be calming and reassuring. Other people who can comprehend their actions still need to be left alone for a while to soothe and calm themselves. Do not speak with them while they are somewhat escalated; wait until later.

Consolidation of Gains

Refer to Chapter 11, Information Processing and Retention: Consolidation of Gains, for more information about how to ensure that your family member learns from the critical incident, and furthermore, how you can assess *if* they have learned.

It is not enough, however, to simply reiterate an agreement. If you have promised some kind of action, let them know clearly what you can do and give them a timetable of when you will do it. If they do not get the results you promised, they will not only feel betrayed, but they will also be much harder to calm in future disputes.

CHAPTER 60

Conclusion

The graph below depicts de-escalation tactics as they apply throughout the cycle of aggression:

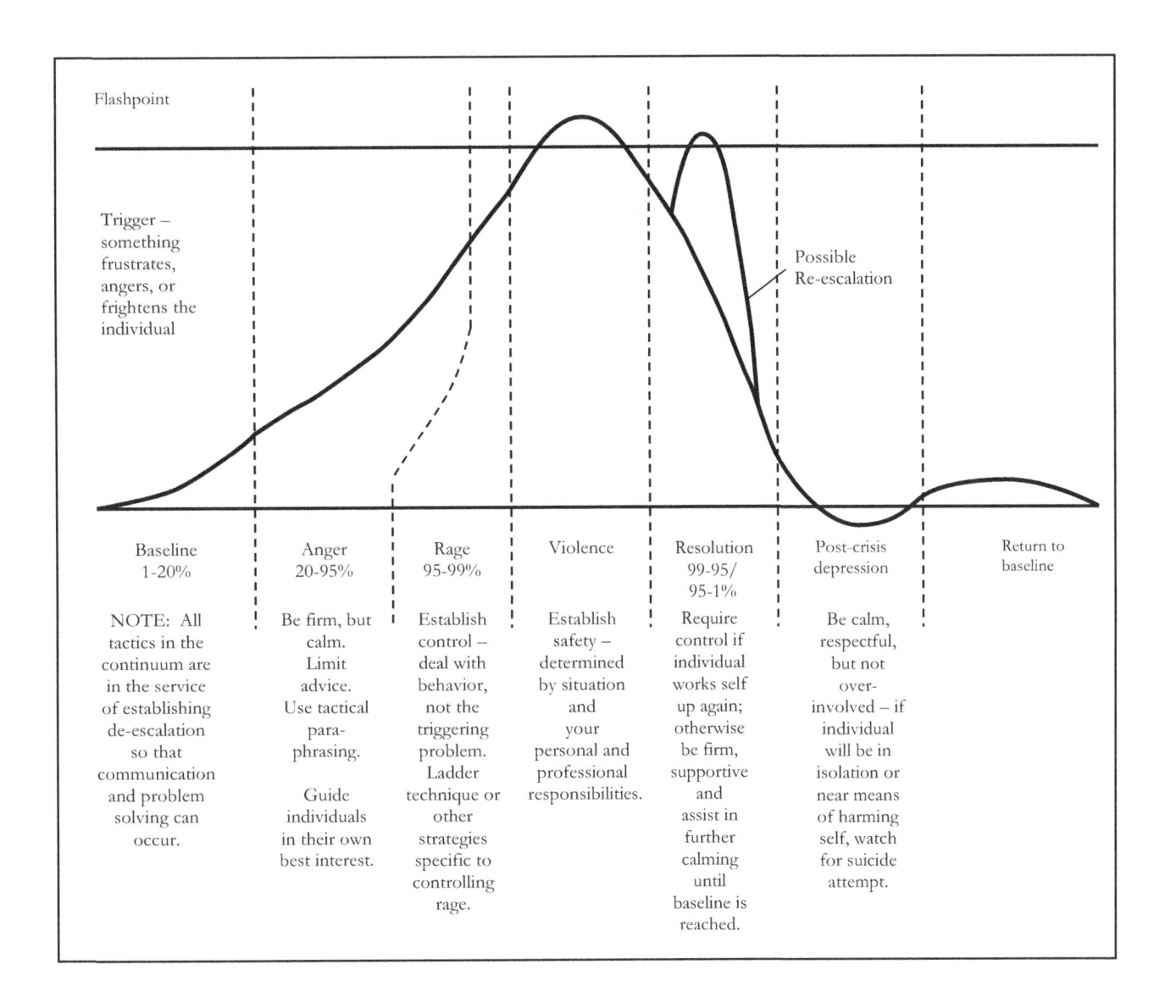

Flashpoint

Trigger – something frustrates, angers, or frightens the individual

Possible Re-escalation

Baseline 1-20%	Anger 20-95%	Rage 95-99%	Violence	Resolution 99-95/ 95-1%	Post-crisis depression	Return to baseline
NOTE: All tactics in the continuum are in the service of establishing de-escalation so that communication and problem solving can occur.	Be firm, but calm. Limit advice. Use tactical paraphrasing. Guide individuals in their own best interest.	Establish control – deal with behavior, not the triggering problem. Ladder technique or other strategies specific to controlling rage.	Establish safety – determined by situation and your personal and professional responsibilities.	Require control if individual works self up again; otherwise be firm, supportive and assist in further calming until baseline is reached.	Be calm, respectful, but not over-involved – if individual will be in isolation or near means of harming self, watch for suicide attempt.	

Now that you have finished this guidebook, you have really just begun. It is important that you regularly review and practice the safety and de-escalation methods in this book. You should be as familiar with this information as you are with the information necessary to drive your car or use your cell phone. Just as you automatically snatch your hand away from a hot stove or blink your eyes when a small object flies toward them, these skills must become as automatic as instincts to you.

It is difficult to consider the subject of potential violence, particularly when it involves a loved one. It can be so painful to realize that a family member may want to hurt or even maim or kill you that you might prefer to pretend it isn't happening. However, aggression, unattended, hurts everyone far more. Skill in de-escalating aggression and establishing a culture of safety within your family will create a sense of spaciousness that makes you a far better caregiver to your mentally ill loved one. Your family members are the ones who will benefit most.

APPENDIX I

When Monitoring Medication is Part of Your Responsibilities

Make sure that the prescribing physician knows what other medical conditions your family member has as well as other medications (prescription, over-the-counter, and herbal) that the person is taking. You must be aware of each drug's intended effect and how the various medications might interact. Furthermore, you must know what to look for should the medications have a negative effect on the family member. If you notice that the drug is not having the hoped-for results, speak to both your family member and other members of their treatment team. We sometimes only know that a medication is not suitable when your relative begins to do poorly. This can be a life-threatening issue.

If monitoring your family member's medications is not part of your responsibilities, you must, nonetheless, notice if their behavior or symptoms change and consider the possibility that they are having trouble with a drug, whether it is prescribed, over-the-counter, or illicit, and urge them to see their doctor. Whenever possible, contact their physician yourself if you believe that there is an emergent issue.

What Should You Know about Your Family Member's Medications?

If you are directly responsible for monitoring your family member, here is what you should know about their medications:
1. Name of medications (generic and brand name)
2. Date prescribed
3. Expiration date of prescription
4. Number of refills
5. Purpose of the prescription
6. Side effects that the medication can cause
7. Side effects that the person is experiencing
8. Palliative measures taken to deal with side effects
9. Potential drug interactions between medications
10. Actual drug interactions and how they are medically being managed
11. History of discontinuing medications
12. Past reasons for discontinuing medications
13. What reasons the family members can give that would lead them to discontinue medications
14. Your observations of the medications' effects
15. Based on your experience, can you think of other helpful information?

A medication log that lists prescribed drugs can help keep you informed about your family member's pharmaceutical treatment. For maximum effectiveness, the log should not only list the drugs by name but also when they were prescribed, what each medication is for, what side effects to watch for, and your observations on how the medications are affecting your family member's behavior and thought processes.

Why Do They Stop Taking Their Psychiatric Medications?

There are very good reasons for people to resist taking their medications, discontinue them, or take them intermittently.

People can experience unpleasant side effects. Among possible side effects are muscle spasms, intolerable itching/crawling sensations in the limbs, tongue thrusting, tremors, impairment of sexual functioning, dry mouth, weight gain, weight loss, skin disorders, even life-threatening disorders that must be monitored through such invasive procedures as regular blood draws, to name but a few.

Many psychiatric medications are not "felt" beyond their side effects. They do not make the person "high," or even "better." In fact, apart from the side effects, the person simply feels like "himself." Feeling good, therefore, they draw the natural conclusion that the drug has done its job – or in other cases, doesn't work – and therefore can be discontinued.

Even apart from noxious side effects, the illness can feel better than the "cure." Many individuals diagnosed with manic-depressive illness experience a well-medicated, stable life as a terrible sacrifice. Yes, one doesn't get into as much trouble, but from the perspective of the person experiencing mania, one sacrifices life as a skylark for that as a ground sloth. Many individuals experiencing psychotic symptoms find that the medications muffle or suppress delusions and/or hallucinations, but they do not make them disappear. Furthermore, the medications often do not touch the belief system around a person's delusions. Medicated life for such people is like living under a sodden blanket. What is reality to them may be muffled and tranquilized, but not otherwise changed. The medications may help them live a more stable, uneventful life, but just as we shake off bedding when we are too hot and constricted, they may discontinue medications, simply to have, in their view, air to breathe. If you believe your perceptions are real and all the medications do is muffle and obscure that reality, then it is quite natural to discontinue them.

APPENDIX II

Crisis Intervention Teams for Law Enforcement

One of the most exciting innovations in law enforcement in both America and Great Britain is the Crisis Intervention Team (CIT) model, in which law enforcement officers get forty hours of training on dealing with mentally ill individuals in crisis. In many law enforcement agencies, 20 to 40 percent of the officers are CIT trained. These are law enforcement officers who work an ordinary shift. However, they are called, whenever possible, when an individual presents somewhere in their jurisdiction with a possibly dangerous mental health crisis.

- Find out if your local law enforcement agency has a CIT team. If they do, ensure that all family members are familiar with its existence and exactly what such a team can do. If not, lobby to get such training made available.
- If there is a CIT team, always ask for a CIT officer when calling 9-1-1 (or the equivalent emergency number in your country) in crisis situations involving a mentally ill or drug-affected individual. You are not guaranteed a response from a CIT officer: this depends on their availability at the time of the call. Nonetheless, if a team exists, always ask.

Endnotes

1 I am grateful to the late Dan Kelleher for introducing me to "the undamaged self," a phrase that has enabled me to name something I had sensed for a long time, but had no words to describe.

2 I first formally learned tracking from the late Ron Kurtz, the developer of Hakomi, a method of body-centered psychotherapy. A second teacher, David Schnarch, has also elegantly described tracking in his new book, *Intimacy and Desire*, New York: Beaufort Books, 2009.

3 Ron Kurtz also gave me the image of the "bubble." Ron focused on the positive moment – when a palpable, nourishing connection has been established between two people. I have taken his image and used it to describe any experience of interpersonal space.

4 I first saw 4-4-4 breathing presented during a seminar by Lieutenant Colonel David Grossman, author of a number of books, including the famous *Stop Teaching Our Kids to Kill: A Call to Action Against TV, Movie and Video Game Violence*, New York, N.Y., Crown Publishers, 1999

5 Schwartz, Jeffrey, and Beverly Beyette. *Brain Lock: Free Yourself from Obsessive-Compulsive Behavior*. New York: Regan Books, 1996. This groundbreaking book will help you understand this extremely troublesome problem and is a good self-help book for your family member.

6 Ron Kurtz also taught me the concept of the "nourishment barrier."

7 Most stalkers are not delusional. Here are other major categories of stalkers:

- **Relational stalkers**. Often an extension of a controlling or violent relationship, the relational stalker is either keeping tabs on his or her partner, or pursuing them once they have left.

- **Obsessive stalkers**. The classic stalker who has a hyper-focus on the victim as prey, not necessarily to kill or even harm, but always to control. Like those with obsessive-compulsive disorder, this stalker can be well aware that the victim does not desire contact, and may be afraid of or hate him. But just as the germ-obsessed obsessive *must* wash his hands 50 times, despite *knowing* that they are clean, the obsessive stalker has to have, has to be near, or has to have the attention of his victim.

- **Psychopathic stalker**. Such an individual may certainly have been in a relationship or be obsessed with his victim. In addition, there is considerable ego involved: this stalker's psychological energy focuses on himself rather than the victim. A true predator, he is doing something he enjoys – because he can (for fun) or because the victim, in some way, offended him (for revenge).

8 Arieti, Silvano. *Interpretation of Schizophrenia*. 2nd edition. New York: Basic Books, Inc., 1974.

9 This image is taken form the work of philosopher Emanuel Levinas.

10 This elegant example is from Seattle firefighter/EMT Aaron Fields.

11 Lest there be any misunderstanding, this crosses all racial lines – it is a trait of "street culture," not any particular ethnicity.

12 Levinas, Emanuel. *Ethics and Infinity: Conversations with Philip Nemo*. Translated by Richard Cohen. Pgh., PA: Duquesne University Press, 1985. Grossman, David. *On Killing: The Psychological Cost of Learning to Kill in War*. Boston: Back Bay Books, 2009.

13 de Becker, Gavin. *The Gift of Fear: Survival Signals That Protect Us From Violence*. New York, NY., Little Brown, and Company, 1997.

14 This is a very crude approximation. The definition of assault is contingent on the circumstances as well as the identity and abilities of you and the menacing other.

15 I owe the image of the hands as a fence to Geoff Thompson, who has authored a number of books on his career as a doorman in very violent British pubs, as well as exemplary books on self-defense.

16 See the work of Dr. John Gottman of the University of Washington for a detailed discussion of contemptuous silence and stonewalling.

17 I am indebted to Dr. John Holttum, child psychiatrist from Tacoma, Washington. I attended a presentation given by Dr. Holttum that influenced me greatly in terms of how to "subdivide" the presenting behaviors of youth and how best to intervene. I must underscore that any treatment and intervention recommendations are my own, and may be at variance to those Dr. Holttum might offer.

18   If you are concerned about the well-being of your child in any respect, and in particular regarding their behavior, a wonderful resource is www.difficultchild.com, which provides powerful yet kind methods of child rearing and discipline.

19   For such debate:

- Louv, Richard. *Last Child in the Woods: Saving Our Children from Nature-Deficit Disorder*. Chapel Hill, NC: Algonquin Books, 2005.
- Sax, Leonard. *Boys Adrift: The Five Factors Driving the Growing Epidemic of Unmotivated Boys and Underachieving Young Men*. Philadelphia: Basic Books, 2007.

20   There is increasing research and evidence that demonstrates the efficacy of a form of therapy called Eye Movement Desensitization and Reprocessing (EMDR) for traumatized children and adults. If you are working with traumatized individuals, juveniles, or adults, referring them to caregivers familiar with this method may be beneficial. http://www.emdr.com/.

21   I owe a debt for some of the basic information in this section to a form of training called Professional Assault Response Training (PART). I have made a number of significant changes in their basic four-part schema and added a significant amount of new data. Some of my approaches are quite different from PART, and my approach should not be confused with their procedures.

ABOUT THE AUTHOR

Ellis Amdur

Edgework founder Ellis Amdur received his BA in psychology from Yale University in 1974 and his MA in psychology from Seattle University in 1990. He is both a National Certified Counselor and a State Certified Child Mental Health Specialist.

Since the late 1960s, Amdur has trained in various martial arts systems, spending thirteen of these years studying in Japan. He is a recognized expert in classical and modern Japanese martial traditions and has authored three iconoclastic books as well as one instructional DVD on this subject.

Since his return to America in 1988, Ellis Amdur has worked in the field of crisis intervention. He has developed a range of training and consultation services, as well as a unique style of assessment and psychotherapy. These are based on a combination of phenomenological psychology and the underlying philosophical premises of classical Japanese martial traditions. Amdur's professional philosophy can best be summed up in this idea: the development of an individual's integrity and dignity is the paramount virtue. This can only occur when people live courageously, regardless of the circumstances, and take responsibility for their roles in making the changes they desire.

Ellis Amdur is a dynamic public speaker and trainer who presents his work throughout the United States and internationally. He is noted for his sometimes outrageous humor as well as his profound breadth of knowledge. His vivid descriptions of aggressive and mentally ill people and his true-to-life role playing of the behaviors in question give participants an almost firsthand experience of facing the real individuals in question.

He has written a number of works regarding de-escalation of aggression. These books are available on his website, www.edgework.info.

Made in the USA
Las Vegas, NV
13 February 2024